Walter Pater

The aesthetic moment

Wolfgang Iser

translated from the German by David Henry Wilson

The right of the University of Cambridge to print and sell all manner of books was granted by Henry VIII in 1534. The University has printed and published continuously since 1584.

Cambridge University Press

Cambridge
London New York New Rochelle
Melbourne Sydney

Published by the Press Syndicate of the University of Cambridge
The Pitt Building, Trumpington Street, Cambridge CB2 1RP
32 East 57th Street, New York, NY 10022, USA
10 Stamford Road, Oakleigh, Melbourne 3166, Australia

Originally published as *Walter Pater: Die Autonomie des Ästhetischen*
by Wolfgang Iser
(Max Niemeyer Verlag, Tübingen 1960)

Printed in Great Britain
at the University Press, Cambridge

British Library cataloguing in publication data

Iser, Wolfgang
Walter Pater: the aesthetic moment. – (European
studies in English literature)
1. Pater, Walter – Criticism and interpretation
I. Title II. Die Autonomie des Ästhetischen. *English*
III. Series
828.'.808 PR5136

Library of Congress cataloguing in publication data

Iser, Wolfgang.
Walter Pater, the aesthetic moment.
(European studies in English literature)
Translation of: Walter Pater, die Autonomie des
Ästhetischen.
Bibliography.
Includes index.
1. Pater, Walter, 1839–1894 – Criticism and
interpretation. 2. Aestheticism (Literature)
3. Aesthetic movement (British art) 4. Aesthetics,
British. I. Title. II. Series.
PR5137.I813 1987 824'.8 86–8264

ISBN 0 521 30962 X

WD

European Studies in English Literature

Walter Pater

Wolfgang Iser's study of Walter Pater (1839–94) was first published in German in 1960. It places the English critic, essayist and novelist in a philosophical tradition whose major exponents were Hegel and Coleridge, at the same time showing how Pater differed crucially from these thinkers to become representative of a late Victorian culture critically poised in transition between Romanticism and Modernism. Professor Iser broadens the aesthetic context from Plato through to twentieth-century writers such as Virginia Woolf, illustrating Pater's ideas with detailed examples from his critical and fictional work. Pater's new definitions of 'beauty' and 'style' in art, his doctrine of 'art for art's sake', his preoccupation with aesthetic existence, his fascination with periods of balance and historical transition – between 'medieval' and 'Renaissance', 'Classical' and 'Romantic' – are seen in the light of his scepticism towards all systematisation and his view of art as countering human finiteness by capturing the intensity of the moment. In practice, Pater's fiction acts out the problems inherent in any attempt to sustain an aesthetic existence, and it shows his awareness of the questions thus raised both for aesthetics and for culture generally.

This important book, which remains as illuminating now as when it first appeared, should be read by those interested in philosophy and aesthetics, as well as by those concerned with the Victorian novel and with nineteenth- and twentieth-century criticism, whether theoretical or art-historical. For the Pater specialist, it provides the first English version of a major landmark in the field.

European Studies in English Literature

SERIES EDITORS

Ulrich Broich, Professor of English, University of Munich
Herbert Grabes, Professor of English, University of Giessen
Dieter Mehl, Professor of English, University of Bonn

This series is devoted to publishing translations into English of the best works written in European languages on English literature. These may be first-rate books recently published in their original versions, or they may be classic studies which have influenced the course of scholarship in their field while never having been available in English before.

To begin with, the series has concentrated on works translated from the German; but its range will expand to cover other languages.

TRANSLATIONS PUBLISHED

Walter Pater: The aesthetic moment by Wolfgang Iser

TITLES UNDER CONTRACT FOR TRANSLATION

Studien zum komischen Epos by Ulrich Broich
Redeformen des englischen Mysterienspiels by Hans-Jürgen Diller
Die romantische Verserzählung in England by Hermann Fischer
Studien zur Dramenform vor Shakespeare: Moralität, Interlude, romaneskes Drama by Werner Habicht
Präraphaeliten und Fin de Siècle by Lothar Hönnighausen
Oscar Wilde by Norbert Kohl
Das Drama: Theorie und Analyse by Manfred Pfister
Die Frauenklage: Studien zur elegischen Verserzählung in der englischen Literatur des Spätmittelalters und der Renaissance by Götz Schmitz
Das englische Geschichtsdrama seit Shaw by Kurt Tetzeli von Rosador
Das englische Theater der Gegenwart by Christian Werner Thomsen
Anfänge und gattungstypische Ausformung der englischen Strassenballade, 1550–1650 by Natascha Würzbach

Contents

Greek Studies

Foreword

The translation of a book that was written almost thirty years ago is bound to cause mixed feelings in its author. If he is no longer satisfied with what he wrote, then he will feel that, despite its occasional reappearance in quotations and references, it should be left buried in the peace and quiet of bibliographies; if he agrees to its resurrection, however, he cannot help viewing his own text as something alien. This need not necessarily be because his interests have changed; the passage of time alone causes a shift in focus, giving the text a different slant. The temptation, therefore, to reshuffle portions of the book is hard to resist. But alterations of any kind would have resulted in a disturbing juxtaposition of viewpoints.

Literary criticism serves to translate a past into terms of a present, and so it is inevitable that present interests should govern and indeed condition the framework of interpretation. These interests in turn are an offshoot of past approaches, which still function negatively by denoting those approaches which are now blocked. The mid 1950s saw the eclipse of the history of ideas and the life-and-letters model as guidelines for criticism, and witnessed in their wake the flourishing of New Criticism with its devotion to close reading which was as widespread then as Deconstruction is now.

In the 1950s a monograph on an author's complete works entailed using the classic form of scholarly positivism in order to bring out one's own intention by shattering the conventions of the genre. Instead of an accumulation of factual information, more often than not compiled for its own sake, and a record of the history and environment of an author and his sources, the focus shifted to the aesthetic dimension of the work. If the work itself came under scrutiny, then inevitably the interpretation veered towards a New Critical approach, which sought to strip the work of all such extraneous factors and grasp it as an autonomous object.

Caught between this Scylla and Charybdis of literary criticism, I found myself attracted to the figure of Walter Pater. An analysis of his work seemed to promise experience of what it meant to make Art the ultimate value of finite existence. Such an experience would bring to light the problems which New Criticism could not cope with, since it was no longer concerned with the consequences of the autonomous object. Pater dealt precisely with these problems, because for him Art was an ultimate value, enabling man to forget the pressure of finite human existence. For Pater autonomous Art and real life joined hands, as it were, under the table – a relationship that could only be anathema to the basic principles of New Criticism. And so by analysing Pater's work I hoped to uncover what had been glossed over by New Criticism and had thus ultimately caused its demise as a paradigm of interpretation.

Anyone whose life is devoted to Art lives aesthetically. Therefore, Pater's work can be read almost as a blueprint for the aesthetic existence which he is attempting to illuminate. I have borrowed the necessary heuristics from Kierkegaard, especially his *Either/Or* – that penetrating analysis of all Romanticism – though with the reservation that the aesthetic existence is not to be viewed as a sign or even as a preliminary stage of any other form of existence. In order to give shape to the constituent elements of the aesthetic life, I have tried to interpret Pater through Pater, by applying his own hermeneutic principle of the 'spiritual form' to himself. 'Spiritual form' is a kind of Aristotelian *morphē* which Pater seeks to detect in every phenomenon that interests him, so that he can grasp the perceivable aspects as a manifestation of this concealed form. It is a principle which he practices with great virtuosity, and by applying it to Pater himself I hoped to lay bare the 'spiritual form' of his own writings. This proved to be the aesthetic moment – the basic constituent of the aesthetic existence, which he so incessantly propagated and which, being the root of all his work, was something that he could not pull to the surface himself. For a transcendental stance towards oneself would mean transcending the aesthetic existence.

If with hindsight I can now say that my approach sometimes seems rather intrinsic, this is because I was striving not to impose a systematic and hence alien frame of reference on an unsystematic and richly faceted body of work. To have done so would have eliminated the vast range of nuances produced by the Paterian brand of repetition. The aesthetic existence, narcissistically turned in upon itself and yet unable to sustain this fixation, seems to require viewing from standpoints outside itself, but to do this would mean blotting out all inherent problems – especially if one were to use the Kierkegaardian reference of the ethical decision or the religious renunciation of self, not to mention the condemnation the aesthetic existence would have suffered if viewed from a sociological angle. Thus my focal point of interest was the aesthetic moment, and as a result I perhaps unjustifiably neglected those elements of the work that might be taken as pointers to the cultural situation of Pater's time.

In historical terms, then, my monograph may be taken to reflect the problems of literary criticism in the 1950s. On the one hand, I was trying to free literature from being taken as evidence for anything other than itself, so that I could focus on its own specific qualities; on the other, I wanted to show through Pater's work what was entailed in the concept of autonomous art.

Today these aspects have faded into the background, and what was at the time not of prime significance for me now seems to link my 30-year-old study with an aspect whose importance is far greater than I had envisaged – namely, the idea of legitimation. Pater's urgent need to legitimise autonomous art sprang from the instability of the aesthetic existence, which he was eager to underpin. Even though the aesthetic existence is nowadays identified with aestheticism – the final fling of a now all but defunct bourgeois culture – the idea of legitimation is still a burning issue. Its current actuality differs, however, from crises of legitimation in the past by its compulsion to grapple with its own necessity. This becomes all the more obvious through a postmodern attitude, which rejects the idea of legitimation altogether. This outright rejection separates it from High Modernism, which regarded Performance as the legitimation for cultural activities. For Pater, legitimation was still not abstract but concrete, since he believed that history and myth were guidelines that gave solid foundations to the enhanced moment. His very search for such legitimation shows that he had anticipated a problem that was to become crucial for the twentieth century, with its crises of legitimation spreading further and further afield, and plaguing social and ideological orders as well as the arts. Pater's concern, though, was to remove instability, and to this end he mobilised the entire past. His invocation of history and myth sought to elevate the intensified moment into a life-line for the aesthetic existence, thus indicating a change in the function of legitimation. In the past, world pictures provided the orientation, whereas Pater sets out to justify both the transitoriness and the in-between state of the aesthetic existence by making the totality of the human past subservient to this end, thus inverting the idea of legitimation. Instead of providing a framework to which cultural and social activities have to be subsumed, legitimation now applies itself to private longings.

It is this aspect of Pater's work rather than his elucidation of the aesthetic existence that makes him more interesting for us today. What haunts twentieth-century thought – a search for an all-embracing legitimation bearing out the diversified intellectual commitments, social requirements, and multiple ideologies – Pater had anticipated in his own way, and to this extent he is a figure of transition in a sense quite different from that which I had discerned thirty years ago.

Equally important was Pater's attempt to use literary fiction in order to overcome difficulties which had proved to be insurmountable for literary criticism. Criticism is hedged in by references to which its statements are to be connected, whereas literary fiction crosses the boundaries marked by these very frames. The boundary-crossing potential of fiction is actualised when referential writing runs up against its inherent limitations. This is borne out in Pater's writings: whenever he reaches an impasse regarding history and myth as sanctions for his ideas, fiction continues the thread, exploring the reasons for failure by imagining situations in which an aesthetic life might – but never does – achieve the longed-for unity with itself. Where cognitive criticism comes to an end, literature begins, for fiction alone can stage that which is inaccessible to referential discourse.

Although Pater remains deeply rooted in the nineteenth century, and so is usually classified as a Late Romantic, there can be no doubt that his work prefigured the problems that have become dominant in our time. And the parallels between his *fin de siècle* and our own fast-fading century make it all the more fitting that he should now emerge again from the shadows to which his aesthetic label has so long confined him.

Some reviews of the original German edition of this book objected that my systematic unfolding of the problem occasionally led me into departing from the chronology of Pater's work. It would indeed have been well worth combining my own scheme with the chronological one, for the resultant overlaps would have helped to convey the finer details of the structure of the aesthetic existence; the latter never finally rejects anything, and so by taking up earlier, problematic forms of legitimation and relating them to later solutions, I could have shown the extent to which the aesthetic existence is poised – though never stabilised – at the intersection of conflicting tendencies. However, this has been the main trend of my argument anyway, and it seemed to me that a pursuit of the nuances to be brought about by a strict observance of the chronological sequence might in the end have told more about Pater as a person than about the features of the aesthetic existence.

The intervening years have brought further research on Pater,* which made me doubt whether I should retain my introductory section on Pater criticism, as some of the items discussed have since been superseded. But when I wrote the book, a scholarly convention – long since abandoned – demanded that the starting-point of a monograph had to be mapped out by a critical discussion of what was extant on the subject concerned. This basically hermeneutic procedure served the purpose of outlining the chosen approach, which in turn was conditioned by the problems thrown up by previous research. My survey of existing Pater criticism served precisely this function, and so it would have been impossible to omit my introductory section without obscuring my starting-point.

* For a detailed bibliography of writings on Pater up to 1973, see Franklin E. Court's *Walter Pater. An Annotated Bibliography of Writings About Him*, De Kalb, Illinois, 1980.

Finally, I should like to express my deep gratitude to David Henry Wilson, who not only translated my text, but also occasionally reshaped it for the sake of brevity and clarity.

W.I.

Konstanz, October 1985

I *INTRODUCTION*

1 Pater criticism

In 1948 the BBC devoted a series of lectures to Victorianism, and in the course of these Christopher Dawson stated, 'we are still too close to the later Victorians – to the generation of Arthur Balfour and Walter Pater – to understand them'.[1] Ten years later Edmund Chandler wrote in the foreword to his study *Pater on Style*: 'I have naturally looked at everything that I could lay my hands on about Pater – the total volume is not large. And I feel bound to say that most of what goes for biography and criticism of Pater is, in my opinion, frankly unsatisfactory . . . there is no single volume devoted to Pater that I found acceptable.'[2] What underlies these two statements is the fact that Pater criticism is for the most part lacking in any overall view. A certain critical distance seems necessary, since Pater's writings tend to resist traditional modes of classification. Saintsbury was among the first to stress how difficult it was to evaluate Pater,[3] since his work is a meeting-place for poetic, critical and philosophical concepts which intermingle in defiance of the conventional ideas of genres and disciplines. So marked is this characteristic that at times his stories resemble philosophical constructions, while his critical writings have the nature of a poetic intuition. Reisdorff reiterated the difficulty in evaluating Pater,[4] and indeed existing studies are notable for the one-sidedness of their approach. It is perhaps easier merely to condemn than to unravel the individual qualities and intentions of Pater's work, and the difficulty of classification has led to a good deal of unjustified criticism.[5] Equally unjustified, however, are the paeans of praise from those who claim spiritual kinship with Pater[6] and offer sycophantic distortions of the picture.

It is largely through awareness brought about by modern literature that we are now beginning to gain the distance necessary to understand the work of the quiet Oxford don. He marks an intersection of divergent trends, and although it cannot be said that he inaugurated the modernism or 'modernity' of which he often spoke,[7] nevertheless he is a transitional figure who highlights both a waning of Classical and Romantic traditions and a yearning for something new.

The growth of critical distance, and hence of more balanced judgement, can be traced through various monographs on the aesthetic movement in England. In 1921 Brie wrote a short study outlining the changes in the 'aesthetic world view' during the last 400 years. He showed how the different aesthetic forms presupposed particular mental states and social situations, but owing to the limited range of the study, these were only summarised and Pater's ideas were merely outlined rather than interpreted. In 1926 Needham sought to explain the aesthetic movement of the nineteenth century as a sociological phenomenon, but Pater was only briefly touched upon, as his writings were of little relevance to such an approach. Then in 1931 came two comprehensive accounts of the aesthetic movement, by Farmer and by Rosenblatt, and these contain an abundance of indispensable material. They used a descriptive method to unravel the historical strands of Pater's work, with the aim of separating influence from appropriation; what they did not do was examine such basic concepts as *l'art pour l'art* and *décadence*. Gaunt's survey of the 'aesthetic adventure' (1945) runs along similar lines; he supplements Farmer's and Rosenblatt's picture of Pater with a series of illuminating views from different angles. It was not until 1949, however, that Pater interpretation took a new turn with Hough's study of the English Late Romantics. Starting from Eliot's essay on Pater, Hough sought to interpret him from the standpoint of his intellectual position within the context of Late Romanticism. Hough was the first to discard the positivistic view of the aesthetic movement, thus gaining insights that were unavailable to Farmer and Rosenblatt.

There is a similar change of approach to be traced in studies devoted specifically to Pater himself. The four biographies by Greenslet (1905), Benson (1906), Wright (1907) and Thomas (1913) contain material of varying quality[8] – only Benson's really brings Pater's personality to life, while the others offer little more than a chronological sequence of facts. There are no genuine insights into the relation between man and work until Cattan's at times illuminating essay of 1936.

The same pattern is to be observed in monographs on individual aspects of Pater's writings. It is this pigeon-holing of different aspects that typifies the earlier interpretation of his work. The first critical studies concern the link with Wilde: Bock (1913) and Bendz (1914) use parallel quotations to try to establish the extent of Pater's influence on Wilde. There is a similarly restricted purpose behind the dissertations of Proesler (1917), Beyer (1931) and Glücksmann (1932), who discuss respectively Pater's links with German literature, France, and Antiquity. Proesler and Glücksmann limit themselves to a general study of corresponding ideas and recurrent motifs, whereas Beyer interprets Pater's interest in French literature and culture as an expression of his aesthetic attitude.

In 1926 Staub sought to interpret *Imaginary Portraits* – a form both peculiar to and typical of Pater's fictive writing – from the standpoint of his intellectual attitude. Although this study is still permeated with the characteristic deficiencies of Pater criticism, as Reisdorff shows so clearly in his dissertation,[9] there is nevertheless a degree of critical insight. Staub goes to great lengths to uncover the intellectual presuppositions that led to this typically Paterian form. The ultimate inadequacy of his account is due to his negative evaluation and to the fact that he confines himself to historical details in his attempt to explain the form and intention that underlie *Imaginary Portraits*. Z. Chandler's dissertation of 1928 on Pater's stylistic technique offers a statistical survey of the main linguistic features, and is as factual and descriptive as Farmer's study of 1931, which simply states the principles operative in Pater's critical work. Eaker's dissertation (1933) breaks new ground in so far as it traces Pater's creative writing back to psychological origins. However, even if one cannot deny the subjective roots of Pater's work, the study of his stories as a key to his personality seems to be of doubtful relevance. Thus Eaker can only end by accusing Pater of various misunderstandings in relation to the treatment of his subjects. Also in 1933 Young published a well-researched thesis on the extent to which Pater's writings mirrored the views of his time. But however useful the individual references may be, the problem cries out for a synthetic solution. Olivero's comprehensive work of 1939 is the first real attempt to present an overall picture of Pater. But although it is in the form of a scholarly thesis, its tone is frequently that of a confession. Consequently it swings from general statements of fact to rank misjudgements, describing Pater as a man pure of heart and spirit, and a writer of greatest *distinzione* simply *per grazia di Dio*.[10] Thus in *Marius the Epicurean* Olivero sees the triumph of Christianity over paganism[11] even though it would be difficult to find any evidence of this in the text itself. The merit of Olivero's work is that he is the first to break away from focusing on isolated aspects of Pater's writings, but his method is still mainly confined to amassing historical material.

A much more sober and objective approach is Huppé's short essay (1948), exposing Pater's misinterpretations of Plato as a means of uncovering basic elements in the formation of the aesthetic attitude. Reisdorff's unpublished dissertation (1952) sets out to define the 'aesthetic idea' that underlay Pater's 'art criticism', and his starting-point is the eminently sensible belief, hitherto ignored, that Pater's work formed a coherent whole.[12] Thus criteria can be extracted from Pater's own writings, a fact which makes this study particularly revealing. Reisdorff grasps the special nature of Pater's criticism in its mutual permeation of the sensual and the spiritual, and even if the framework devised for conceiving this peculiar interpenetration appears to be rather blurred – the study often degenerates into a mere inventory of these combinations – Reisdorff's choice of perspective is certainly the right one. The year 1955 saw the publication of David Cecil's paper, whose subtitle *Scholar–Artist* denotes Pater's curious in-between quality. This short essay confines itself to summing up the features of this quality, leading into a metaphorically fashioned thesis that Pater represents the contrast between 'broadcloth' and 'apple-green silk tie',[13] which is meant to explain the juxtaposition indicated by the subtitle. Edmund Chandler's meritorious study (1958) deals mainly with the textual history of *Marius*, bringing out the discrepancy between Pater's demands in his essay on style and his actual practice.

This brief survey of Pater criticism necessitates a few words on the problem of method. Clearly the historical approach, focusing on motives, parallels, and influences, lacks criteria that would enable us to assess Pater's work comprehensively. For the most part it is descriptive, ignoring the distinction between influence and appropriation, which is after all the hallmark of Pater's relation to the past. It uses categories inherited from the positivistic tradition in order to define a form of writing whose main thrust is to break down all cognitive pigeon-holing. It is only in more recent studies that we find a fruitful search for a new and more adequate method. The need is summed up by Norman Foerster's *cri de coeur*: 'The tradition of aestheticism running from Keats to Wilde needs fresh exploration, fresh evidence, and, above all, a fresh critical insight.'[14]

The present study is an attempt to meet this need, to the extent that Pater's work is an important and representative landmark in aestheticism. There would be little point in adding to the list of descriptive and historical studies; it will therefore be assumed that the reader is familiar with Pater's writings, and the quotations – sometimes given at length – are meant only to facilitate an understanding of the argument.

The problems to be dealt with here have scarcely been touched on in earlier studies, and so there will be relatively little discussion of other positions. Our concern instead will be to work out the nature of aestheticism, asking first what were the conditions that led to art being hypostatised and endowed with ultimacy, and then how to conceive of the autonomous art which arose out of this transfiguration. If art becomes the ultimate value of finite human existence, it can never be subservient to any reality outside itself. This claim, however, gains credence only when there is sufficient evidence to support it, and so art stands in need of being 'sanctioned'. It is surprising how often Pater uses this term. 'The sanction of so many ages of human experience'[15] is the basis of his doctrine, and as autonomous art cannot be subjected to any normative concepts, he finds his 'sanction' in history and myth. Chapters 3 and 4 will examine this idea in detail. Above all, our aim will be to show the limitations of this concept, and it is in his fiction that Pater shows his awareness of the deficiencies of the historical and mythical sanctions. Thus the final chapter will seek to grasp the nature of aesthetic existence by way of an interpretation of *Marius the Epicurean* and *Imaginary Portraits*. Human life that is orientated by art will experience the insecurity of this basis through continually changing moods which will only resolve themselves in death.

In examining the nature of Pater's ideas, we shall not merely be interpreting but will also be striving after an analysis of the aesthetic. Indeed, since Pater's writings are representative examples of aestheticism, we shall be aiming for a definition of the aesthetic whose validity will extend beyond Pater. Since neither condemnation nor adulation can capture the evanescence of the aesthetic, what is needed is a dispassionate study, and it is in this spirit that we shall endeavour to formulate concepts which will help us to distinguish between different manifestations. The order of the chapters should not be construed in terms of development, for aestheticism is not an ordered phenomenon. The chapters deal successively with ideas that preoccupied Pater simultaneously, and for this reason the chronology of his writings is also of minor significance.[16] We are first and foremost concerned with an investigation of the aesthetic, and it is this analysis that has conditioned the sequence of the chapters.

2 Historical preliminaries

Art as creation

The following observations are in no way meant as an account of nineteenth-century English aesthetics, for this would be a major task in itself. We are concerned only with those trends that will lead to a better understanding of Pater's point of departure. Although there have been a few revealing studies,[1] no one has yet produced a comprehensive analysis of nineteenth-century aesthetics, and indeed the highly significant replacement of rhetoric by aesthetics at the end of the eighteenth century still stands in need of a theoretical explanation. In this respect Burke is an important figure, marking a juncture not to be overlooked, for with him aesthetic feeling frees itself from given rules and aesthetic objects and becomes a subjective quality of the percipient.[2]

It was Young whose doctrine of the genius broke with traditional poetics, but it is only with Blake that this change took on a revolutionary fervour. The passionate claim that 'To Generalize is to be an Idiot'[3] marks the final break with the old Aristotelian function of art as mimesis.[4] But this break is just the starting-point for Blake's attempt to formulate what is for him the true meaning of art. In *Marriage of Heaven and Hell* there is a revealing passage in which the visionary author is dining with Ezekiel and Isaiah and discussing the existence of God:

> Then Ezekiel said: The philosophy of the east taught the first principles of human perception: some nations held one principle for the origin, and some another: we of Israel taught that the Poetic Genius (as you now call it) was the first principle and all the others merely derivative, which was the cause for our despising the Priests & Philosophers of other countries, and prophesying that all Gods would at last be proved to originate in ours & to be the tributaries of the Poetic Genius.[5]

Blake's concept removes not only the hallowed distinction between art and nature, but also that between art and life. For him the Poetic Genius is a universal principle. There are two vital elements in Blake's aesthetics. First there is the radical repudiation of mimesis; secondly there is a visionary drive towards a hitherto inconceivable notion of art. This new idea, ushered in with concomitant revolutionary pathos, is marked by a high degree of subjectivity. Traditional concepts can no longer embrace the function of art, and so subjectivity replaces them. Blake's approach is typical of the nineteenth century. The greater the emphasis on subjectivity, the swifter the changes in principles of art, for now the yardstick is individual intention and not universal convention. Hence the variety of concepts that arise during the nineteenth century in the attempt to give art an irrefutable foundation.

Blake also seeks to consolidate his concept by representing the Old Testament prophets as harbingers of the Poetic Genius; they invoke the artist as the new God, they perceive the origins of the world in him, and they regard all other gods as enslaved to him. This subjugation of biblical figures to a totally alien purpose shows just how far Blake's concept of art is to be taken, for it embodies the very substance of the world and is the beginning and the end of all things. 'The Poetic Genius may overthrow the bounds of "finite organical perception". The artist in society strives to regain Eden for all men, to leave behind that state of delusion characterized by Lockean nature and spiritual forms fallen into material. Art is thus prophetic in the religious sense.'[6]

The moment art is freed from its traditional function, it is defined as the creation of the world. Its forms are those of prophecy, which forces Blake to invent a myth whose purpose is the regaining of the Paradise that lies behind the duality of the world as mythicised by him. He defines art in terms of the attributes of God, and thus leads the way into the nineteenth century, which began to transfer the attributes of God to the world itself.

Towards the end of the eighteenth century, Samuel Taylor Coleridge confessed: 'I do not like history.'[7] Instead he loved poetry, metaphysics and dreams. In this respect he is closely akin to Blake, but it is the differences between the two that are most revealing. The visionary character of Blake's aesthetics is cast in cognitive language by Coleridge, which allows for the difference to be perceived in their respective conceptions of art. From German transcendental philosophy Coleridge derived the following definition of art in its relation to nature:

> In the objects of nature are presented, as in a mirror, all the possible elements, steps, and processes of intellect antecedent to consciousness, and therefore to the full development of the intelligential act; and man's mind is the very focus of all the rays of intellect which are scattered throughout the images of nature. Now so to place these images, totalized, and fitted to the limits of the human mind, as to elicit from, and to superinduce upon, the forms themselves the moral reflexions to which they approximate, to make the external internal, the internal external, to make nature thought, and thought nature, – this is the mystery of genius in the Fine Arts. Dare I add that the genius must act on the feeling, that body is but a striving to become mind, – that it is mind in its essence! In every work of art there is a reconcilement of the external with the internal; the conscious is so impressed on the unconscious as to appear in it.[8]

Nature for Coleridge is not an independent entity of the human mind – it rather embodies a stage on the journey towards self-consciousness in which the mind has not as yet recognised its ultimate aim. Nature is the sum of the mind's unconscious forms. The old Aristotelian concept of nature, which was still adhered to in the eighteenth century, is subverted by exposing nature as nothing but a condition of the mind – it fades away in proportion to the mind's consciousness of itself. Thus the dividing line disappears between nature and thought, thereby ensuring the predominance of the creative genius. Coleridge identifies the process of becoming conscious with art, whose perfection lies in the final removal of the supposed differences between nature and mind. The mastery of art is to be seen in the merging of external and internal, of nature and thought, and by means of art nature becomes a mirror for the mind to see itself as *natura naturans*.[9] 'Art . . . is the mediatress between, and reconciler of, nature and man.'[10]

For Coleridge art, as an abstract entity, is a dialectical concept, and in this respect he diverges from Blake's Poetic Genius, for while the latter is the origin preceding all opposites, Coleridge's art only achieves unity once it has bridged the cleft of opposites. Thus art as 'mediatress' and 'reconciler' presupposes awareness of opposites which provide the starting-point for its efficacy. Blake's visions therefore fade into terms of abstraction, and his revolutionary fervour gives way to heightened reflection. Art, then, for Coleridge is no longer a priori, but a posteriori. While Blake mythologises the world through his revelations, Coleridge seeks to come to grips with essence or being in terms of German idealism. Blake's Poetic Genius is a divinity, but for Coleridge art is the means whereby the totality of what is can be made tangible, and so Blake's art as origin gives way to Coleridge's art as a process of unending mediation. For Coleridge, art serves the 'great eternal I AM'.[11] 'In other words, it is a subject which becomes a subject by the act of constructing itself objectively to itself; but which never is an object except for itself, and only so far as by the very same act it becomes a subject.'[12] Art for him is not the ultimate,[13] because it serves to make visible the efficacy of the self-creating mind – unlike Blake's Poetic Genius, which *is* the ultimate reality.

The Platonism of Percy Bysshe Shelley's *Defence of Poetry* and his concepts of 'Reason' and 'Imagination' tie up with Coleridge's aesthetics,[14] but despite this idealistic basis, Shelley's main concern is the task and the achievement of the poet. Even if this shift of emphasis is attributable to the apologetic origins of the treatise, one cannot help being struck by the extraordinary definition of the poet which he offers at the end: 'Poets are the hierophants of an unapprehended inspiration; the mirrors of the gigantic shadows which futurity casts upon the present; the words which express what they understand not; the trumpets which sing to battle, and feel not what they inspire . . . Poets are the unacknowledged legislators of the world.'[15] This priestlike function of the poet suggests that he has contact with some supernatural reality that speaks through him. But he is not a passive medium, merely passing on sacred inspiration – he activates the unworldly reality within the world. He is the legislator because the ethos of the world grows out of the discoveries of the poet,[16] who creates an indestructible order out of chaos, forms language, drafts laws, and so with his fellow poets becomes 'founders of civil society'.[17] These for Shelley are the consequences of the poet's role as mediator between Platonic transcendence and reality.

A substantial part of the *Defence of Poetry* consists of the evidence for this idea. Shelley finds it in history, for it is in history that the spirit of poetry is given tangible form by the poets.[18] Poetry needs the chaotic and the transient in order to take effect, precisely because it gives permanence to the transitory. Shelley is aware of his own obsession with history, and pulls himself up short: 'But let us not be betrayed from a defence into a critical history of poetry and its influence on society.'[19] From the past he moves to the poet's revelations of the future, for the poet's access to another world enables him to step beyond the temporal limitations of this world. Shelley's concept of poetry differs from that of Coleridge principally through the fact that it is historical rather than abstract, providing social orders rather than mirrors for the mind. His preoccupation with poetry's impact on reality is illustrated by his much-quoted claim that 'Poetry redeems from decay the visitations of the divinity in man.'[20] But art as redemption does not refer to man's liberation from pedestrian reality, as is the case with Pater later on; for Shelley, art ensures the restoration of the divine within a disfigured world order. Yet the very fact that the divine is threatened with decay shows the degree of significance now assumed by the historical world. For both Coleridge and Shelley, then, art is a process of creation, but for the one it is conceived normatively, and for the other historically.

Thomas Carlyle's pronouncements about the hero as poet are perhaps not directly related to aesthetics, but they do bring out some of the consequences implicit in Shelley's concept: ' . . . the Hero can be Poet, Prophet, King, Priest or what you will, according to the kind of world he finds himself born into'.[21] This dependence of the hero on historical circumstances takes Shelley's ideas on the relation between art and history one step further, for history virtually determines what the hero is to do (since his task is to change history). For Carlyle, history ceases to be a neutral arena in which poetry can display its powers, because historical situations must be resolved by the redeeming and healing qualities of the 'great man'. Instead of creating human order by virtue of his contact with another world, the poet now restores, through his moral resolve, the orderliness and totality that have been shattered by history. Carlyle's poet is a being 'once more, in earnest with the Universe, though all others were but toying with it'.[22] This 'once more' shows the poet's opposition to a decaying world, and only he 'communicates an Unendlichkeit'.[23] Shelley's legislator now becomes the hero who must restore meaning to the universe.

This hero for Carlyle is the 'Man of Letters'. But the writer is forced into the position of the apologist, for he lives in a 'godless world',[24] where he must bring out 'the True, Divine and Eternal, which exists always, unseen to most, under the Temporary'.[25] What transforms the man of letters into a hero are his efforts to withstand and to counteract the 'paralysing scepticism' of the modern world. Earnestness and uprightness become essential qualities of the hero, whose incorruptible sincerity alone elevates him to the ranks of genius.[26]

The more art is related to history, the less important becomes the idea of art as creation. Instead it turns into a haven promising redemption from the growing malaise of ordinary reality. Thus the man of letters is now less the creator than the healer of the sick historical world.

Carlyle's view of the great man as hero contains two highly significant aspects: (1) man becomes a hero by overcoming the historical world; (2) his designation as hero entails possible failure, in which case the great man is a potentially tragic figure. Writers, who must endure the 'paralysing' modern world, are therefore potentially heroes and tragedians.

With Carlyle the concept of art as creation reaches a point of crisis: art no longer builds the world but instead can only restore what has been lost; its function is no longer to create but is to overcome existing reality.

Art as mimesis

The traditional concept of art as imitation of Nature was in no way discarded by the conception of art as creation, let alone by the assumption that it originated in the inspired genius. It was a concept that – in spite of changing definitions – survived long into the nineteenth century, though it was to undergo considerable changes. William Wordsworth's '*Note on Ode. Intimations of Immortality*' contains an interesting observation. Recalling his childhood, he says: 'I was often unable to think of external things as having external existence, and I communed with all that I saw as something not apart from, but inherent in, my own immaterial nature. Many times while going to school have I grasped at a wall or tree to recall myself from this abyss of idealism to the reality.'[27] This attitude is different from Coleridge's in that Wordsworth has to save himself by reaffirming the physical existence of the outside world. For him, Nature is a reality,[28] whereas for Coleridge it was an unconscious form of the mind. The child's actions show clearly, however, the extent to which idealistic concepts threatened awareness of the physical world's independence.

Wordsworth's endorsement of the Aristotelian function of poetry is a logical consequence of this attitude:

> Aristotle, I have been told, has said, that Poetry is the most philosophic of all writing: it is so: its object is truth, not individual and local, but general, and operative . . . Poetry is the image of man and nature.[29] . . . the Poet . . . considers man and nature as essentially adapted to each other, and the mind of man as naturally the mirror of the fairest and most interesting properties of nature.[30]

Both Wordsworth and Coleridge use the image of the mirror, but whereas the latter sees the mind reflected in Nature, the former sees Nature reflected in the mind. For Wordsworth, Nature is independent and exemplary, and in poetry man and Nature adapt to one another, with Nature no longer meaning human nature, as it did in the eighteenth century. It now takes on divine attributes, whose imitation in art leads to a transformation of man. In her study of Romantic poetry, Powell stresses that 'Because the spirit of Nature is the divine spirit, Wordsworth cares about the common life of her several creatures.'[31] It is the poet's task to imitate Nature and so to restore the original forms of human conduct that Nature now teaches him.

Wordsworth, then, remains committed to the idea of mimesis, but his pantheism extends the concept of Nature prevalent in the eighteenth century. Indeed, the divinity of Nature, as he saw it, enabled him to imitate it more truly through art, in consequence of which he attacked the ideas of the Enlightenment as being *un*natural. And so at the beginning of the nineteenth century, art, still viewed as mimesis, itself determines the attributes of Nature, and the traditional concept of mimesis is extended by an individual idea of that which Nature is meant to be.

This attitude received its first powerful support from the pen of John Ruskin, whose concept of Nature was, in Townsend's words, 'a striking testimony of the dissemination of the ideas of the Lake School'.[32] Ruskin's links with Wordsworth are borne out by his view of Nature as being the model: 'For young artists nothing ought to be tolerated but simple bona fide imitation of nature.'[33] In *Modern Painters*, as Evans points out in her biography of Ruskin, the liveliness of Nature is starkly contrasted with the lifelessness of man.[34] This establishes a hierarchical relationship between man and Nature which forms the basis of Ruskin's aesthetics. In *Modern Painters* he demands the absolute authenticity of clouds, rocks, trees, etc.,[35] which at the time gave rise to the reproach that he expected the landscape painter to be botanist and geologist as well.[36] This attempt to explore the truth of natural phenomena, however, was no more a matter of science than was Wordsworth's:

> it is not possible for a Christian man to walk across so much as a rood of the natural earth, with mind unagitated and rightly poised, without receiving strength and hope from some stone, flower, leaf, or sound, nor without a sense of a dew falling upon him out of the sky . . . It seems to me that the real sources of bluntness in the feelings towards the splendour of the grass and glory of the flower, are less to be found in ardour of occupation, in seriousness of compassion, or heavenliness of desire, than in the turning of the eye at intervals of rest too selfishly within.[37]

Nature for Ruskin is a Christian revelation, and elsewhere he says that God is the soul of Nature.[38] Expressions like 'glory of the flower' underline this theological concept of the *liber creaturarum*, and so it is clear that man must look outwards at Nature, and the moment he begins to look inwards he will shut himself off from the divine. Thus the mimetic and individualistic concepts of art are poles apart for Ruskin. 'According to Ruskin's theory, art was the interpreter of nature, and unless the artist saw nature through the eyes of religion, he could not show the beneficence of God, and thus he could not attain to truth in his interpretation.'[39] He did not view imagination as a means of expressing what the artist saw or what lay hidden in himself. For him 'Imagination is a pilgrim on the earth – and her home is in heaven.'[40] Ruskin's theologically enhanced Nature gave new dignity to art as mimesis. He used the Aristotelian concept to link art to religion, and for him only the pious man was capable of great art.[41] He replaced Wordsworth's pantheism with Christian theology and evangelical fervour, making art into a moral phenomenon that reflected God's presence in the world. He and Wordsworth may have had the same starting-point, but their concepts of Nature varied considerably, and these variations take on their true significance when seen against the background of tradition. In the past, Nature had seemed to be something fixed, but now it is viewed ever more individually; consequently art as mimesis loses what for centuries had been its stable precondition.

Since the basis of art was already subject to different interpretations, it was inevitable that the concept of art should also change. Dante Gabriel Rossetti's tale 'Hand and Soul' is a vivid illustration of how art was to take on new functions. In their programme, the Pre-Raphaelites declared that art was an imitation of Nature,[42] but for Holman Hunt and Millais – who regarded Ruskin as their prophet[43] – Nature was no longer the *liber creaturarum*; it was, rather, identified with those qualities that had been made tangible during the history of painting. Rossetti's story starts from this premise, but moves on to a new orientation for the artist. The young painter Chiaro dell'Erma grows up among the old Florentine masters.[44] He strives 'from early boyhood towards the imitation of any objects offered in nature'.[45] He is soon himself a master in the imitation of Nature, and quickly outstrips the earlier masters.[46] His desire to equal or exceed them is a sign of the secret ambition that drives him on,[47] and whenever he hears of a greater artist, he endeavours to surpass him.[48] Imitation of Nature, then, is no longer an end in itself, but serves to advance the artist's personal glory. Thus Chiaro diverges from the original purpose of art as grasped, at least theoretically, by Ruskin and the Pre-Raphaelites. Within Chiaro there develops a dichotomy which cannot be resolved even by the fame he achieves.[49] There is an unbalanced relationship between his art and his ambition, and it is aggravated by 'a feeling of worship and service'[50] which drives him to paint. These were qualities which Ruskin demanded of the artist so that he should have the right attitude towards divine Nature and its moral forces, but Chiaro cannot orientate his feelings properly because Nature for him is only an object which he must copy in order to attain glory.

In his distress, Chiaro decides to set himself a new goal: 'From that moment Chiaro set a watch on his soul, and put his hand to no other works but only to such as had for their end the presentment of some moral greatness that should influence the beholder: and to this end, he multiplied abstractions, and forgot the beauty and passion of the world.'[51] He tries to rectify the false relationship between hand and soul by excluding the soul from his representation of objects, hoping in this way to endow his pictures with moral exemplariness. But the hand can only multiply abstractions, and art stiffens into mere technique which can grasp neither beauty nor passion. Thus the moral concept of art, which for Ruskin was the basis of all art, is equated by Rossetti with technique *sans* soul, *sans* beauty, *sans* passion. Chiaro's separation of hand and soul is to be fulfilled through a work of exemplary moral art – an allegory of peace, which is placed before the portal of the church. When the warring factions in the town meet in front of this picture, there is a bloody conflict, and the allegory of peace is stained with the blood.[52] Chiaro's efforts have failed, and he condemns himself as totally reprehensible.[53] Suddenly, in a dream, he has a vision of his own soul. He falls on his knees before this vision, which addresses him in biblical tones. He is overwhelmed with shame and sorrow that he has cut himself off from the demands of the soul.[54] Finally the apparition commands him: ' "Chiaro, servant of God, take now thine Art unto thee, and paint me thus, as I am, to know me: weak, as I am, and in the weeds of this time; only with eyes which seek out labour, and with a faith, not learned, yet jealous of prayer. Do this; so shall thy soul stand before thee always, and perplex thee no more".'[55]

Now Chiaro has found the true object of his art, and the hand enters into the service of the soul. Art ceases to represent natural phenomena or moral forces as Ruskin had demanded; instead it becomes the self-expression of what lies hidden within. It is only through this awareness that Chiaro's confusion is resolved and his art set in the right direction. The new function in turn affects the concept of mimesis, for the soul which is now to be represented has no exemplariness. It confesses that it is weak and dressed in the clothes of the transient world. Art as mimesis aimed to be an exemplary representation, but art as expression can only illustrate subjective experience. Rossetti's 'Hand and Soul' thus illuminates the process through which mimesis turned into expression.

At the end of his tale, Rossetti spotlights the loss of exemplariness suffered by art as self-expression. With a touch of irony he reports his observations when seeing the picture of Chiaro's soul during his stay in Florence in 1847.[56] The people looking at the painting produce a series of misunderstandings, owing to the fact that each of the beholders comes up with a different explanation both of it and of his fellows' interpretations. As each interpretation stems from a purely subjective viewpoint, there seems to be no common ground for assessing the significance of Chiaro's picture. Finally a Frenchman suggests that something which cannot be understood cannot have a meaning. Rossetti then remarks: 'My reader thinks possibly that the French student was right',[57] and this is the end of the story. It is clear from Rossetti's attitude, which can be extrapolated from the misunderstandings of the different observers, that art triggers multifarious responses. It ceases to set up moral and intellectual standards,[58] such as Ruskin had demanded, detaches itself from the hitherto all-important object, and instead makes itself subservient to subjectivity. This radical change within the conception of art has repercussions on its functions. As mimesis, art fulfilled itself by bestowing an exemplary status on the represented; as expression, art finds its meaning in the revelation of what lies submerged beneath the surface of the artist. The need for expression may turn into compulsion when the hidden life yearns for redemption.

II *AUTONOMOUS ART*

3 The starting-point

Scepticism

Literary debuts are often more than the chance beginnings of a new activity – frequently they contain a whole programme. A programme is not necessarily the same as a manifesto, and the more complex the problems to which the author addresses himself, the more cautious will his intentions be. In 1866 Pater published an essay on Coleridge. The one systematic thinker among nineteenth-century English poets intrigued Pater into systematising *his* thoughts. Pater sought to explain Coleridge's speculative thinking as a direct outcome of his personal dejection. Thus Coleridge's attempt at an all-embracing philosophical synthesis in itself held no further fascination for Pater; he conceived of it as no more than an answer to the modern situation, and it was the situation itself that attracted him.

The essay offers a sketch of the modern situation as Pater saw it:

> Modern thought is distinguished from ancient by its cultivation of the 'relative' spirit in place of the 'absolute'. Ancient philosophy sought to arrest every object in an eternal outline, to fix thought in a necessary formula, and the varieties of life in a classification by 'kinds', or *genera*. To the modern spirit nothing is, or can be rightly known, except relatively and under conditions.[1]

The relativity and conditionality of knowledge are not something negative, for through its awareness of them, the modern mind will be able constantly to observe[2] an abundance of phenomena which the absolute spirit would be forced to shut out. The absolute spirit reduces the world to a set of hierarchical categories, whereas the relative spirit registers an expansion of things and an obliteration of dividing lines. The flexibility and freedom of the relative from any preordained commitments offers a vastly wider range of connections than the absolute, which constantly imposes restrictive patterns on what is.

These introductory remarks of Pater's take on added significance as they provide guidelines for an interpretation of Coleridge. Pater intends to draw different conclusions from the very same situation to which Coleridge responded, and it seems as if Coleridge served Pater to substantiate his own assessment of the modern situation. For this reason he sees Coleridge's literary work as 'a disinterested struggle against the relative spirit . . . It was an effort, surely, an effort of sickly thought, that saddened his mind, and limited the operation of his unique poetic gift.'[3]

According to Pater, Coleridge was resisting the necessity of the relative, and his resistance manifested itself through his increasing dejection. Systematically encompassing the world of appearances in order to grasp the absolute[4] is for Pater self-violation, which even destroys genius. All Coleridge's intellectual efforts point to the fact that an all-embracing grasp of the world has become impossible, and from this Pater draws the following conclusion:

What the moralist asks is, Shall we gain or lose by surrendering human life to the relative spirit? Experience answers that the dominant tendency of life is to turn ascertained truth into a dead letter, to make us all the phlegmatic servants of routine. The relative spirit, by its constant dwelling on the more fugitive conditions or circumstances of things, breaking through a thousand rough and brutal classifications, and giving elasticity to inflexible principles, begets an intellectual *finesse* of which the ethical result is a delicate and tender justice in the criticism of human life.[5]

What Pater illuminated at the start of his Coleridge essay as opposing attitudes of mind revealed in history is now given an evaluation. The relative spirit is ranked above philosophical dogmatism because it grasps the dynamism and the associative multiplicity of experience. The absolute spirit cannot allow for this all-important flexibility of experience because it has to impose a rigid pattern of cognition upon it.

In counteracting such patterns, scepticism has a vital role to play – but it is scepticism in the old classical sense of 'spying out, investigating, searching, examining',[6] without the more modern attribute of resignation[7] which can only arise if scepticism is a response to human cognition viewed from the standpoint of faith. As Kierkegaard wrote, human finiteness could only be comprehended by way of 'infinite resignation'.[8] Pater's scepticism, however, is not conditioned by an all-exceeding faith – or at least not in his first essay – but is a reaction against a dogmatism that imposes a structure on the world. He dismisses the workings of the absolute spirit as 'routine', and to scepticism falls the task of rejecting all that is rigid and fixed. This task can only be performed through the vital driving force behind the relative spirit – namely, experience. The absolute spirit is orientated by the idea and therefore must conceal the many complexities and contradictions of the concrete experience; the relative spirit works through a revelational scepticism, which sets the pure appearance of things above any interpretation of those things, no matter how comprehensive it may be. Reality then is at best approached, not with a compulsive imposition of norms, but with a keen sense of observation, catching the multifariousness of its experiential nature.

Pater's form of scepticism is an active force whose dual effect is to counter the absolute spirit and to open up the mind to experience. It preserves experience from distortion by ideas and systems, and at the same time it keeps the mind actively aware of the complexity of reality, which for Pater is the sole source of the world of appearances. This is why he regards any normative explanation as merely a reification of experience. The brand of scepticism he advocates consists precisely in the ability to break through such reifications, thereby pushing aside the known and hitherto valid reality, and making way for one that is new. Pater would accept no all-embracing theory of life, for by definition such theories could only be reductions, ignoring the basic conditionality of reality. Unconditional reality could only be sought in experience itself and could only be defined in negative rather than in positive terms. It is that which is and not an interpretation of that which is, and therefore 'according to the scepticism, latent at least, in so much of our modern philosophy, the so-called real things themselves are nothing but *spectra* after all'.[9]

The sceptical, relative spirit, then, is a countervailing force,[10] subverting and undoing all frameworks set up by the filing system of the human mind. It releases the facts from their subservience to general principles to which they have been yoked by the absolute spirit. In undercutting all normative ordering, it highlights open-endedness as the hallmark of experience. The relative spirit is no longer committed to a cognition of reality, but mobilises the human mind to face up to an open future, so that it will follow the unpredictable road of experience as its sole route to knowledge. Whatever explanations are formed on the way must therefore be undone,[11] and Pater calls this lack of finality the 'salt of truth'.[12] His scepticism, it is true, depends on global explanations of the world, but only in so far as by rejecting these explanations it can open up access to the multifariousness of experience. Such an endeavour presupposes a keen sense of history and can only be pursued by someone deeply imbued in European culture, because the revelatory impact of the relative spirit takes on its proper functions when directed against the system-building efforts permeating the European past. It is the polemics against closed systems which throw the liberating impulse of the relative spirit into proper relief. Pater's scepticism is negative (rejecting the norms of the absolute spirit) and positive (bringing to light the undefined and undefinable). It is therefore no coincidence that a critical but entirely well-disposed study of Coleridge led Pater to a concrete formulation of his own ideas. In this encounter with English Literature's last speculative systematist, Pater proclaims his own originality.

The essay

The scepticism of Pater's first essay remained fundamental to all his writings. It also raised the problem of presentation, for he had to find a form that would capture the uncatchable nature of experience. His awareness of this problem is evident from his reflections on the differences between forms. The form that he needed was one that would have to run counter to the very purpose of form – removing the basic dissonances of experience.[13] For scepticism only searches for the possibilities of experience but does not try to mould them. Pater therefore needed, paradoxically, a form that could convey experience unformed:

> The poem, the treatise, the essay: you see already that these three methods of writing are no mere literary accidents, dependent on the personal choice of this or that particular writer, but necessities of literary form, determined directly by matter, as corresponding to three essentially different ways in which the human mind relates itself to truth. If oracular verse, stimulant but enigmatic, is the proper vehicle of enthusiastic intuitions; if the treatise, with its ambitious array of premiss and conclusion, is the natural out-put of scholastic all-sufficiency; so, the form of the essay . . . [is] . . . the literary form necessary to a mind for which truth itself is but a possibility, realisable not as general conclusion, but rather as the elusive effect of a particular personal experience; to a mind which, noting faithfully those random lights that meet it by the way, must needs content itself with suspension of judgment, at the end of the intellectual journey, to the very last asking: *Que scais-je?*[14]

For Pater the essay is a form that reflects the loss of totality and 'all-sufficiency', and in their place follows the unpredictability of real life. It captures the elaborate effects, possibilities and individual moods which mirror personal attitudes and experiences that defy comprehension through any overarching reference. The essay, typologically related to oracular verse and treatise as mythical and scholastic visions of the world, signifies an important change in man's consciousness, the manifestation of which demands its own particular form. Just as the relative spirit used the absolute in order to grasp its own otherness, the essay is for Pater the modern form that gains its shape against the background of earlier shapes to be discerned in the history of forms. In essence it reflects the mind on its journey, and registers its movements, meandering without destination. Truth pales into a possibility as the mind moves from random light to random light, and the form which captures this groping movement conveys the impression of endlessness within a finite world.

> The essay is the medium for a mode of writing that seeks to be not a result but a process, just like thought which here unfolds itself through writing. The special character of this particular type of thinking – scepticism – has found its ideal vehicle in the essay . . . As scepticism replaces an overall view with the vision of the individual, the flexible essay opens itself up to the sensual and the inner vision; it describes, narrates, articulates, and thus testifies to its capability of articulating truth more adequately and less imposingly than any discursive analysis is able to achieve.[15]

As the essay moves the welter of experience into focus, it shows realities in a constant and unending process of formation, which marks it off from the treatise as a form destined to present results:

The treatise, as the instrument of a dogmatic philosophy *begins* with an axiom or definition: the essay or dialogue, on the other hand, as the instrument of dialectic, does not necessarily so much as conclude in one; like that long dialogue with oneself, that dialectic process, which may be co-extensive with life. It does in truth little more than clear the ground, as we say, or the atmosphere, or the mental tablet, that one may have a fair chance of knowing, or seeing, perhaps: it does but put one into a duly receptive attitude towards such possible truth, discovery, or revelation, as may one day occupy the ground, the tablet, – shed itself on the purified air; it does not provide a proposition, nor a system of propositions, but forms a temper.[16]

The essay, then, is distinguished from the treatise not only historically, but also functionally. It holds open that which the treatise seeks to close, for truth *is* not – at best, it can only *become*. If this process of self-discovery is dialectic, this is not in the Hegelian sense of an integrating synthesis, but rather as a fanning-out of perspectives: 'in that long and complex dialogue of the mind with itself, many persons, so to speak, will necessarily take part; so many persons as there are possible contrasts or shades in the apprehension of some complex subject'.[17] Pater conceived of the dialectics operative in the essay as a matter of collecting impressions and sharpening observation; it was not a form for presenting systematically organised inferences. Thinking and inferring proceed associatively, for it is the associative establishment of connections that embraces the two vital poles of the essay: the randomness of experience and the subjectivity of perception. The individual perceiver directs his limited vision towards the limitless potential of the experience, and the essay brings to life the ever-changing area between the two. The essay is 'that characteristic literary type of our own time, a time so rich and various in special apprehensions of truth, so tentative and dubious in its sense of their *ensemble*, and issues'.[18] This gives rise to the essay as an open form, which is unique in so far as the other forms mentioned can only bear witness to what the essay is able to tackle head-on. In presenting intimate observations, inarticulate emotions, fleeting impressions and disjointed observations, the essay appears to be the form of formlessness, which makes it necessary for Pater to contrast it with the treatise as a paradigm of the closed form. The essay, then, is a form which deconstructs itself in order to represent open-endedness, unrelatedness and endlessness as facts of experiential reality. It is a half-way house between treatise and fiction; in registering the facts of life it has the same reference as the treatise; in making their interconnections ambivalent and opaque it approaches fiction. The essay is a discourse simultaneously renouncing a discursive tackling of its findings, thereby casting doubts on the efficacy of discursive thinking.

Defining human existence

Since scepticism undermines any attempt at an a priori definition of world and man, how did Pater formulate the relation between the two? His inquiring spirit was directed towards man's self-discovery through experience, but although his essays are full of observations about the problem, the relationship is most vividly brought to life through his fictional characters. The very fact that he did not confine himself to theoretical considerations shows the special nature of the problem.

The tension between man and experience is particularly apparent in the Imaginary Portrait 'Emerald Uthwart',[19] one of the tales in *Miscellaneous Studies*. Emerald's life is recounted in an extraordinary manner. At the very beginning we are told about his death.[20] This technique of anticipating important moments is carried on right through the story. For example, when Emerald eagerly goes to war – he had regarded the soldier's life as his ideal – we are immediately told of his failure, and only afterwards do we learn of the reasons for this.[21] By presenting conclusions first, Pater prevents any tension as regards outcome, and instead directs his reader's attention to the forces that resulted in that outcome. There is no linear time development, but instead – to use Lugowski's terms – a concentration on 'how' rather than 'whether',[22] epitomising the tension of the epic, in which the outcome is always present throughout the story. The narrative therefore remains static, for the interest lies not in any progress but in the basic forms of human life.

This technique is reinforced by another narrative trick: the turning-points are not recounted directly by the author. The military tribunal[23] and Emerald's death[24] are reported by means of diaries, the writers of which play no part in the events themselves. Thus Emerald's involvement in the various actions is neutralised by these distant reporters, so that attention is never allowed to stray from the all-important question of 'how'.

The suppression of temporal tension and dampening down of action enable Pater to bring his basic interest to the fore: man's relation to the world, as it can be perceived prior to any distortion caused by time and action. In this respect the 'portrait' of Emerald Uthwart leads to significant disclosures. When he goes to King's School, Canterbury, in the shadow of the great cathedral, we read:

> Here, from morning to night, everything seems challenged to follow the upward lead of its long, bold, 'perpendicular' lines. The very place one is in, its stone-work, its empty spaces, invade you; invade all who belong to them, as Uthwart belongs, yielding wholly from the first; seem to question you masterfully as to your purpose in being here at all, amid the great memories of the past, of this school; – challenge you, so to speak, to make moral philosophy one of your acquirements, if you can, and to systematise your vagrant self . . . In Uthwart, then, is the plain tablet, for the influences of place to inscribe.[25]

Pater's desire to generalise rather than particularise the definition is shown by the different levels of address, as Uthwart recedes behind 'one' and 'you'. Pater sees man empirically as a *tabula rasa* for experience to make its marks upon. It is a vital function of scepticism to protect man from all idealising distortions, and so man is no longer set above reality but is placed in association with it. Reality is the situation of experience in which man finds himself, and however varied the experiences may be, they have one thing in common: man sees them as a continual challenge. Thus reality has a strange dual aspect: on the one hand it fashions him by writing on the 'white paper'[26] and by thus showing him his ability to change in accordance with the arrival and disappearance of new situations; on the other hand, the now apparently defined man will feel reality as a ceaseless challenge demanding answers from him. The relation of man to reality is therefore dialectic, for the forming nature of reality is not purely defining but also challenging. The answers to the challenge are in themselves problematic, since for Pater the self is no longer a substance in the way Hegel, Coleridge or Shelley saw it; it merely embodies a *tabula rasa* that can only be given form by a challenging reality.

Emerald initially reacts to the problem by being overwhelmed and incapable of any answer: 'If at home there had been nothing great, here, to boyish sense, one seems diminished to nothing at all, amid the grand waves, wave upon wave, of patiently-wrought stone.'[27] But this boyish sense, almost completely bewildered by the mighty impressions made on it, must still somehow find an answer to the challenge, and this answer is: 'Submissiveness! – It had the force of genius with Emerald Uthwart.'[28] Accepting the given and giving way to what is expected – this becomes the basis of Emerald's conduct. He sees himself increasingly absorbed 'into the world of peremptory facts',[29] and responds by being submissive.[30] Only once does he follow a spontaneous whim – in the heat of war he refuses to obey, and this event leads him to disaster.

Pater has prepared the way for this dramatic switch. He points out directly that such submissiveness cannot encompass the whole person. Of the discipline Emerald submits to in his schooldays, we learn: 'He found himself in a system of fixed rules, amid which, it might be, some of his own tendencies and inclinations would die out of him through disuse.'[31] This explicit indication is illustrated by the characterisation of Emerald all through the 'portrait'. His unconditional acceptance prevents all self-reflection – he remains totally unaware of his own personality, predilections and indeed existence. What he is is only known to us through the observations of people around him – either in diaries or in relation to friends and fellow pupils at the school. The fact that he can be identified only through such observations shows what little direct contact he has with a challenging reality, and indeed the technique of characterisation is at pains to remove the tension of any such contact. Even his liking for the army, his final choice of career, is not narrated but indirectly mirrored from a position outside himself.[32] The lack of conflict inevitably gives his submissiveness 'the force of genius', which leads ultimately to catastrophe when apparently forgotten inclinations spontaneously rise to the surface and, as it were, short-circuit his conduct. One is forced to conclude from the structure of the tale that Pater does not regard his hero's relation to the world as finalised. It was, of course, a possibility inherent in the fact that man is a *tabula rasa* and is therefore open to a reality which will determine him. But the challenging nature of that reality also denotes that man's relations to the world are not deterministic, for anyone who sees them as such can only submit to reality. By submitting, he must suppress those elements of himself that could respond to the challenge, and so if man were to be totally determined by his environment, he would lose that ability to reflect which might make it possible for him to survive the perils of experience.

With scepticism in the background, we cannot expect any final definitions, but by examining the problem from different angles we can extrapolate certain tendencies that make Pater's basic position clearer. His tale 'The Child in the House', for instance, goes even more deeply into the interrelationship between man and world. Florian Deleal searches nostalgically in his childhood memories for those things that were important to him 'in that process of brain-building by which we are, each one of us, what we are'.[33] He, too, opens himself up completely to the impressions of his immediate environment – the quiet old house and the resplendent garden – and he notes in wonderment: 'How indelibly, as we afterwards discover, they affect us; with what capricious attractions and associations they figure themselves on the white paper, the smooth wax, of our ingenuous souls.'[34] The indelible impressions, then, are not mere copies of the reality, but are extended by the 'capricious attractions and associations', the linking of which defies explanation. There is clearly a process of transformation that takes place in between the reality and the soul, 'and the early habitation thus gradually becomes a sort of material shrine or sanctuary of sentiment; a system of visible symbolism interweaves itself through all our thoughts and passions'.[35]

Experience ceases to determine man, but instead arouses feelings that are not inherent in experience itself. Increasingly Florian discovers a strange relationship with the outside world which is reflected by an intensification of his inner world as he becomes conscious of the changes undergone by what is experienced: 'Also then, for the first time, he seemed to experience a passionateness in his relation to fair outward objects, an inexplicable excitement in their presence, which disturbed him, and from which he half longed to be free.'[36] Thus experience leads to the discovery of strange, hitherto unfelt emotions. He resists experience, which sometimes amounts to a 'tyranny of the senses over him'[37] and places an intolerable burden on his sensitivity. Evidently there are emotions in man that have no equivalent in experience, which therefore have the effect of confusing, tyrannising and ultimately arousing the desire for escape. He tries to select only those elements of experience that suit him, but even then he must remain subject to the unpredictable forces of chance,[38] which sow insecurity into human life.

> And he remembered gratefully how the Christian religion, hardly less than the religion of the ancient Greeks, translating so much of its spiritual verity into things that may be seen, condescends in part to sanction this infirmity, if so it be, of our human existence, wherein the world of sense is so much with us, and welcomed this thought as a kind of keeper and sentinel over his soul therein.[39]

The sanctioning power of religion offers a kind of idealisation of experience, and this idealisation of a world to which he feels himself inescapably tied appears to be necessary if the palpable imbalance between world and man is to be evened out.

> His way of conceiving religion came then to be in effect what it ever afterwards remained – a sacred history indeed, but still more a sacred ideal, a transcendent version or representation, under intenser and more expressive light and shade, of human life and its familiar or exceptional incidents, birth, death, marriage, youth, age, tears, joy, rest, sleep, waking – a mirror, towards which men might turn away their eyes from vanity and dullness, and see themselves therein as angels, with their daily meat and drink, even, become a kind of sacred transaction – a complementary strain or burden, applied to our every-day existence, whereby the stray snatches of music in it re-set themselves, and fall into the scheme of some higher and more consistent harmony . . . Some ideal, hieratic persons he would always need . . . And he could hardly understand those who felt no such need at all, finding themselves quite happy without such heavenly companionship, and sacred double of their life, beside them. Thus a constant substitution of the typical for the actual took place in his thoughts.[40]

This last stage of 'brain-building' brings out the burdensome aspect of experience, whose fragile insecurity is countered by the solid system provided by religion. For Florian the actual is replaced by the typical because only the ideal continuity of the typical can make reality bearable.

In this respect there are fairly substantial differences between Pater and the anthropologically orientated philosophy of the nineteenth century as represented, for instance, by Feuerbach. Feuerbach conceived the typical as man's projection of his actual need.[41] He thus undermined the very substance of religion, whereas Pater in the 'portrait' of Florian Deleal attempts to idealise reality through a religious elevation of experience. Unlike Feuerbach, he does not wish to confirm or ordain the sovereignty of man;

he wishes only to balance out the evident discrepancy in the relations between man and world. If man, who is shaped by experience, needs the idealising effect of religion, it is evident that self and reality are in total disharmony, and Pater therefore senses a longing that cannot be satisfied by experience and that drives the self beyond the limitations of the given world.[42]

The two imaginary portraits of 'Emerald Uthwart' and 'The Child in the House' represent man's spiritual development, and the slow formation of these characters is permeated by a reflection of Pater's own personal experience.[43] Pater did not include them in the volume *Imaginary Portraits*, for even though their lay-out is similar, thematically they are different: these two characters never come to grips with their respective worlds, whereas in *Imaginary Portraits* this is the prime concern of the characters portrayed. Emerald and Florian highlight only the way in which experience imprints itself on their receptive minds, and they convey their feelings of what happens while they are being shaped by a world outside themselves. Emerald submits himself to reality, thus revealing its challenging nature and his own inability to respond properly to the challenge. Florian selects what he likes best from the passing pageant of experience, but he too becomes aware of an indefinable and inexorable imbalance which he seeks to remove through an idealisation that goes beyond and is not derived from experience.

These reactions of submission or idealisation show that man's dependence on experience creates fundamental gaps, though these can only be perceived as it were negatively. The incompatibility of man and world turns out to be a dynamic force in so far as man is constantly set at odds with the world by way of the experiences that shape him, and he must therefore be at odds with those experiences themselves; this discrepancy brings out not only the fragility of the man–world relationship, but also the constant necessity to counteract that fragility.

Expression

'It is of such diagonal influences, through complication of influence, that expression comes, in life, in our culture, in the very faces of men and boys.'[44] Although Pater is talking here about traditional English education, what he has in mind is a contradiction that is sublimated into expression. By transplanting the discrepancies of everyday appearance into another setting, expression reconciles contradiction, and in the realm of art, the irreconcilable is, so to speak, outplayed. 'What mankind, pressed on all sides by the boundaries of his purely terrestrial life, in fact requires is that region of more essential reality, in which every opposition and contradiction is overcome, and freedom can finally claim to be wholly at peace with itself.'[45] This for Hegel is the 'position of art relatively to finite reality'. Pater's starting-point is similar to Hegel's[46] in so far as real-life oppositions demand resolution, whose 'more essential reality' is to be found in expression. Expression becomes freedom because it enables the challenge of reality to be met. The reconciliation of opposites takes place in art, for scepticism prevents it from taking place in thought, although the discrepancies constantly demand sublimation.

What quality does Pater find in expression that enables it to achieve such a balancing out?

The essence of all artistic beauty is expression, which cannot be where there's really nothing to be expressed; the line, the colour, the word, following obediently, and with minute scruple, the conscious motions of a convinced intelligible soul. To make men interested in themselves, as being the very ground of all reality for them, *la vraie vérité*, as the French say: – that was the essential function of the Socratic method: to flash light into the house within, its many chambers, its memories and associations, upon its inscribed and pictured walls.[47]

For Pater expression plays a central role because it arises from man's inner world, his soul. This inner world, however, has no substance of its own, no given character – on the contrary, the 'inscribed and pictured walls' indicate the fact that its nature is formed by experience. The Socratic light flashing within results in a self-illumination of the mind that will enable man to fashion multifarious experience into ideas. Here, all the elements discussed so far begin to interlink. Being shaped by the workings of experience is only part of a process whose culmination is the aesthetic composition of that experience. Only through the transformations wrought by the inner world and through their translation into expression can the indiscriminate workings of the outer world be pinned down.

It is the object of art, on its more noble plane, to give external shape to the inward content of Spirit. This content we discover in the conscious life of men realized in the world. As such it possesses – we include with it our conscious human experience generally – an external semblance directly presented in and through which it finds expression.[48]

Expression, then, is a continual objectification of inwardness, which in turn subjectifies neutral experience into a form which will at least modify, but more often actually change, the experience. Thus expression reflects reality but at the same time cancels its basic law of inconsistency.

The art of Luca della Robbia exemplifies for Pater the outcome of this struggle for expression. His sculptures

bear the impress of a personal quality, a profound expressiveness, what the French call *intimité*, by which is meant some subtler sense of originality – the seal on a man's work of what is most inward and peculiar in his moods, and manner of apprehension: it is what we call *expression*, carried to its highest intensity of degree.[49]

Here expression has become almost a counter-movement, for Pater sees it as a relentless subjective invasion of the typical and the general. It is the unique and unmistakable seal of inwardness, manifesting itself simultaneously in a triumphant gesture.

Once more it is Pater's fictional characters that give concrete form to the ideas he expounds theoretically. In his one completed novel, *Marius the Epicurean*, the struggle for expression is embodied in Marius's friend Flavian, who shows him the way to the world of imagination. In the chapter evocatively entitled 'Euphuism', Pater reveals the hidden driving-force of expression:

The secrets of utterance, of expression itself, of that through which alone any intellectual or spiritual power within one can actually take effect upon others, to overawe or charm them to one's side, presented themselves to this ambitious lad in immediate connexion with that desire for predominance, for the satisfaction of which another might have relied on the acquisition and display of brilliant military qualities. In him, a fine instinctive sentiment of the exact value and power of words was connate with the eager longing for sway over his fellows.[50]

For Pater expression means self-expression, but the aim is not self-revelation so much as influence on the outer world,[51] and the achievement of power. Flavian wishes to impose his inner world onto the outer world and so subjugate it through the power of expression.

This new dimension of expression can only be fully appreciated if one recalls that throughout the eighteenth and early nineteenth centuries, right up to Ruskin, no distinction was made between expression and communication. Ruskin saw no aesthetic difference between them:

In his earlier period it is the representative character of painting which appeals to him – though his glorification of Nature and God often carries him away with evangelical fervor into a half-expressionistic attitude. In his middle years, society held his interest; the social function of art was to express the noble feelings of great personalities. Yet even here, art is still conceived as the conveyer of truth, moral and factual. Thus, in both periods, art is a language the purpose of which is to communicate truth of appearance and the nature of which is an expression of 'moral emotion' or personality . . . communication and expression were complementary ends.[52]

Expression always has the character of communication when it relates to a given reality, for what it illustrates is a world accessible to all. So long as there are shared thought and social systems, it will represent something that arises from a common and all-embracing basis. And so long as expression is equated with communication, the artist can do no more than modify existing reality, and cannot make himself the object of representation.[53] The moment he begins to express himself, the communicative aspect of expression will be eclipsed. This was what underlay Dante Gabriel Rossetti's new concept of self-expression as the one and only precept of art. The ironic twist at the end of 'Hand and Soul' has Chiaro's picture of his own soul defying the comprehension of the on-lookers.[54] Expression here has ceased to communicate, and instead turns into a manifestation of a self-experience that tends to become hermetic. Communication gives way to mystification, and Rossetti leaves no doubt that mystifying expression is to be the polemic counterpart to the mimetic concept of art.

Pater's 'secrets of utterance' also spring from impenetrable inwardness, but unlike Rossetti he is not content merely to confirm expression's loss of its communicative function; he also tries to endow self-expression with a new and concrete force as a means of exercising impact and achieving mastery. When there is no common and binding order of things, expression no longer communicates a specific and graspable vision, but instead becomes compellingly active, replacing comprehension with subjugation.

Pater's demand for self-expression is not to be confused with the Croce and Collingwood concept of expression as central intuition.[55] Croce's view of artistic expression is tightly bound to the time-honoured conception of the artist as creator.[56] For Pater, however, the inwardness that is objectified by expression still remains linked to experience. What is expressed is experience transformed by the alchemy of subjectivity, and not inspiration preceding experience. This comes out especially clearly in Flavian's quest for power. Reality in the Pater concept has a central importance in so far as it is to be changed by expression, with inwardness seeking to establish superiority over the 'burdensome character' of experience. This effort can only be properly objectified through the impact exercised. Expression implies correction of the world, and it will only reproduce those parts of experience that accord not with the patterns of outside reality but with the secret wishes of the expresser.

The inner world whose walls are inscribed by experience finds freedom through expression: 'It is in aesthetic expression that we discover imagination as a means to genuine and meaningful freedom, understandable in terms both of choice and originality.'[57] In the great art of the Renaissance, Pater saw expression as originality, but for himself the freedom became actual through selection from the passing pageant of experience. The idea of expression as potential power implies a desire to give binding form to an inner world that draws its life from experience and yet at the same time transcends it, and this form is to stand level with, if not above, the real world.

The submissiveness and idealisation depicted in 'Emerald Uthwart' and 'The Child in the House' bring out the fact that, for all its dependence on the world of experience, the inner world can never be totally equated with what is. Expression opens up a region that transcends the given and proclaims the freedom of the individual. This freedom can only come about by way of art, for, as Pater's scepticism shows most clearly, the gap between man and world cannot be bridged by ideas.

4 Defining art

'Art for art's sake'[1]

Since scepticism prevents the individual's experience from ever cohering into an overarching pattern, the question arises as to what form experience actually had for Pater. Only if we can answer this question will we be able to grasp the basis of the imbalance between man and world. In his 'Conclusion' to *The Renaissance*, Pater outlines the situation. Human life, he says, both physical and spiritual, is woven together in a ceaseless movement of experience:

> if we begin with the inward world of thought and feeling, the whirlpool is still more rapid, the flame more eager and devouring . . . At first sight experience seems to bury us under a flood of external objects, pressing upon us with a sharp and importunate reality, calling us out of ourselves in a thousand forms of action.[2]

This flood of experience naturally demands a response.

> But when reflexion begins to play upon those objects they are dissipated under its influence; the cohesive force seems suspended like some trick of magic; each object is loosed into a group of impressions – colour, odour, texture – in the mind of the observer.[3]

Individual experiences, then, do not range themselves into some universal order,[4] but they remain amorphous. The only thing that limits the flood of experiences is the fact that they are perceived only as impressions.

> And if we continue to dwell in thought on this world, not of objects in the solidity with which language invests them, but of impressions, unstable, flickering, inconsistent, which burn and are extinguished with our consciousness of them, it contracts still further: the whole scope of observation is dwarfed into the narrow chamber of the individual mind.[5]

The world of experience therefore depends on the individual mind for its reality, since the impressions that it makes will vary from one observer to the next.

> Analysis goes a step farther still, and assures us that those impressions of the individual mind to which, for each one of us, experience dwindles down, are in perpetual flight; that each of them is limited by time, and that as time is infinitely divisible, each of them is infinitely divisible also; all that is actual in it being a single

moment, gone while we try to apprehend it, of which it may ever be more truly said that it has ceased to be than that it is.[6]

If time is the all-pervading quality of these fleeting impressions, reality, then, can only be conceived as pure temporality, which defines itself by an increasing acceleration of change. All perceptions turn into an endless series of moments which can never be pinned down to any consequential sequence as they are imbued with an uncontrollable temporality. Hence 'not the fruit of experience, but experience itself is the end'.[7] It is only through the onward movement that our inner world can be enriched with the precious momentary impressions of experience that come and swiftly go.

The transitoriness of these moments makes us increasingly conscious of the shortness of our lives. Time as a negative factor now takes on an overriding significance, providing common ground between man and his experience, and through its own infinity driving home to him his all too finite nature.

Well! we are all *condamnés* . . . we are all under sentence of death but with a sort of indefinite reprieve . . . we have an interval, and then our place knows us no more. Some spend this interval in listlessness, some in high passions, the wisest, at least among 'the children of this world', in art and song. For our one chance lies in expanding that interval, in getting as many pulsations as possible into the given time. Great passions may give us this quickened sense of life, ecstasy and sorrow of love, the various forms of enthusiastic activity, disinterested or otherwise . . . Only be sure it is passion – that it does yield you this fruit of a quickened, multiplied consciousness. Of such wisdom, the poetic passion, the desire of beauty, the love of art for its own sake, has most. For art comes to you proposing frankly to give nothing but the highest quality to your moments as they pass, and simply for those moments' sake.[8]

Only passions – preferably those aroused by art – can momentarily cover the pain of finiteness by capturing the intensity of the passing moment.

Pater's aesthetic creed finds its ideal manifestation in the school of Giorgione:

Such ideal instants the school of Giorgione selects, with its admirable tact, from that feverish, tumultuously coloured world of the old citizens of Venice – exquisite pauses in time, in which, arrested thus, we seem to be spectators of all the fulness of existence, and which are like some consummate extract or quintessence of life.[9]

Art composes experience anew, giving it a density that enables us to forget the otherwise destructive dimension of time.

Every phenomenon conveyed through the senses points to a becoming, a movement into itself (change) . . . Imposing 'order' on a movement – of whatever sort, whether it be of body, colour, sound – will mean, however, removing it from its 'natural' context, setting it within a human pattern, and so preventing it from fading into featurelessness.[10]

The observer can only snatch impressions of things as they pass, while art seizes these impressions and transplants them into a new context of heightened life. For Pater the transplanting and the heightening are two vital functions of art, which can thereby transcend the fleeting experience and offer its devotee a feeling of detachment from the ravages of time.

Pater's concept of *l'art pour l'art* differs subtly from that of Gautier,[11] for he does not see his hypostatised art as a protest against a specific sociological reality; for him, art is not an attitude towards a given outside world, it is a heightening, an intensification of reality. *L'art pour l'art* is a transformation of human experience into a 'fulness of existence', and while Gautier demanded a total separation of art from life, Pater saw the one as a 'consummate extract' of the other. T. S. Eliot seized on this difference between Pater and the Frenchman,[12] and called Pater's concept a moral theory.[13] There are substantial grounds for this in the precepts Pater laid down in *The Renaissance*:

> To burn always with this hard, gemlike flame, to maintain this ecstasy, is success in life. In a sense it might even be said that our failure is to form habits . . . Not to discriminate every moment some passionate attitude in those about us, and in the very brilliancy of their gifts some tragic dividing of forces on their ways, is, on this short day of frost and sun, to sleep before evening. With this sense of the splendour of our experience and of its awful brevity, gathering all we are into one desperate effort to see and touch, we shall hardly have time to make theories about the things we see and touch. What we have to do is to be for ever curiously testing new opinions and courting new impressions, never acquiescing in a facile orthodoxy of Comte, or of Hegel, or of our own. Philosophical theories or ideas, as points of view, instruments of criticism, may help us to gather up what might otherwise pass unregarded by us.[14]

Art, then, is conceived as the countervailing power to the temporality of human existence. Its basic definitions are given in negative terms owing to the fact that time and death are its frames of reference. Yet to transmute the fugitive moment into enraptured ecstasy makes art the ultimate value of human existence. Art therefore is hypostatised, and the slogan of 'art for its own sake' is meant to indicate that it is not subservient to any overriding reality. On the contrary, by constantly selecting from the pageant of experience the precious, the incomparable and the inimitable, it endows human existence with a seeming perfection which in reality it lacks. If temporal experience is transformed into aesthetic, all philosophical concepts and notions have to be rejected, because they eclipse the uniqueness inherent in each individual phenomenon. The only ideas tolerated are those that help us to be ecstatic and allow us forever to be open to new experiences. This aesthetic way of life is dependent on what emerges in the constant flux of time, and to shut oneself off from the workings of chance is to shut oneself off from life itself. Thus the aesthetic attitude is opposed to any notion of a finalised reality – it thrives on possibilities.[15]

Time, then, is experienced as infinite possibility, and art, by weaving together the strands of the extraordinary, appears to overcome the contingency of time. It idealises secular life and therefore contains its own criteria within itself. It

> rips the object of its contemplation out of the flowing stream of the world and holds it out in isolation. And this one thing, which was a tiny disappearing part of that stream, now through art becomes a representative of the whole, an equivalent of the infinite plenty in time and space; and so that is how art keeps it – halting the wheel of time.[16]

Thus art is 'fulfilment everywhere'.[17]

Owing to the intricate relationship between art and time, time itself imparts something of its endlessness to art. In constantly selecting precious and extraordinary moments, surfacing in the flux of time, art creates a haven resembling an earthly paradise. Thus real life becomes aesthetic life, and real conduct becomes aesthetic conduct to the degree in which autonomous art functions as an escape from the melancholy of human finiteness.

Autonomous art, then, was not conceived as a form of protest by Pater. Nevertheless, it does represent a detachment from and a contradiction to man's ordinary modes of existence, and these negative qualities are integral to a definition of art in the Paterian sense. What remains difficult is to reach a definition in positive terms. As a consummate reality, art embraces the infinity of the possible, and as a world complete in itself, it provides its own basis for meaningful existence – but infinite possibility and meaningful existence in relation to autonomous art are expressions that defy positive definition. In discussing a late-nineteenth-century anthology of verse, Sternberger summed up very vividly the emotions vibrating behind the propagation of hypostatised art:

> These rambling, errant and sensitive nerves, these senses, which ceaselessly grope for and follow contours and consistencies – cool and 'heartless' gems, metals, the velvety or taut or thin and translucent skin of the female body – they search as if with a wishing wand for the hidden sources of a life that must be lived and perhaps also must be patterned on the far side of inherited conventions.[18]

But what is this hidden life? And what is the frame of reference for an art that is meant to counter ordinary modes of existence? Benjamin sums up an all-important nineteenth-century answer: 'Art that begins to doubt its task and ceases to be "inséparable de l'utilité" (Baudelaire) must make the new into its highest value.'[19] Newness becomes the goal of all aesthetic striving.

> The basis of all artistic genius lies in the power of conceiving humanity in a new and striking way, of putting a happy world of its own creation in place of the meaner world of our common days, generating around itself an atmosphere with a novel power of refraction, selecting, transforming, recombining the images it transmits, according to the choice of the imaginative intellect.[20]

It is impossible to say in what direction the selecting, transforming and recombining is to proceed, and so Pater uses history to illustrate his meaning. Not least for this reason the Renaissance becomes for him one of the most illuminating periods in history, marked by 'the divination of fresh sources . . . new experiences, new subjects of poetry, new forms of art'.[21] 'Perhaps the utmost one could get by conscious effort, in the way of a reaction or return to the conditions of an earlier or fresher age, would be but *novitas*.'[22] Against the background of history, the new becomes concrete through its otherness, constantly exceeding the given, and this is precisely what Pater demands of art. Hypostatised art cannot be defined by norms if it is to retain its autonomy, and thus it is epitomised by newness as otherness. History for Pater bears out this conception; in its incessant drive for change, the constant emergence of otherness is never subjected to any unifying norm. What is new is what is different, and it arises as a potential from traditions and conventions that have lost their validity. Freed from the binding force of such conventions, art can give access to territories hitherto concealed by them, and so at one and the same time the new means freedom from the old and also the uncovering of the extraordinary in what has so far been taken for granted.

> It was only decadence (a European process) that made . . . the smouldering fire burst into flames: one would have to call it a revolution of the senses, if senses could have a revolution. At all events, in this sudden upheaval of all the nerves discoveries were made, and in that respect this 'decadent' art was not so much an ending or running-down as a beginning.[23]

If art is now to be conceived as a search for the new, clearly it can no longer be defined by the classic norm of mimesis. John Ruskin was the last great champion of mimesis: 'as I have already so often repeated, all beautiful works of art must either intentionally imitate or accidentally resemble natural forms'.[24] For Ruskin, Nature is the *liber creaturarum*. 'And so it is with external nature: she has a body and a soul like man; but her soul is the *Deity*.'[25] Townsend sums up Ruskin's aesthetics as follows: 'Scripture is one manifestation of God, and the preacher expounds it; nature is another manifestation of God, and the artist expounds it.'[26] For Ruskin, the task of art was to seek out and depict the presence of God in Nature, and for this complex process he constructed a tangled and at times rather quaint system. Pater was not only opposed to all such systems, but he also rejected the exclusively theological concept of art. For him, art had no fixed place in the hierarchy of a fixed world order, and its function was not to imitate but to extract experiences and impressions from the flow of time. Ruskin's Nature was conceived as a manifestation of the divine creator, and this concept needed ideas to define the business of art as mimesis. But ideas are helpless in the 'whirlpool' of time, and so art for Pater can no longer be pinned down as mimesis, breaks free from its traditional shackles and proclaims itself to be an end in itself.

Pater's acute awareness of this development is to be found at the beginning of his essay on Mérimée:

> Art: the passions, above all, the ecstasy and sorrow of love: a purely empirical knowledge of nature and man: these still remained, at least for pastime, in a world of which it was no longer proposed to calculate the remoter issues: – art, passion, science, however, in a somewhat novel attitude towards the practical interests of life.

For nineteenth-century man has been cut off from the old traditional hopes that guaranteed order and stability, and so his relationship to reality, hitherto taken for granted, now seems to have crumbled.

> Deprived of that exhilarating yet pacific outlook, imprisoned now in the narrow cell of its own subjective experience, the action of a powerful nature will be intense, but exclusive and peculiar. It will come to art . . . to the experience of life itself, not as to portions of human nature's daily food, but as to something that must be . . . exceptional; almost as men turn in despair to gambling or narcotics, and in a little while the narcotic, the game of chance or skill, is valued for its own sake. The vocation of the artist, of the student of life or books, will be realised with something – say! of fanaticism, as an end in itself, unrelated, unassociated. The science it turns to will be a science of crudest fact; the passion extravagant, a passionate love of passion . . . the art exaggerated, in matter or form, or both.[27]

With the real world now orderless, interest[28] can only be held by the unusual, and by the stimulating effect of things.[29] If art were to be seen as mimetic, at best it could only convey the senselessness of this world, but this would run counter to Pater's view of the healing effect of art. And so instead of imitating a given world, art defamiliarises in order to arouse new interest. Defamiliarisation entails abstraction from the given, to such an extent that in the work of art the imagination triumphs over the compulsion exercised by reality. While Ruskin believes that the artist attains piety[30] by imitating nature, Pater hopes that the dejected self exposed to the demands of pedestrian reality will be stimulated to a new freedom[31] by restructuring the given:

> What modern art has to do in the service of culture is so to rearrange the details of modern life, so to reflect it, that it may satisfy the spirit. And what does the spirit need in the face of modern life? The sense of freedom.[32]

Art for Ruskin is praise of the eternal divine order;[33] for Pater it is freedom within the framework of temporal experience. Mimetic art seeks to grasp the significance of the given, whereas autonomous art seeks out the new, whose essence is otherness. Consequently this concept of art was anathema to Ruskin:

> it is to be remembered that the love of change is a weakness and imperfection of our nature . . . it will be found that they are the weakest-minded and the hardest-hearted men that most love variety and change . . . the hardest-hearted men are those that least feel the endearing and binding power of custom, and hold on by no cords of affection to any shore, but drive with the waves that cast up mire and dirt.[34]

Ruskin rails against the 'aesthetic cliques of London',[35] and so by implication against the concept outlined by Pater in the 'Conclusion' to *The Renaissance*.[36] Here custom has lost its binding power, since autonomous art rejects the fundamental norms of classical aesthetics, according to which art had to represent the constituent forms of Nature and the ideals of the respective culture.[37] However, when temporality has become the be-all of human existence, all cultural ideals pale into insignificance. Temporality highlights the flux of time: what has been is gone, what is to come is not here yet, and what is here constantly disappears. Thus temporality is the hallmark of life's deficiencies, which instead of being imitated have to be transcended. The difference between life and its representation in art is that art overcomes destiny: 'l'art est un antidestin'.[38] It is related, not to God but to life, whose basic quality for Pater is that it is a motion towards death.

It follows, then, that *l'art pour l'art* means the triumph of art over reality. The aim is not imitation but transformation of life, and the aim of this in turn is not to present the ideal but to relieve man of the burden of his finiteness. Art is not a translation of the world, as Ruskin believed, but a treatment of it.

> That the end of life is not action but contemplation – *being* as distinct from *doing* – a certain disposition of mind: is, in some shape or other, the principle of all the higher morality. In poetry, in art, if you enter in their true spirit at all, you touch this principle, in a measure: these, by their very sterility, are a type of beholding for the mere joy of beholding. To treat life in the spirit of art, is to make life a thing in which means and ends are identified: to encourage such treatment, the true moral significance of art and poetry.[39]

Art removes the 'end' from life, in both senses, and by dispensing with all teleology it not only relieves the burden of finiteness, but also liberates those elements of life that would otherwise be only 'means' to the end. Their loss of direction enables them to gain a multitude of possible new directions, and the contemplation of these is a 'higher morality' for Pater in that their sterility allows the beholder to forget the transitoriness of time and life. The beholder is released from activity and may bask in aesthetic quietism. Thus art becomes a kind of privileged world to which are devoted 'the wisest, at least among "the children of this world" '.[40]

Impressionism

We have so far discussed what might be called the programme of autonomous art, but now the question arises as to what are its qualities. These must be such as to lend concrete form to the abstract idea of the new. Pater's 'Conclusion' designates impression as the ultimate point of contact between man and world, and so clearly impression must be a highly significant factor, but it is one that cannot be defined with any degree of precision. It is not identical to experience, for it only registers the impact of experience, but this fact in itself entails a principle of selection which is in no way inherent in the thing experienced. On the other hand, impression is in no way pure imagination, for it depends at least partly on elements that are outside the imagination. Impression, then, is a mixture of subjective perception with objective perceptibility. One might say that the imagination is the frame into which experience puts the picture, for it is the subject that holds the picture, but what is held will depend on the contingency of experience. The problem of distinguishing the one from the other is raised in Pater's 'Preface' to *The Renaissance*.

> Our education becomes complete in proportion as our susceptibility to these impressions increases in depth and variety. And the function of the aesthetic critic is to distinguish, to analyse, and separate from its adjuncts, the virtue by which a picture, a landscape, a fair personality in life or in a book, produces this special impression of beauty for pleasure, to indicate what the source of that impression is, and under what conditions it is experienced. His end is reached when he has disengaged that virtue, and noted it as a chemist notes some natural element, for himself and others.[41]

Pater strives to break down impressions into their constituents, and the scientific image indicates his intention to pin down the 'power' that underlies the interaction between subject and experience. His method can only be inductive. From the multiplicity of impressions arises the density of the aesthetic experience shaped by contingent reality, and here scepticism is a vital integrating factor, for it prevents conceptualisation of what is concealed in these impressions and instead points the way to what Pater calls 'that virtue', which in its indeterminacy is potentially far richer than the monovalent idea. Pater's analysis seeks to open up the impression, not to close it. And what he finds is a community of subject and experience that is not confined simply to art itself, but through its unity actually lifts the barrier between art and life.[42] Impression is all-embracing, and for Pater is a branch of knowledge itself. 'In enunciating the particularity of an impression, we also give expression to the disposition, the particular attitude to life in which the impression makes its appearance.'[43]

What Pater is searching for in the impression is its basic constituent quality, the 'virtue' that takes it out of the 'permanent flux' and enables it to defy time by freezing the transient into a permanent image. The need for such a quality is directly connected to Pater's awareness of ever-increasing secularisation:

Fundamental belief gone, in almost all of us, at least some relics of it remain – queries, echoes, reactions, after-thoughts; and they help to make an atmosphere, a mental atmosphere, hazy perhaps, yet with many secrets of soothing light and shade, associating more definite objects to each other by a perspective pleasant to the inward eye against a hopefully receding background of remoter and ever remoter possibilities.[44]

This groundswell running through the latter half of the nineteenth century made the adoption of an aesthetic attitude of paramount concern to Pater. The cult of art not only arose from the ruins of beliefs, creeds and thought systems of yore, but it also had to assume some of the functions once fulfilled by them. The aesthetic attitude as an answer to the existing challenge was promulgated as the new horizon encompassing all the remnants of former conceptualisations of life. An atmosphere had to be distilled out of these fragments, formed neither by laws of dogma nor concepts of philosophy, but by the contingency of association. It could never be clearly defined, but within it all reality was sublimated to a selection of fascinatingly uncommitted possibilities. Max Picard described this impressionistic situation as follows, though his observations were drawn from a standpoint hostile to the aesthetic sphere, so that he felt bound to denigrate the phenomenon:

Impressionism is the formal expression of an age that believes nothing. That distrusts its own unbelief. That does not even believe that it believes nothing. An age that believes nothing is afraid of all that is to come . . . (It could perhaps not exist at all without this doubt . . .) Such an age always wants to be ready for the jump. The present must be swiftly leavable. The meaning and purpose of an appearance demand too much commitment. But it is easy to free oneself from the surface.[45]

Through this lack of involvement and purpose, Impressionism for Picard was an anticultural modernistic movement.[46] Impressionism, however, did not question the culture from which it emerged;[47] what it did, through its particular mode of perception, was to lift appearances out of their defining contexts and so free them from the normative interpretation imposed on them in different cultural periods.

In his studies of the Renaissance, Pater provides a vivid idea of how the impression as he conceives it is to be turned into a category of cognition.

He starts out with an investigation of two late medieval French *contes*, which for him typify the upsurge of a new attitude towards life.

> One of the strongest characteristics of that outbreak of the reason and the imagination, of that assertion of the liberty of the heart, in the middle age, which I have termed a medieval Renaissance, was its antinomianism, its spirit of rebellion and revolt against the moral and religious ideas of the time. In their search after the pleasures of the senses and the imagination, in their care for beauty, in their worship of the body, people were impelled beyond the bounds of the Christian ideal.[48]

Pater questions the idea of the Middle Ages being a period of uniform faith.[49] What interests him is the forces at work beneath an apparently uniform surface, preparing for a sudden breakthrough. He sees the new intoxication with beauty as a rebellion, as something illegitimate and forbidden, and he regards the aesthetic as being comprehensible only in terms of contradiction to the norms of the age. It is this contradiction that he seeks to bring out in the first essay in *Renaissance*, 'Two Early French Stories'. The essential and fascinating quality of the aesthetic is its 'antinomianism'. However, to run counter to the Christian character of the Middle Ages does not mean to negate it; on the contrary, it filters through to the new aesthetic feeling for life, whose inherent dynamism is propelled by the mounting tension of countervailing forces. What mainly concerns Pater is not the difference between Middle Ages and Renaissance as two separate and distinct periods in cultural history; his interest lies in the telescoped qualities that arose from the meeting of two opposites. Thus he coins the term 'medieval Renaissance' long before modern historians begin to talk of a Renaissance in the twelfth century.[50] He does not set out to condemn the Middle Ages to the greater glory of the Renaissance, but indeed in the essay on Joachim du Bellay it is the enduring presence of the Middle Ages that actually constitutes the charm of the French Renaissance:

> What is called the *Renaissance in France* is thus not so much the introduction of a wholly new taste ready-made from Italy, but rather the finest and subtlest phase of the middle age itself, its last fleeting splendour and temperate Saint Martin's summer.[51]

Pater always focuses, not on the basic ideas which define a period, but on those moments when the old begins to be effaced by the new, when contradictions begin to break through the hitherto smooth surface of fixed beliefs. When this happens, the determinate becomes vague and permeated by a dark and still uncertain future, giving rise to a discernible moment of transition in which the old loses its validity and the new is not as yet firmly established. The two must interact, since the new depends on the old for its shape, gaining determinacy to the degree in which it erodes the old. The moment of transition brackets the two together and thus encompasses what in terms of philosophical and moral definitions can only be conceived as separate entities.[52]

This is the vital area that Pater explores in his studies of the Renaissance, and already in the second essay, on Pico della Mirandola, we find him concentrating on the nature of the moment of transition:

> No account of the Renaissance can be complete without some notice of the attempt made by certain Italian scholars of the fifteenth century to reconcile Christianity with the religion of ancient Greece. To reconcile forms of sentiment which at first sight seem incompatible, to adjust the various products of the human mind to one another in one many-sided type of intellectual culture, to give humanity, for heart and imagination to feed upon, as much as it could possibly receive, belonged to the generous instincts of that age . . . For that age the only possible reconciliation was an imaginative one, and resulted from the efforts of artists, trained in Christian schools, to handle pagan subjects.[53]

For Pater the significance of the Renaissance is not that the individual was freed from the 'veil . . . woven of faith . . . prejudice and folly',[54] but that it offered such rich variations on the theme of transition. In this he differs radically from an ethically orientated cultural philosophy which conceived of the Renaissance as a major shift from the past, giving birth to a new ideal of man. For Pater, however, the driving force is one of reconciliation, not of rupture, for the latter would imply conceptualising the new beginning, which would be totally alien to Pater with his deep distrust of any kind of philosophical concept. It was art that brought about the reconciliation, and so the transitional quality was only to be understood in aesthetic terms. Reconciliation was not a dialectic movement towards synthesis; it was, rather, an interaction of opposites, a telescoping of incompatibles, resulting in a syncretic and synchronic perception of what was and what had been:

> the essence of humanism is that belief . . . that nothing which has ever interested living men and women can wholly lose its vitality – no language they have spoken, nor oracle beside which they have hushed their voices, no dream which has once been entertained by actual human minds, nothing about which they have ever been passionate, or expended time and zeal.[55]

Through the co-existence of opposites, reconciliation makes it feasible for the vast variety of human possibilities to be embraced, and this is the meaning of art, which, however, can only open up this play of possibilities in a realm that lies beyond challenging realities.

What links the different elements of Pater's syncretic vision together is the frequently invoked quality of the 'interesting',[56] which proved to be a category for all latter-day Romantics focusing on art. It implied that no particular concept of art – not even the achievements of Greek antiquity –

could claim exclusive validity. On the contrary, the quality of the interesting as a subversive force against hierarchies of any kind is that it seeks to rescue all human possibilities from being subsumed under overriding concepts. For Pater, then, the Renaissance reconciles Christian and pagan elements by making each relative to the other as interacting appearances. When they lose their claim to validity by being telescoped into one another, reconciliation becomes possible, and this turns out to be a purely aesthetic process. Pater gives a vivid illustration of this interpenetration in his essay on Botticelli. First there is a reference to Dante, through which he points to a new and special form of art:

> To him, as to Dante, the scene, the colour, the outward image or gesture, comes with all its incisive and importunate reality; but awakes in him, moreover, by some subtle law of his own structure, a mood which it awakes in no one else, of which it is the double or repetition, and which it clothes, that all may share it, with visible circumstance.[57]

Exposed to the same challenging reality as Dante, Botticelli perceives a completely different structure whose representation is achieved not by means of a hierarchically patterned world order, but by being cast as a mood. And mood as an ultimate is one of the most vital driving-forces in art.

> So just what Dante scorns as unworthy alike of heaven and hell, Botticelli accepts, that middle world in which men take no side in great conflicts, and decide no great causes, and make great refusals. He thus sets for himself the limits within which art, undisturbed by any moral ambition, does its most sincere and surest work. His interest is neither in the untempered goodness of Angelico's saints, nor the untempered evil of Orcagna's *Inferno*; but with men and women, in their mixed and uncertain condition, always attractive, clothed sometimes by passion with a character of loveliness and energy, but saddened perpetually by the shadow upon them of the great things from which they shrink.[58]

Art, then, is an in-between region of undecidedness, separating itself from a single metaphysical interpretation of the world without being committed to rejecting such an interpretation. For religion also has its part in the humanity portrayed, though feelings of insecurity, sadness and terror reflect the in-between state of man. Mood has replaced metaphysical hierarchies, and for Pater it is mood that determines art.

> Moods have no particular object. They are states, colourings permeating human existence, in which the self turns in a special way inwardly in order to be at one with itself, and thus they do not point towards anything outside themselves.[59]

Art removes the intentionality of a challenging reality, and replaces it with a transitional reality that neither rejects the old nor defines the new, but remains a mood in which contrasts lose their firm outlines and begin to merge into one another.

Pater uses Botticelli's paintings of the Madonna and of Venus to illustrate this merging:

I have said that the peculiar character of Botticelli is the result of a blending . . . He paints the story of the goddess of pleasure in other episodes besides that of her birth from the sea, but never without some shadow of death in the grey flesh and wan flowers. He paints Madonnas but they shrink from the pressure of the divine child, and plead in unmistakable undertones for a warmer, lower humanity.[60]

In the blending of opposites, Pater sees 'the temper in which he [Botticelli] worked'.[61] The inherent contradictions impair the symbolic qualities of the paintings. Yet this seems to have been done deliberately; the gradual effacing of the symbolic significance gives expression to an emerging mood. And so the shadow of death accompanies the goddess of love, and the Madonna longs for 'the gipsy children, such as those who, in Apennine villages, still hold out their long brown arms to beg of you'.[62] Out of these blended opposites arises mood, which harks back to the 'original unity that preceded the split between man and world'.[63] Here autonomous art takes on a new dimension. It arises from mood, the deepest layer of man's being, for there had been a 'breakdown of faith in reason as man's essence . . . now thought and at the same time the other loftier achievements of the spirit could no longer be considered as regions resting within themselves and understandable by themselves'.[64] Now only mood – in which the split between self and world had not as yet occurred – could remove life's dissonances and create the illusion of totality. This is why Pater claims that even ethics is in the final analysis shaped by art, as he indicates in his rather strange assessment of Plato:

And Platonic aesthetics, remember! as such, are ever in close connexion with Plato's ethics. It is life itself, action and character, he proposes to colour; to get something of that irrepressible conscience of art, that spirit of control, into the general course of life, above all into its energetic or impassioned acts.[65]

Hence in a scattered and fragmented world only art, as a portrayal of moods, promises to flash illusory totalities before the mind's eye. In describing a basic quality of Michelangelo's sonnets, Pater epitomises the intrinsic interconnection of art and mood: 'the spirit of the sonnets is lost if we once take them out of that dreamy atmosphere in which men have things as they will, because the hold of all outward things upon them is faint and uncertain'.[66] The 'dreamy atmosphere' restores man's identity with the world, removing once again the boundaries between subject and object, and making invisible a fundamental substratum 'that had . . . become invisible in the theoretical approach, and could never have been uncovered so long as one proceeded only theoretically'.[67]

Mood is the revolutionary element in autonomous art, and the uniqueness of its promise of totality lies in the fact that it imposes no binding obligations.

The opposing elements of the mood are far easier to grasp than the mood itself, for it is the very lack of a determinate object[68] that endows the mood with its special character. By integrating its elements, it distances itself from each of them individually, and this distancing is an integral part of what Pater sees as a reaction against the temporality of human existence. Mood as a passive state reflects the calm of timelessness, and even where there is passion and animation, the lack of intention takes away the destructive force of time:

> Above the more massive forms of temporality . . . rises, with a more fragile perfection, the realm of these new temporalities that are experienced as timeless. And so the former are the primary forms which alone provide a base for the latter to build on, and to which the latter must always refer back. And in turn both are only extreme cases, between which there is a multitude of mediating transitions.[69]

In his essay on Michelangelo, Pater goes deeper into the nature of mood when he considers the symbolic figures of *Dusk* and *Dawn*, *Night* and *Day* in San Lorenzo:

> They concentrate and express, less by way of definite conceptions than by the touches, the promptings of a piece of music, all those vague fancies, misgivings, presentiments, which shift and mix and are defined and fade again, whenever the thoughts try to fix themselves with sincerity on the conditions and surroundings of the disembodied spirit. I suppose no one would come to the sacristy of San Lorenzo for consolation; for seriousness, for solemnity, for dignity of impression, perhaps, but not for consolation. It is a place neither of consoling nor of terrible thoughts, but of vague and wistful speculation.[70]

The vagueness of the impact made by these sculptures can hardly be captured in words. The welter of nouns and verbs here tends to blur more than to clarify, and the intentional nature of language appears to obstruct Pater's quest for expression. The objects he is describing are of less significance to him than the associations that they arouse. The sculptures give way to impressions of the sculptures, marble gives way to mood. Even the mention of 'consoling' and 'terrible thoughts' serves only to provide negative extremes that will help give some shape to the quality that resides between them. Furthermore, the impression moves in no particular direction – it is simply itself, 'wistful' but with no indication of what is desired. This indeed is Pater's image of Michelangelo, as a man whose last hope lay in the 'consciousness of ignorance – ignorance of man, ignorance of the nature of the mind, its origin and capacities'.[71] This consciousness of the impermeable made Michelangelo immortal – he was 'in possession of our inmost thoughts'.[72]

Since the world can no longer be encompassed by a single concept, the aesthetic attitude adopted towards all phenomena will feel itself constrained to derive as many associations as possible from the objects around it,[73] for only in this way can the finite world take on the illusion of infinity. Appearance is never seen merely as appearance. It 'serves to unfurl other appearances. The ideal experience of this time is to dissolve a single appearance into so many connections that one can thereby gain the whole world.'[74] The connections free themselves from the objects, and thus change the nature of the objects themselves. The focus is not on the individual identity of phenomena, but on the contacts between them – on the multifariousness of their potential relations. This makes the character of the object dwindle to insignificance, giving way to the penumbrae which are to be observed and related to those of other appearances. Therefore any unequivocal idea will rank as an obstacle to the aesthetic expansion of associations. Reality must lose its determinacy, so that it can be broken up into mood.[75] This idea finds its culmination in Pater's description of the *Mona Lisa* – a passage dismissed by some critics as merely a purple patch.[76]

> The presence that rose thus so strangely beside the waters, is expressive of what in the ways of a thousand years men had come to desire. Hers is the head upon which all 'the ends of the world are come', and the eyelids are a little weary. It is a beauty wrought out from within upon the flesh, the deposit, little cell by cell, of strange thoughts and fantastic reveries and exquisite passions. Set it for a moment beside one of those white Greek goddesses or beautiful women of antiquity, and how would they be troubled by this beauty, into which the soul with all its maladies has passed! All the thoughts and experience of the world have etched and moulded there, in that which they have of power to refine and make expressive the outward form, the animalism of Greece, the lust of Rome, the mysticism of the middle age with its spiritual ambition and imaginative loves, the return of the Pagan world, the sins of the Borgias. She is older than the rocks among which she sits; like the vampire, she has been dead many times, and learned the secrets of the grave; and has been a diver in deep seas, and keeps their fallen day about her; and trafficked for strange webs with Eastern merchants, and, as Leda, was the mother of Helen of Troy, and, as Saint Anne, the mother of Mary; and all this has been to her but as the sound of lyres and flutes, and lives only in the delicacy with which it has moulded the changing lineaments, and tinged the eyelids and the hands. The fancy of a perpetual life, sweeping together ten thousand experiences, is an old one; and modern philosophy has conceived the idea of humanity as wrought upon by, and summing up in itself, all modes of thought and life. Certainly Lady Lisa might stand as the embodiment of the old fancy, the symbol of the modern idea.[77]

The Paterian mode of perception comes to full fruition in this rhapsodic encounter with Leonardo's picture. He describes not the work but the impression the work makes on him. The painting becomes the source of a diversified chain of impressions, the fashioning of which takes us further and further away from the picture itself, and deeper and deeper into Pater's own imagination. His focus is almost exclusively on the potential relations of what can be seen, extending the figure portrayed into an unbounded realm of associations. As each association engenders a new one, the impressionistic mode of perception becomes discernible. It transforms the object through the act of grasping it. The transformation, however, is not due to any governing idea; it is triggered by the potential interconnection of the phenomena and executed by the mind's eye of the beholder. It expresses his yearning to transmute given objects into a limitless expanse.

This approach entails the evocation of different realms each of which is marked by a stereotype. Thus 'the animalism of Greece, the lust of Rome, the mysticism of the middle age' are amalgamated with the Renaissance as an historical phenomenon and with individual characters such as the Borgias. The chthonic secrets of death and resurrection are interwoven with the idea of unimaginable longevity, and Mona Lisa's doubling as Leda and Saint Anne brings together pagan mysteries and Christian redemption. Once more the contrasts create a mood. No single element can exclusively capture the essence of Mona Lisa, and indeed it is the very exclusion of exclusiveness that permits the intermingling of associations, with each element losing its autonomy and simply adding tone and colour to the kaleidoscopic collection of nuances. It is noticeable that Pater's language here consists of blocks of nouns mainly linked by the neutral verbs to be and to have. He is clearly at pains not to give any one element precedence over another. The absolute parity of the association is essential for the creation of the mood, and in order that there should be no distraction from their evocativeness, Pater even avoids placing them in any historical sequence: he seems to jump arbitrarily from one period and one context to another, so that all the spheres become, as it were, foreshortened. The arbitrariness seems almost to be a law underlying the formation of impression, and the resultant accumulation of images endows the mood with ever greater intensity. Neither Leonardo's picture nor the historical and mythical figures are alluded to for their own sakes; they serve to establish the mood. The intensity of this mood is an artistic quality that transcends the norms of classical aesthetics, for instead of leading the observer deeper into what the work of art represents, it subjugates the work in order to represent itself. Even philosophy and religion must serve the same purpose, and the surprising montages to which they are subjected are striking indications of man's changed and changing view of himself. Although Pater's arrangement of history and tradition is not to be compared to that found in *Waste Land* or *Ulysses*, it does already foreshadow the upheavals in literary techniques that were later to be wrought by Eliot and Joyce.

This conception of mood as a form of heightened intensity has a further consequence to be discerned in the Paterian description of the *Mona Lisa*. The way in which the different images are interconnected tends to blur their respective outlines, decreasing their visual vividness. Vivid perception, however, is an integral quality of art and literature as long as it is devoted to making meaning conceivable. Fading perceptibility is closely linked to a dispersal of meaning, which in turn is a basic condition for establishing mood. And as mood is no longer a perceivable entity, the picture of Leonardo ceases to be representation and is instead 'the fancy of a perpetual life, sweeping together ten thousand experiences [and it is] expressive of what in the ways of ten thousand years men had come to desire'.[78] The object of the painting evaporates into a hazy dream, the portrayal of which demands an eradication of perceptibility and determinacy in order to prevent disillusionment. Ten thousand experiences and ten thousand years of desire articulate an inconceivable yearning which not only leaves the *Mona Lisa* far behind, but also blots out what can be seen and so gives free rein to the triumphant observer's imagination. Seeing is no longer perceiving, but is projecting. In Maugham's gently ironic words, 'Walter Pater is the only justification for Mona Lisa.'[79]

This fading away of the picture itself should not be mistaken for a formalistic game. It is evident from the ever-expanding chain of impressions brought about by Pater's montage of images that the mood created is coloured by a particular expectation. Therefore his description of the *Mona Lisa* amounts to an epiphany of eternal life, though his longing for the all-embracing and the unending is never articulated by a concept, but is transmitted as a sequence of 'resurrections'. Pater assembles all the human voices which have responded to challenging realities and all the archetypes in which these problems have found a solution in order to convey the infinity inherent in human finiteness. Art has to make us conscious of this dream that lies within all of us, but to do so, it cannot allow itself to be bound to any single idea or culture. Instead ideas and cultures serve to adumbrate an all-encompassing horizon that is forever widening.

The relativising of normative aesthetics that took place at the beginning of the nineteenth century triggered a series of 'resurrections' and renaissances which has continued right up to the present. First the Middle Ages were resuscitated, then chthonic Antiquity, and after that the art of Polynesia, Oceania and Africa, with fetishes and totems. From the beginning of the nineteenth century, the downgrading of concepts in aesthetics and art criticism corresponded to a drive towards resurrecting manifestations of art which lay buried or seemingly lost in human history.

Art does not deliver man from being only an accident of the universe; but it is the soul of the past in the sense that every ancient religion was a soul of the world. It ensures for its followers, while man is born to solitude, that profound bond which is abandoned by the gods receding into the distance.[80]

Pater's desire 'to treat life in the spirit of art'[81] is a desire to establish inviolable continuity in a temporal world. Art as 'the soul of the past' preserves all human solutions from oblivion, and welds them into an illusion of totality. 'In us is everything'[82] is the message behind Pater's Mona Lisa, which indicates that only art allows for a perpetual recurrence and resuscitation of whatever has been of human concern.

Style

Into the mind sensitive to 'form', a flood of random sounds, colours, incidents, is ever penetrating from the world without, to become, by sympathetic selection, a part of its very structure, and, in turn, the visible vesture and expression of that other world it sees so steadily within, nay, already with a partial conformity thereto, to be refined, enlarged, corrected, at a hundred points; and it is just there, just at those doubtful points that the function of style, as tact or taste, intervenes.[83]

This quite vivid description of the impressionistic processing of perception directs attention to that area where self and world blend together – an area that Pater calls 'doubtful', because it is one that cannot be defined theoretically. Self and world enter into a relationship which eludes definition when viewed from either of the two poles, in spite of the fact that there is a tilt in favour of the self. As theory appears incapable of penetrating this 'fusion', style as a means of elucidating it assumes an overriding significance.

Style 'intervenes' in order to make the indefinable more tangible. It manifestly balances out the relationship between reality and the subjective observer of reality. It is therefore no coincidence that the essay on style, regarded by many as one of Pater's greatest literary achievements,[84] is the longest of his theoretical essays[85] and contains what might be seen as his creed. It is not without significance that here, as E. Chandler's painstaking study has shown, Pater's own style tends to fall short of the programmatic demands of the essay.[86]

The importance of style lies in its linking subjectivity to the given, and Pater begins by examining this link:

just in proportion as the writer's aim, consciously or unconsciously, comes to be the transcribing, not of the world, not of mere fact, but of his sense of it, he becomes an artist, his work *fine* art.[87]

This 'imaginative sense of fact'[88] is for Pater the basis of all art, representing as it does the feelings aroused by the facts.

Literary art, that is, like all art . . . is the representation of such fact as connected with soul, of a specific personality, in its preferences, its volition and power[89] . . . wherever the producer so modifies his work as, over and above its primary use or intention, to make it pleasing (to himself, of course, in the first instance) there, 'fine' as opposed to merely serviceable art, exists.[90]

Pater sets off his own principles against those concepts of art that find their ideal in the service of Nature through faithful imitation. There is a clear allusion here to Ruskin's view of art as a participation in the whole, requiring pious submission to Nature. Pater rejects this view, for he sees art as personal perception, which focuses on given objects only in so far as they trigger the projections which they have stimulated.

Unlike Ruskin, Pater could never believe in Nature as substance, because for him even an overall coherence of things appeared inconceivable – a situation that had inevitable repercussions on the apparent factualness of fact. At the very beginning of his essay, he says: 'The line between fact and something quite different from external fact is, indeed, hard to draw.'[91] This statement is not surprising coming from someone who rejects overriding principles which organise the world of experience by imposing patterns on it. Facts and objects are bound to lose their distinctness and solidity when subjective perception endows them with qualities and properties which in turn have to be processed in a subjective manner. Whoever is aware of this will give 'an expression no longer of fact but of his sense of it, his peculiar intuition of a world, prospective, or discerned below the faulty conditions of the present, in either case changed somewhat from the actual world'.[92] What style makes tangible is the artist's individuality, not a reality made classifiable through a norm. 'Art is born . . . from the fascination of the ungraspable, from the refusal to copy sights; from the desire to seize forms out of the world man suffers, in order to make them enter the world he governs.'[93] Thus style reduces things to their human dimension, not copying reality but filtering it. What style represents must always be the individual's perspective, and for the individual it is only this perspective world that is real. 'The style, the manner, would be the man, not in his unreasoned and really uncharacteristic caprices, involuntary or affected, but in absolutely sincere apprehension of what is most real to him.'[94]

Since style gives form to subjective reality, it is ultimately to be identified with art – an identification that becomes possible when art is no longer devoted to a particular service, whether sacred or profane. For Pater, style had freed itself from the task of elaborating and decorating a given reality, and had instead become a means of transforming and so mastering reality: 'it was a refuge, a sort of cloistral refuge, from a certain vulgarity in the actual world . . . a religious "retreat" '.[95] It remains the handwriting of the individual, but now it is much more, for rather than serving an overall convention, it is a means of possessing the world by composing it anew.[96]

The synonymy of art and style is given particular prominence in Pater's essay 'The Beginnings of Greek Sculpture'. In this, Pater traces the development from the old craftsmen through to the great masters, and the distinction between the two is clearly the emergence of personal style.

> Mere fragment as our information concerning these early matters is at the best, it is at least unmistakeably information about men with personal differences of temper or talent, of their motives, of what we call *style*. We have come to a sort of art which is no longer broadly characteristic of a general period, one whose products we might have looked at without its occurring to us to ask concerning the artist, his antecedents, and his school. We have to do now with types of art, fully impressed with the subjectivity, the intimacies of the artist.[97]

Style is a decomposition of Nature to the degree in which the artist's vision imprints itself onto the given. With the great masters, style took on an inimitable subjectivity,[98] not only of form but also of the manner in which they transformed reality.

Subjective transfiguration of the world as the hallmark of style automatically demands that the critic pay closer attention to the subject in whom perceiving as transforming takes place. An inquiry into this activity works back upon the subject in the sense that the latter has to gain clarity about itself, and so Pater is soon delving into the interaction between man and world as evinced through style:

> The one word for the one thing, the one thought, amid the multitude of words, terms, that might just do: the problem of style was there! – the unique word, phrase, sentence, paragraph, essay, or song, absolutely proper to the single mental presentation or vision within.[99]

By 'vision' he does not mean optical sight, like the uninvolved eye of Flaubert, so much as the transforming sight of the mind's eye, from which arises the 'imaginative sense of fact'. Pater did not realise that he was diverging from Flaubert – to whom he refers directly – but the distinction is clear: Pater's vision is interested and involved,[100] whereas the claim of Flaubert's stylistic vision is impersonality.[101] And although they both grapple with the same problem of finding *le mot juste*, their intentions differ, too. Pater demands from his writer 'a vocabulary faithful to the colouring of his own spirit',[102] whereas Flaubert sought a passionless reproduction of the facts. Pater exclaims: 'Well! all language involves translation from inward to outward',[103] while for Flaubert the inward process of observation was for the most part excluded as he wished to confine his observations to the pure phenomenality of the world. Pater's problem was how to objectify the inner vision, and the search for the right word, phrase etc. is the result of this need. It is this search, and not the cause for the search, that links Pater to Flaubert, who originally inspired Pater's essay.[104]

The importance of the right word can be gauged by the fact that Pater equates a correspondence between word and vision with truth: 'It will be good literary art not because it is brilliant or sober, or rich, or impulsive, or severe, but just in proportion as its representation of that sense, that soul-fact, is true.'[105] To define truth in terms of a formal relationship is in keeping with the aesthetic attitude; yet to qualify the adequate translation of inwardness into language as truth shows a sense of commitment in the otherwise uncommitted realm of the aesthetic that reveals much of Pater's way of thinking. He sees the search for the right expression as a many-layered process, and the distinction between these layers will help us to understand Pater's own vision more clearly. The lowest level in this complex process consists of the word, which provides the basis of the vision that is to be objectified.

Pater demands a high degree of scholarship from his writer: 'The literary artist is of necessity a scholar, and in what he proposes to do will have in mind, first of all, the scholar and the scholarly conscience.'[106] In order to ascertain the full implications of this demand, it will be useful to glance again at Pater's *Marius* which has a chapter significantly entitled 'Euphuism'. Flavian, the literary revolutionary, subjects language to a

> serious study, weighing the precise power of every phrase and word, as though it were precious metal, disentangling the later associations and going back to the original and native sense of each, – restoring to full significance all its wealth of latent figurative expression, reviving or replacing its outworn or tarnished images. Latin literature and the Latin tongue were dying of routine and languor; and what was necessary, first of all, was to re-establish the natural and direct relationship between thought and expression, between the sensation and the term, and restore to words their primitive power.[107] What care for style! what patience of execution! what research for the significant tones of ancient idiom![108]

The inner vision needs all the manifold connotations of words in order to objectify itself, and so their forgotten and hidden nuances must be revived and their historic significance and richness restored.

Language is not, however, confined to representing the inner vision; it also contains 'that true "open field" for charm and sway over men',[109] the study of which should lead – as far as Flavian is concerned – to the restoration of its primitive power. The inner vision, then, is not merely satisfied by gaining a tangible appearance; it strives for authenticity by means of impact on the external world in the form of power. This aim makes it necessary for the utmost attention to be paid to the invocatory character of the word. If the effect of language is to be ensured, its old magic functions must be revived. Flavian felt, together with his

> fastidious sense of a correctness in external form . . . something which ministered to the old ritual interest, still surviving in him; as if here indeed were involved a kind of sacred service to the mother-tongue. Here, then, was the theory of

Euphuism, as manifested in every age in which the literary conscience has been awakened to forgotten duties towards language, towards the instrument of expression: in fact it does but modify a little the principles of all effective expression at all times.[110]

Pater makes it clear that Flavian's efforts to revive these 'forgotten duties' are not merely personal, but typify 'Euphuism' throughout the ages. This quest for style reflects a commitment to Mannerism,[111] which for Pater entails contrast to current and ordinary language, with 'love of novelty' as its main characteristic[112] powered by an interplay between archaism and neologism.[113] The word regains its ability to challenge and provoke when its forgotten nuances of the past are restored to depict man's present. Thus the lonely individual – exposed to the threat of temporality – may find in the historically sedimented connotations of words as well as in the magic spell of language a means both of externalising his inwardness and of wielding power. And it is power which endows inwardness with authenticity.

What makes the quest for style mannered is the fact that meanings are removed from their historical context and transferred to the self. This shift is necessary because the spiritual uncertainty and scepticism of the self reject any philosophical frameworks for its self-conceptualisation.

That mannerism is a striking medium for signalling both inauthenticity and lack of independence in human existence is . . . already clear from everyday language. With 'se guinder' [guinder = to hoist with a windlass, and se guinder = to give oneself airs] . . . it falls back on a technical manoeuvre in order to compensate through its stiltedness for the individual's inability to sustain himself without recourse to a technical aid outside himself.[114]

In Pater's imaginative portrait 'The English Poet', which has been almost totally ignored by critics, the main strands of Mannerism are woven together:

Having nothing else to live on, he [i.e. the English Poet] extracted all they could yield from words, and in his sense of them came to be curiously cultivated at all points . . . To his poetic nature, sick like Hamlet, in a world partly 'out of joint', words by themselves win not indeed more than daily food, yet sufficient to satisfy the cravings of that appetite in him which lives not by bread alone.[115]

As a *poète maudit*, he finds himself in a world without any reliable orientation.[116] When all systems have fallen apart, his last chance of capturing the inner vision – even if only indirectly and cryptically – lies in the word. Gottfried Benn once described the word as a 'totem',[117] and indeed its overpowering spell arises out of its capacity to store magic, mythical and historical meanings which the poet has both to discover and to resuscitate. This is why the poet must be a scholar, for the lost power must be reclaimed through research and intuition. This reverence for scientific research was a pious superstition rampant in the nineteenth century, and propelled by the hope that the empirical sciences might one day arrive at final solutions and total explanations. Pater, so it seems, did at least share some of that hope.

The intention behind Pater's advocacy of scholarship and research was twofold: to uncover in language a means of expressing the inner vision, and to activate the forces of language in such a way that this inner vision could exercise an indelible impact. Thus we read of Pater's young poet:

> Afterwards, when he was understood to be a poet, this, a peculiar character as of flowers in metal, was noticed by the curious as a distinction in his verse, such an elastic force in word and phrase, following a tender delicate thought or feeling as the metal followed the curvature of the flower, as seemed to indicate artistic triumph over a material partly resisting, which yet at last took outline from his thought with the firmness of antique mastery.[118]

The image illustrates the resistance that the inner vision had to overcome: the feelings are soft and tender, whereas the mode of their presentation is as hard as metal. Once again, interest is focused exclusively on the mode – we are given no indication as to what the thoughts and feelings actually are, and the effect is only described aesthetically: the fragile inner images impose themselves firmly on the resistant metal. For the young poet, these filigree flowers take on an almost symbolic value; he feels 'a sensuous longing for that warmer soil out of which exotic flowers or flowers of metal would naturally grow'.[119] This is tantamount to a longing for the triumph of art, whose perfection would lie in the naturalness of an artificial appearance.

The mannered style meets resistance because it is no longer applied to a graspable object but to an intangible subject. One might say that the subject becomes its own object. The word can never capture the whole, but by restoring its old magic the poet can surprise and stimulate, thereby indirectly illustrating the particular.[120]

Mannerism marks the demise of the Platonism inherent in all styles up until the nineteenth century. Style ceases to represent a given context and now becomes a compulsion to express the incommensurable subject. The metal flowers typify a new desire to transcend the vulgarity of the world by artificial means.[121] 'The form and rule of literary language' must therefore become 'a language always and increasingly artificial'.[122] Nietzsche also recognised this phenomenon:

> What is the hallmark of all literary decadence? The fact that life no longer dwells within the whole. The word becomes sovereign and leaps out of the sentence, the sentence spreads out and obscures the sense of the page, the page gains life at the expense of the whole – the whole is no longer a whole.[123]

The page as life at the expense of the whole sums up the essence of the mannered style, by means of which the artist's manner triumphs over the non-subjective world. 'He is really vindicating his liberty in the making of a vocabulary, an entire system of composition, for himself, his own true manner; and when we speak of the manner of a true master we mean what is essential in his art'.[124]

The search for the past magic of words is not the only feature of the mannered style. The richness of the word's layered meanings, mythically and historically accumulated, can be so seductive that it can distract from the actual intention of the style if it is not controlled by some counter-movement.

Parallel, allusion, the allusive way generally, the flowers in the garden: – he knows the narcotic force of these upon the negligent intelligence to which any *diversion*, literally, is welcome, any vagrant intruder, because one can go wandering away with it from the immediate subject. Jealous, if he have a really quickening motive within, of all that does not hold directly to that, of the facile, the otiose, he will never depart from the strictly pedestrian process, unless he gains a ponderable something thereby. Even assured of its congruity, he will still question its serviceableness. Is it worth while, can we afford, to attend to just that, to just that figure or literary reference, just then? – Surplusage! he will dread that, as the runner on his muscles. For in truth all art does but consist in the removal of surplusage.[125]

Dazzled by the diversification of nuances contained in every word, the poet is in danger of being enthralled by his discovery and cherishing the word for its own sake. It is the 'really quickening motive', however, that controls the flood of language, and its jealousy is necessary if the seductive power of words is to be resisted. For the decorative 'is rarely content to die to thought precisely at the right moment, but will inevitably linger awhile, stirring a long "brainwave" behind it of perhaps quite alien associations.'[126] Pater's openness to words 'rich in "second intention"'[127] and the impossibility of defining what is to be expressed, make the *mot juste* a real problem. The less concrete the desire for power, the more seductive will be the hidden meanings that consolidate themselves as decorations. Indeed the irrelevant ornament and the undefinable inner vision seem almost to converge in Pater's vague 'ponderable something', though he quickly calls on a sporting metaphor – later he changes the allusion to the world of Sparta – in order to restore the predominance of subjectivity and the 'serviceableness' of the word. And to make matters crystal clear, he then defines the function of art as the removal of 'surplusage'. This, however, is a purely negative definition. Subjectivity does not take on a solid form through style, but the true artist can be recognised by 'his tact of omission'.[128] This is another way of saying that inwardness can never become real and can only remain a potential reality. Thus the opaque quality of indeterminacy actively underpins Pater's concept of style.

The search for the *mot juste*, then, embraces two mutually exclusive though interlinking features: enrichment and asceticism.[129] Since we are never told what principle is to govern the ascetic 'tact of omission', style assumes a configurative disposition, with the factual being transformed in its contact with the inner world, although the intention of this transformation is never made apparent. As Kassner had indicated, in configurations the personality has the upper hand over the dignified object in art,[130] which simultaneously indicates the dissolution of canonical conventions as guidelines for the production of art.

This trait is to be seen even more clearly in Pater's central concept of style as structure.

So far I have been speaking of certain conditions of the literary art arising out of the medium or material in or upon which it works, the essential qualities of language and its aptitudes for contingent ornamentation, matters which define scholarship as science and good taste respectively. They are both subservient to a more intimate quality of good style: more intimate, as coming nearer to the artist himself. The otiose, the facile, surplusage: why are these abhorrent to the true literary artist, except because, in literary as in all other art, structure is all-important.[131]

Once again Pater seizes on a formal characteristic as basic to style – it is structure that enables the artist to express the intimate depths of subjectivity.

Structure is impelled by two forces, which Pater designates as 'mind' and 'soul'.[132] 'Mind' embodies an architectonic principle that reconstructs but also transforms the given.

With some strong and leading sense of the world, the tight hold of which secures true *composition* and not mere loose accretion, the literary artist, I suppose, goes on considerately, setting joint to joint, sustained by yet restraining the productive ardour.[133]

'Mind' is not so much a grasping, but a composing and therefore a mastering of the world, and the extent of this mastery is to be gauged by the extent to which the end can already be seen in the beginning, and to which the end gathers together the threads that have led to it.[134] The laws of logic and of architecture are the images Pater uses to elucidate this element of style.[135]

To explain the element of 'soul', Pater uses images from religion. The qualities of soul are fanatical conviction, the fire of language, mysticism, magic and prophecy. The Bible, the Book of Common Prayer, Swedenborg and *Tracts for the Times* (Newman, Keble *et al.*) serve as outstanding examples of 'widely different and largely diffused phases of religious feeling in operation as soul in style'.[136]

These two elements of mind and soul work together to create the structure of style, and common to both is

a drift towards unity – unity of atmosphere here, as there of design – soul securing colour (or perfume, might we say?) as mind secures form, the latter being essentially finite, the former vague or infinite . . . it does but suggest what can never be uttered, not as being different from, or more obscure than, what actually gets said, but as containing that plenary substance of which there is only one phase or facet in what there is expressed.[137]

The drift towards unity means that each element loses its independence. Logic and philosophical thinking as well as religious fervour and conviction are turned equally into component features of style. Indeed style can only take on its structure if these elements lose their determinacy, for only then can they merge into one another to meet the demands of style whose function is of a dual nature: to externalise the distinctness of subjectivity, and to endow it with a dynamic power of suggestion. Thus style is the means through which subjectivity realises itself. Style, then, provides a coherent form for what has emerged in the struggle for the *mot juste*. The autonomous subject arrogates to itself not only the richness of nuances sedimented in the word, but also the compelling stringency of logic and the fervent ardour of religion, in order to equate itself with the impact it is able to exercise.

Since logic and religion lose their original significance and become elements of a technique enabling the subject to externalise itself, this coalescence is clearly of an aesthetic nature. It is an embodiment of the aesthetically ideal state, making the forces which organise the world subservient to subjectivity. Therefore, to Pater, this unity appears to be the pinnacle of all style:

To give the phrase, the sentence, the structural member, the entire composition, song, or essay, a similar unity with its subject and with itself: – style is in the right way when it tends towards that. All depends upon the original unity, the vital wholeness and identity, of the initiatory apprehension or view.[138]

The identity of subject and object in the work . . . is the eternalising of a subjectivity which posits itself as the absolute; it entails a nullification of its 'arbitrariness', which is bound to cling to every 'subjective' act as such, though fashioned in such a way that it is objectified precisely as arbitrariness. What is intended is therefore not the absolute, but a form of positing whose nature renders the question of absoluteness quite meaningless – a level of validity on which absoluteness simply cannot arise. Something absolute *is* to be achieved, but in no way is it absoluteness itself. It is, rather, a sphere in which the absolute can be neither thought nor experienced, a sphere in which there are only ultimate complexes, complete in themselves, independent of one another, unconnected to one another and to the 'outside world' of no matter what kind of objectivity (to which the absolute also belongs) – complexes that one can only leave by stepping out of the whole sphere.[139]

Style, for Pater, indicates the consummation of the aesthetic attitude; the 'imaginative sense of fact' makes subjectivity tick.[140] In a world where meaning has faded, ordering systems have been dismantled and philosophic concepts are distrusted by a rising scepticism, style becomes an all-encompassing fiction which allows the self – perhaps for the last time – to be at one with itself and the world. In the fiction of style, Pater finds a replacement for the ordering function of 'great' subject-matter. This insight leads him to end his essay with a carefully considered study of what constitutes good art and great art. Surprisingly, only good art will be produced by the mode of perception and the self-representation that he has described in the essay.

The distinction between great art and good art depending immediately, as regards literature at all events, not on its form, but on the matter . . . Given the conditions I have tried to explain as constituting good art; – then, if it be devoted further to the increase of men's happiness, to the redemption of the oppressed, or the enlargement of our sympathies with each other, or to such presentment of new or old truth about ourselves and our relation to the world as may ennoble and fortify us in our sojourn here, or immediately, as with Dante, to the glory of God, it will also be great art.[141]

Great art, then, is not merely a matter of style, which is the handwriting of the artist, the purely technical mastery of the object. What makes good art into great art is above all the dignity of the object. In modern reality, however, the drive to tackle basic questions of life is considerably weakened, and the modern world is to be characterised by the 'chaotic variety and complexity of its interests, making the intellectual issue, the really master currents of the present time incalculable'.[142]

Since incalculability is the keystone of modern man's contact with the world, inevitably style, which must cope with this situation, can only provide a formalistic circumscription of it. Good art, as stylistic technique, thus emerges from man's helplessness when faced with basic questions of existence. In a world with 'fundamental beliefs gone', there remains only the possibility of grasping what is left, and the more complex and chaotic that world appears, the more emphasis must be laid on style, which permits not only the unity between self and world, but also the mastery of the incalculable. In view of this goal, style can be nothing but a formal strategy, ridding itself of all its ties to dignified objects and thus turning into a purely aesthetic phenomenon. Here style divests itself of its Platonic function, for it is no longer the individual representation of the general – which for Pater was the essence of great art; now it subjugates the general in order to bring to the fore the individual. It remains to be seen how Pater maintains this reversal in his interpretation of Plato.

If great art derives its greatness from its content, it would seem that for Pater great art was no longer possible: 'artistic law . . . demands the predominance of form everywhere over the mere matter or subject handled'.[143] Although every form of art has its own special features, what they all have in common is an 'Anders-streben – a partial alienation from its own limitations'.[144] This 'Anders-streben' finds its purest expression in music.

All art constantly aspires towards the condition of music . . . That the mere matter of a poem, for instance, its subject, namely, its given incidents or situations – that the mere matter of a picture, the actual circumstances of an event, the actual topography of a landscape – should be nothing without the form, the spirit, of the handling, that this form, this mode of handling, should become an end in itself, should penetrate every part of the matter: this is what all art constantly strives after.[145]

But if this applies to *all* art, it must surely apply to great art, and so there appears to be a contradiction in Pater's argument. He goes on to say that 'art, then, is thus always striving to be independent of the mere intelligence, to become a matter of pure perception, to get rid of its responsibilities to its subject or material'.[146] Again, a direct contradiction to his definition of great art. The contradiction, however, is of less significance than the way of thinking that gave rise to it. Clearly such terms as 'good' and 'great' had begun to lose their relevance in a world in which there were now neither dignified objects nor fundamental questions. The frame for great art had vanished beyond hope in a world which had become impermeable. Art was no longer representational, and therefore could no longer master great subject-matter in the traditional sense; instead, it had changed into 'pure perception'.

Pater's fusion of form and content entails the transformation of the world through the imagination. The dominance of form denotes the dominance of subjectivity, which by subjugating matter irradiates the world as an 'aesthetic phenomenon'. But this aesthetic attitude does not lead to an aesthetic idea that might consolidate the 'Anders-streben' into a tangible symbol, for postulating an idea would mean leaving the aesthetic sphere and entering the metaphysical, with its hierarchical order.[147] Pater is aware that a unifying concept of the arts is only possible through the 'alienation' of the individual arts, but if this were to relate to an idea, instead of to music, the alienation would be holistic, and so the inner laws of the aesthetic sphere that Pater sought to establish would lose their validity. Nevertheless, he had to find a central aesthetic standpoint, and this was his concept of style as a new aesthetic principle which not only displaced all traditional norms, but also and above all made it possible for the subjective self to master the world of objects. Thus he equates all art with the style that brings about the transformation.

In order to illustrate this new concept of style, we shall now look at a couple of examples. The fact that these will be in the nature of very short extracts may be justified by Pater's view of the sentence as a paradigmatic entity of expression. His revision of *Marius* gives ample evidence of this, as Chandler's investigations have shown, for all his revisions relate to the expressiveness of individual sentences and not to the overall conception of the novel.[148] This concentration on the sentence accords with the principles laid down in his essay on style, and it is clear that he regarded changes to this all-important inner unit as being bound to have an effect on the whole.

The examples that follow have been taken from Pater's critical writings, since these seem to demand a greater objectivity than fictional 'genres'. The departure from the concrete will afford a deeper insight into the nature and intention of Pater's style. The essay 'The Beginnings of Greek Sculpture' starts with a description of the heroic age of art, which Pater saw as springing from the skill of the craftsmen. Amongst other things, he considers the shield of Achilles:

> The shield of Achilles, the house of Alcinous, are like dreams indeed, but this sort of dreaming winds continuously through the entire *Iliad* and *Odyssey* – a child's dream after a day of real, fresh impressions from things themselves, in which all those floating impressions re-set themselves. He is as pleased in touching and looking at those objects as his own heroes; their gleaming aspect brightens all he says, and has taken hold, one might think, of his language, his very vocabulary becoming *chryselephantine*. Homer's artistic descriptions, though enlarged by fancy, are not wholly imaginary, and the extant remains of monuments of the earliest historical age are like lingering relics of that dream in a tamer but real world.[149]

The one given, concrete object here is Achilles's shield, which is merely the starting-point for a whole sequence of impressions which, in turn, relegate it to the background. It ignites the 'imaginative sense of fact' until imagination triumphs over fact. The impressions thus become detached from the object, and take on a life and an interest of their own.[150] Pater uses involved sentences, mainly hypotactic, in order to grasp the complexity of the impression, and his sentence structure conveys the various nuances that are meant to build up and differentiate the image of the dream. The dream then gives way to the glamour of the heroes, which reaches its peak in the precious 'chryselephantine'. The movement of these sentences and images is centrifugal, diverging away from their object through a constant accumulation of new associations. Thus the mainly hypotactic structure follows the demands not of logic but of association, the course and consistency of which are impossible to rationalise. The individual images are not rounded off by determinate ideas, but lead to further images and associations in a swift and arbitrary progression which deprives the hypotaxis of its basically logical function, and substitutes the freedom of fantasy. Pater himself explains the purpose of these impressions before going on to a more factual description of the shield:

In speaking of the shield of Achilles, I departed intentionally from the order in which the subjects of the relief are actually introduced in the *Iliad*, because, just then, I wished the reader to receive the full effect of the variety and elaborateness of the composition, as a representation or picture of the whole of ancient life embraced within the circumference of a shield.[151]

It is basic to Pater's style and to the aesthetic approach generally that the variety of nuances should aim to build up a whole. Elsewhere he states that 'objects, real objects, as we know, grow in reality towards us in proportion as we define their various qualities'.[152] Pater's style breaks down given objects into their qualities and shades of meaning which, by their overlapping and interweaving, lead to a dynamically shifting configuration which makes the object expand beyond its limits. The object has to pass through the imagination, which alone is able to open it up and reveal it in all its potentialities. In the passage we have been dealing with, the description of the shield is enshrouded in the dream image, which engenders new images and so endows the impression with an ever-changing, almost exploratory quality – intended to suggest more than can be said or to mean something that is beyond saying. But even this intention remains unclear in the volatility of the configuration. If there is a positive quality to be found in the latter, it is not the assembly of a new meaning but the gesture of evocation, the practice of magic which Pater has always sought to restore to the word. He uses style to conjure up the unknown and ungraspable whole.

This magic is even more evident in the following sentences taken from Pater's discussion of William Morris's poetry:

The English poet . . . has diffused through King Arthur's Tomb the maddening white glare of the sun, and the tyranny of the moon, not tender and far-off, but close down – the sorcerer's moon, large and feverish. The colouring is intricate and delirious, as of 'scarlet lilies'. The influence of summer is like poison in one's blood, with a sudden bewildered sickening of life and of all things.[153]

Instead of an analysis, Pater offers a sequence of impressions that leave the original subject far behind. The metaphors do not in any way build up a complete picture, but leap surprisingly from one sphere to another in a manner reminiscent of Hegel's description of imagery:

The metaphor, in fact, is always an interruption to the logical course of conception and invariably to that extent a distraction, because it starts images and brings them together, which are not immediately connected with the subject and its significance, and for this reason tend to a like extent to divert the attention from the same to matter cognate with themselves, but strange to both.[154]

In Pater's discussion of Morris, the movement away from the subject-matter is intended to denature it until it is unrecognisable. The unexpected juxtaposition of images leads to a build-up of intensity which, as a subjective mood, *can* only arise from the defamiliarisation of the subject-matter, for intensity is generated from within and not from without. The dominant trend in this passage is that of an artificial arrangement, intended to stimulate the extraordinary. What Pater does is to dislocate individual elements from their normal context, comparing the incomparable, and so opening all of them up to the intention underlying his style. The sun, for instance, is 'maddening' – in contrast to its usual positive value – while the 'tyranny' of the moon, which is a 'sorcerer's moon', clearly denotes that it is not the pale and beatific light of the Romantics. Pater's image is meant to take shape in the recipient's imagination, which is guided to conceive the moon in terms totally alien to common expectations so that it may be experienced in its otherness. Similarly, the 'delirious' colours suggest a totally new realm of perception whose qualities have to be divined rather than realised. It is the same with summer as 'poison'. In each of these instances, vividness of perception fades into a contrived stratagem of floating signifiers which are not meant to designate a definite signified.

The style here is mannered, and the more incongruous the images become the more strongly one feels the surge of subjectivity that transforms objects into impressions. As the object fades away behind the accumulation of metaphors, so paradoxically the subject emerges. The inner self, however, is not definable, for it is an ultimate that is unrelated to any overall supra-individuality against which it might be measured, and so its emergence spreads darkness rather than light. It assumes the aura of a divine creator, uncovering new modes of awareness through which the world may be newly constructed. Style, a perspective mode of perception, is the instrument used to stimulate this process.

The mannered poets of the late nineteenth and twentieth centuries exhibit similar stylistic gestures to those observable in the passage quoted above. They, too, juxtapose incongruous images, but they differ from Pater in so far as their mannerisms head in a particular direction: with Yeats, for instance, it is a resuscitation of myth and folklore, and with Eliot a totalising of cultural experience. It is this lack of direction that makes the structure of Pater's style paramount, for it brings about the indefinable triumph of imagination over reality by means of an artificial contrivance.

In this respect Pater also differs from his immediate contemporaries, the symbolists, although they all had a similar starting-point. R. L. Stevenson wrote:

> Life is monstrous, infinite, illogical, abrupt and poignant; a work of art, in comparison, is neat, finite, self-contained, rational, flowing and emasculate. Life imposes by brute energy, like inarticulate thunder; art catches the ear, among the far louder noises of experience like an air artificially made by a discreet musician . . . The novel, which is the work of art, exists, not by its resemblances to life, which

are forced and material, as a shoe must still consist of leather, but by its immeasurable difference from life, a difference which is designed and significant, and is both the method and the meaning of the work.[155]

To the extent that art contradicts vulgar experience and so seeks to transcend pedestrian reality, Pater and Stevenson stand together. Stevenson put his ideas into practice by distancing himself from the world of the merely factual. His fairy-tales and even his detective stories were permeated by a touch of otherworldliness, and therefore the world he created was in no way a 'resemblance to life', but symbolised the requisite distance from life.

Pater never achieved such a symbolisation of the aesthetic experience. He was never able to turn away from the temporal flow of reality. His style therefore remains basically a technique for the mastering of experience, with facts transformed by fantasy into a configuration that is never consolidated into symbols. Nor does it ever seek to capture a particular hidden meaning, but remains a kind of in-between world, to be felt, not interpreted. This may well explain why his work is mainly critical. He is far more concerned with illuminating the conditions to which man is subjected, in a world which the gods have vacated long ago, than with creating a new, self-contained and symbolic world. What motivated Pater was the desire to get to grips with empirical reality through an approach orientated by autonomous art. In his quest and his questioning he is clearly a forerunner of Virginia Woolf.[156] For him, art transcends ordinary human experience, and snatches perfection from the passing currents of time. As a configurative arrangement it freezes the moment, and with its ever-changing imagery it makes itself felt as a longing for the eternally different.

5 The problem of orientation

Beauty

In defining art, Pater's main concern was to set it free from reality, and the concept of *l'art pour l'art* lays emphasis on the contrast between art and human experience. By distancing it from any determinacy derived from the real world, he moulded it into a kind of negative theology,[1] which arises from the fact that art is rooted in temporal experience but has the task of transcending its basis. This transcendence is to be achieved through impressionistic mood and style, both of which have negative starting-points: mood invalidates the various contrasts, thus enabling them to merge into one another, and style turns away from the given world in order to transform it through modes ranging from configuration to evocation. It is this negative basis of *l'art pour l'art*, and of impressionistic mood and style – the fact that art lives by contradicting the real world – that makes art so difficult to define. The inadequacy of reality may endow it with its significance, but this does not help us to grasp its qualities. If we *are* to understand the true nature of this subjective transformation of the world, we need an objective referent. So long as art remained orientated by great subject-matter and canonical conventions, the problem did not arise. It was only when art disconnected itself from mimetic representation that it needed to look elsewhere for its justification. Was there a frame of reference which would sanction the claims of autonomous art, and how could there be a guarantee that its transformation of the world was nothing more than self-delusion?

The answer to this question may lie in the concept of beauty. The quest for harmony leads both Classic and Romantic writers and artists to beauty, and in his *Ode on a Grecian Urn* Keats used the ancient Platonic identification of beauty and truth as a rallying cry. Pater applies the same formula, though with a somewhat different interpretation of the terms.[2]

Pater's obsession with beauty is mentioned by George Moore: 'Pater cut himself off from many readers . . . by insisting on a certain unfailing sense of beauty'.[3] In his 'Preface' to *Renaissance*, Pater outlines some important aspects of his concept of beauty. The fact that this discussion takes place so early on is significant, for his study of the Renaissance brings out the special nature of mood, culminating in the famous 'Conclusion', showing that art is to be conceived in terms of the temporality of human experience. He begins by asking what beauty is.

> Many attempts have been made by writers on art and poetry to define beauty in the abstract, to express it in the most general terms, to find some universal formula for it . . . Beauty, like all other qualities presented to human experience, is relative; and the definition of it becomes unmeaning and useless in proportion to its abstractness. To define beauty, not in the most abstract but in the most concrete terms possible, to find not its universal formula, but the formula which expresses most adequately this or that special manifestation of it, is the aim of the true student of aesthetics.[4]

There can, then, be no general definition, but only expression of individual manifestations. It is the differences that are paramount. What is revolutionary in this concept is its rejection of the Platonic notion of beauty that had dominated aesthetics far into the nineteenth century. Although earlier in the century the Platonic correlation between idea and copy was split dialectically, the Platonic structure of beauty remained untouched. Hegel defined beauty in art 'as one of the means which resolve and bring back to unity that antithesis and contradiction between the mind and Nature as they repose in abstract alienation from each other in themselves'.[5] This balancing operation is based on the 'beautiful . . . as the *sensuous semblance* of the Idea'.[6] For Hegel, beauty is the embodiment of the idea, with a simultaneous sublimation of physical reality. Even if this departs from Plato's idea and copy relationship, Hegel leaves no doubt that beauty assumes its power of mediation from the idea which becomes graspable through that mediation. Beauty is seen as the effect of an idea – an effect represented by art.

Ruskin, whom Graham Hough once called an unconscious Hegelian,[7] has a similar concept of beauty, even though its application is somewhat different. He attributes to beauty the same mediating function as does Hegel, except that it serves to vivify God's qualities in the world.[8] Ruskin, even more than Hegel, felt himself constrained to derive the natural world from the idea, because for him art had to convey an impression of God's work. Where he and Hegel both departed from the Platonic concept of beauty was in their refusal to distinguish qualitatively between idea and copy. They replaced the concept of linkage with that of reconciliation. For Ruskin, perception of 'divine types of beauty' promised a union of man and God,[9] and neither he nor Hegel leaves any doubt that the dialectical balance between man and Nature can be achieved by beauty only because this is seen as a special embodiment of the idea. The movement away from the linkage and towards mediation is typical of the nineteenth-century quest for totality by means of reconciliation.

The same quest is to be found in Pater, but his definition of beauty neither achieves nor seeks to achieve such a balance. He sees beauty as something relative; the abstract definition that Ruskin was still seeking, Pater rejects as meaningless. And what had previously been stressed as the constitutive idea of beauty is now viewed by Pater as the negation of the real qualities of beauty.

Pater's justification for this standpoint is the fact that time has the last word in all human affairs, and so invalidates all abstract values. Beauty and truth are mutually exclusive. For Pater beauty exists only as a particular form of appearance, and while Hegel defines it as the sensuous appearance of the Idea, Pater reduces the formula to the sensuous appearance, the definition of which will vary from one case to another. Thus it is the task of the student of aesthetics to find not an abstract and general definition, but a concrete and particular one for every manifestation. There is a polemic undertone in this task, and it is to be observed in the explicit contrast between relative and absolute as defining qualities of beauty. In this context, Pater's discussion is deliberately set against the background of the hitherto seemingly self-evident Platonic structure of aesthetics. His argument that beauty is pure appearance assumes its full force in opposition to the traditional concept, and instead of representing the universal, beauty becomes a special mode in which the percept is cast; it is the rare and select, the 'distinct within the immediate'.[10]

Thus beauty loses the synthetic character which Hegel and Ruskin had still taken for granted. It ceases to be an idea of balance, and so renounces its classical defining feature of harmony. Beauty as harmony presupposed the eradication of contrast through a universal ideal to which it gave presence. It therefore marked a transcendence of the aesthetic sphere to which Pater was unable to reconcile himself, in spite of the fact that beauty as harmony spread peace and assurance. But if beauty is regarded as pure appearance, then harmony can no longer be a defining feature, for what counts in the realm of pure phenomenality is difference.

> With a passionate care for beauty, the romantic spirit refuses to have it, unless the condition of strangeness be first fulfilled. Its desire is for a beauty born of unlikely elements, by a profound alchemy, by a difficult initiation, by the charm which wrings it even out of terrible things; and a trace of distortion, of the grotesque, may perhaps linger, as an additional element of expression, about its ultimate grace. Its eager, excited spirit will have strength, the grotesque, first of all – the trees shrieking as you tear off the leaves.[11]

This marks a complete break with the Platonic structure. The grotesque is the absolute antithesis of harmony, not least because it can only be defined through the different forms of appearance, whereas harmony is an a priori concept. For classical aesthetics beauty was the sensuous appearance of the Idea; for Pater it is the unusual appearance, most visible in the grotesque. Through this transvaluation, the world of appearances takes arms against the world of ideas, and beauty becomes an esoteric phenomenon, accessible only 'by a difficult initiation'. The alchemy metaphor captures the mysterious nature of this beauty, which resists illumination by directing us into shadowy darkness. This again is in contrast to the classical concept, which linked beauty to light. It is the impenetrableness of beauty that brings about its extraordinary fascination. In all its deformity it bursts upon the world of appearances without ever allowing us to take full possession of the forces concealed behind its strangeness. It is dependent upon appearance, and yet life is only seen as beautiful when it is defamiliarised. Thus it is not the trees that are beautiful, but their grotesque distortion as they shriek. 'What unites our art to the sacred arts is in no way that it is, like them, sacred, but that, like them, it only considers as valuable the forms that are completely different from those of appearance.'[12] Here we have a concept that runs completely counter to that of Nature and the ideal, which can no longer be equated with the totality of life. The grotesque seeks out that which in classical aesthetics would either be outlawed or rejected as unartistic and contingent; it tries to uncover the significance of the dark, out-of-the-way appearances, reacting aggressively against classical harmony, which is a provocation rather than a reassurance.

The aesthetic experience of beauty is now possible only by way of an ever-changing pageant of extraordinary appearances, and so beauty can no longer be defined through a concept. There are no longer any aesthetic objects with an existence of their own – there are only aesthetic potentials in the empirical world which must each be realised individually. Beauty will vary from one observer to the next, and the classical consensus has gone for ever. Becker calls the structure of the aesthetic sphere 'Heraclitan':

> i.e. the 'same' experience by the 'same' person in relation to the 'same' aesthetic object cannot be repeated with any certainty. And so ultimately the aesthetic is to be found only in the extremely vulnerable 'momentary' experience of what in turn is an extremely vulnerable and also merely 'potential' object. This is what conditions the 'fragility' of the aesthetic.[13]

Classical 'harmony' and anti-classical 'fragility' are concepts of beauty that spring from totally different sources: the idea and time. That which is extraordinary in life is perishable and ungraspable, and these are qualities that endow art, which filters out these transient moments, with its endless fascination.

Pater gives life to these critical insights through his fictional characters. Florian Deleal, intoxicated by all things beautiful, has a strangely correlative experience: 'For with this desire of physical beauty mingled itself early the fear of death – the fear of death intensified by the desire of beauty.'[14]

Beauty stems from the physical character of things, and so awakens fear of death, for it is only to be perceived through transient appearance.[15] Thus instead of comforting the beholder with the illusion of permanence, as did the classical concept, beauty confronts the beholder with its and therefore his own temporality, and ultimately death.

Pater's heroes embody the fragility of beauty. They must always remain open to the ever-changing pageant, burning as 'a hard gemlike flame', but slowly fading away in the ecstasy of their quest. Beauty, for them as for Pater, is to be grasped only as the moment of triumph locked between appearance and disappearance. 'The artist's existence is . . . incomparably adventurous.'[16] Marius's 'adventure' has almost cultic dimensions: 'In his scrupulous idealism, indeed, he too feels himself to be something of a priest, and that devotion of his days to the contemplation of what is beautiful, a sort of perpetual religious service.'[17] The perpetuity of this service and the religious vocabulary stress the agonising awareness of the threat to which the cult of beauty is exposed owing to the inseparability of beauty and time. The religious metaphor simultaneously elevates beauty to an ultimate within the aesthetic sphere, and indicates the necessity to cover up beauty's transient nature. The consolation remains that beauty is not to be encountered in one manifestation of itself, as every manifestation offers a different nuance; consequently the variations are infinite, and this coerces the human mind to be forever awake to beauty's multifarious appearances.

It is the indefinableness, self-concealment and sheer mystery of beauty that gives it this religious dimension. Marius experiences it for himself when he reads Apuleius's *Cupid and Psyche.*

> The *hiddenness* of perfect things: a shrinking mysticism . . . the fatality which seems to haunt any signal beauty, whether moral or physical, as if it were in itself something illicit and isolating: the suspicion and hatred it so often excites in the vulgar: – these were some of the impressions, forming, as they do, a constant tradition of somewhat cynical pagan experience, from Medusa and Helen downwards, which the old story enforced on him.[18]

The hiddenness of perfection and the fatality of beauty are interrelated concepts that form the basis of anti-classical Mannerism. The source of Marius's insight – the work of Apuleius – is itself part of late classical Mannerism. The disturbing quality is essential to beauty, for it defies and challenges the everyday world – not in the service of an idea that would legitimise it, but as an end in itself. Beauty can only reveal itself through its countless manifestations, each of which is unique and exclusive, because any access to it by means of cognition or explanation is sealed off forever; thus the inexplicable is the generative matrix of all the opaque appearances.

Beauty conceived in this manner is the governing quality of the aesthetic existence, which can never reach behind appearances (beyond which emptiness dwells). Needless to say, beauty is also free from all practical and utilitarian criteria, however important these may have been in the contemporary Arts and Crafts Movement. It embodies a quality which belongs to a region halfway between empirical reality and a transcendent world, and whose vague attributes are continual change and fragile impermanence. It is a reflection of the aesthetic condition, but it is not a legitimation. And so the question remains, how can this ever-changing, fragile quality be given objective expression without having an idea imposed upon it? Pater sees this legitimation in history.

'Postscript'

Appreciations ends with an essay modestly entitled 'Postscript', in which Pater takes a fresh look at the terms 'Classic' and 'Romantic'. He not only refrains from defining them, but also cautions against their reification, as they seem to be not so much concepts as 'real tendencies in the history of art and literature'.[19] He removes them from their traditional context by arguing against the idea that Classicism designates particular historical situations in art, and Romanticism a longing for the past. The art of Antiquity, and latter-day enthusiasm for the Middle Ages, are for him simply illustrations of 'tendencies' that extend far beyond the historical borderlines imposed on them.[20] Each historic epoch is nothing but a representation of a particular driving force of the time, and therefore embodies the tendencies operative in it:

> however falsely those two tendencies may be opposed by critics, or exaggerated by artists themselves, they are tendencies really at work at all times in art, moulding it, with the balance sometimes a little on one side, sometimes a little on the other, generating, respectively, as the balance inclines on this side or that, two principles, two traditions, in art, and in literature so far as it partakes of the spirit of art.[21]

Pater not only stretches the received notions of Classicism and Romanticism considerably, but he also delves below the surface of their respective manifestations in order to uncover the interplay out of which art arises. The interlinkage of these 'tendencies' endows art itself with a dialectic character represented in a constant interpenetration of Classicism and Romanticism.

This slant given to the traditional concepts applies especially to Romanticism, which Pater reassesses in the light of French Romanticism.

> Outbreaks of this spirit . . . come naturally with particular periods – times, when, in men's approaches towards art and poetry, curiosity may be noticed to take the lead, when men come to art and poetry, with a deep thirst for intellectual excite-

ment, after a long *ennui*, or in reaction against the strain of outward, practical things.[22]

The romantic longing here is not directed towards the past but towards an as yet unknown future. It frees itself from the shackles of the present, and searches for excitement in a realm beyond. Pater defined nineteenth-century Romanticism as a perpetual and unresting break with the familiar:

what in the eighteenth century is but an exceptional phenomenon, breaking through its fair reserve and discretion only at rare intervals, is the habitual guise of the nineteenth, breaking through it perpetually, with a feverishness, and incomprehensible straining and excitement, which all experience to some degree, but yearning also, in the genuine children of the romantic school, to be *énergique, frais, et dispos.*[23]

Such a break can only assume its outline when set against the familiar world it opposes, and so according to Pater Romanticism grows out of contradiction, which gives rise to the exploration of new realms.

There are the born romanticists, who start with an original, untried *matter*, still in fusion; who conceive this vividly, and hold by it as the essence of their work; who, by the very vividness and heat of their conception, purge away, sooner or later, all that is not organically appropriate to it, till the whole effect adjusts itself in clear, orderly, proportionate form; which form, after a very little time, becomes classical in its turn.[24]

Here, both the new correlation and the transvaluation of the traditional concepts are made apparent. Romanticism, in its quest for absolute otherness, is an avant-garde movement, and Pater quotes the opening sentences of Rousseau's *Confessions* to summarise the nature of this tendency.[25] Romanticism constantly seeks out new and hitherto concealed possibilities for art, but since the search must always lead into the unknown, its nature can only be defined at that point where it departs from a closed and formulated world. Thus Classicism is a necessary complement, marking off the area from which Romanticism departs. This in no way involves a devaluation of classical ideas, which in view of Pater's enthusiasm for the Greeks would be unthinkable; what it does point to is the dialectic nature of art. For despite its forward movement, Romanticism does not generate forms of art which, even after centuries, could still be clearly distinguished from classical achievements. On the contrary, whenever Romanticism has raided the inarticulate, the processing and shaping of the discoveries has turned them into classical form. And therefore Pater can echo Stendhal in claiming that: 'all good art was romantic in its day'.[26]

This marks the demise of the normative element in Classicism–Romanticism. The classical is no longer synonymous with perfection achieved by following rules, and is no longer confined to the exemplarity of ancient art. It now merely embodies a manner of writing striving after perfection, the nature of which eludes definition. Romanticism is no longer just a yearning for the Middle Ages, but instead is an avant-garde movement that looks forward with an indefinable longing to a future which will, in turn, render it classical in form – a Classicism which a new Romantic movement will then strive to break away from. The alternation between contrast and reconciliation which constitutes this interplay between Romanticism and Classicism is integral to art. And since 'all critical terms are relative',[27] neither the one nor the other can ever be understood as a prescriptive concept. No matter how far Romanticism distorts or transcends the familiar, the time will always come when the new will become the old and thus turn into Classicism.

This has far-reaching consequences for the definition of art, as Pater indicates in his essay.

> To be interesting and really stimulating, to keep us from yawning even, art and literature must follow the subtle movements of the nimbly-shifting *Time-Spirit*, or *Zeit-Geist*, understood by French not less than by German criticism, which is always modifying men's taste, as it modifies their manners and their pleasures . . . To turn always with that ever-changing spirit, yet to retain the flavour of what was admirably done in past generations, in the classics, as we say – is the problem of true romanticism.[28]

Since Classicism and Romanticism cease to be abstract concepts for Pater, their effects can only be grasped through their alternating movement in history; normative concepts are transmuted into historical ones. Art draws life from their interaction, and hence its 'essence' is through and through historical. As an historical phenomenon it reflects the inherent dialectic of the ever-changing 'Zeit-Geist', and therefore it is history which legitimises art or, in Pater's own words, provides the sanction for it. The successive movements of Classicism and Romanticism are the form in which the historicity of art embodies itself. In view of this interaction, art could never be equated with any ideal; instead it breaks up what has been solidified, and it preserves what has been perfected, and so history becomes the objective record of its endless mutations. Art for Pater is therefore no longer tied to a definite sacred or profane setting or service, but allows instead a perception of the manifold forms of human self-realisation, the endlessness of which is symbolised by the '*House Beautiful*, which the creative minds of all generations – the artists and those who have treated life in the spirit of art – are always building together, for the refreshment of the human spirit.'[29] The treasure chest can never be filled, because the human spirit will always be on the look-out for new effects.

History, then, sanctions Pater's idea of art. It animates man's urge to change the familiar and at the same time to preserve it. His redefinition of Classicism and Romanticism also objectifies his own position, which might otherwise have seemed precariously arbitrary without the backing of history. Art is now to be seen as an intermediate realm, situated between an experiential and an intangible reality, and this realm takes on a tangible reality in history. 'When becoming or destiny replaces being, history replaces theology, and art appears in its plurality and in its metamorphosis.'[30]

III *ART AND HISTORY*

6 What is history?

Hegelian schematism

The Greek mind had advanced to a particular stage of self-reflexion, but was careful not to pass beyond it. In oriental thought there is a vague conception of life everywhere, but no true appreciation of itself by the mind, no knowledge of the distinction of man's nature: in its consciousness of itself, humanity is still confused with the fantastic, indeterminate life of the animal and vegetable world. In Greek thought, on the other hand, the 'lordship of the soul' is recognised; that lordship gives authority and divinity to human eyes and hands and feet; inanimate nature is thrown into the background. But just there Greek thought finds its happy limit; it has not yet become too inward; the mind has not yet learned to boast its independence of the flesh; the spirit has not yet absorbed everything with its emotions, nor reflected its own colour everywhere. It has indeed committed itself to a train of reflexion which must end in defiance of form, of all that is outward, in an exaggerated idealism.[1]

These ideas, expounded by Pater in his essay on Winckelmann, form the basis of his view of history. The Hegelian structure is unmistakable, and indeed Pater actually quotes him.[2] For both of them, history is identical to a particular view of the mind, which stage by stage increases its awareness of itself. The dialectic movement of this self-propelled mind lies in the fact that at the different stages it gradually breaks free from its entanglement with Nature. It is still confused with Nature in oriental thought, achieves a happy balance in Greece, and then reacts against that balance as being its own opposite. By their contradictions to one another, the historical periods become integrating factors in a dialectical process whose overall goal is externalisation of inwardness. History is a continual individualisation of the mind, which gains increasing independence and complexity as it embraces more and more opposites. In short, it is the mind's process of self-perfection.

Pater's approach is not free from value judgements. He is fascinated by the balance unique to the Greek period – a balance that is subsequently destroyed by what for him is an 'exaggerated idealism', boasting its 'independence of the flesh' and ruining perfection by discovering and hence concentrating on inwardness. For Pater the highlights of history are the periods of balance, which would seem to indicate an immanent purpose independent of any philosophy of history and only to be fulfilled by the workings of history itself. The mind's awareness of itself can only be captured by its historical manifestations, since the mind is not subordinate to any overriding principle outside itself. The self-perception of the mind through its history is the purpose underlying Pater's concept of art, and so it is not Hegel's *Phenomenology of the Spirit* or his *Philosophy of World History* that make their mark on Pater's conception of history, but it is his *Aesthetics*.

The self-revelation of the mind entails an abstract problem which, in view of man's dependence on the physical world of experience, demands a concrete solution. Pater draws from Hegel's *Aesthetics*:

> The arts may thus be ranged in a series, which corresponds to a series of developments in the human mind itself. Architecture, which begins in a practical need, can only express by vague hint or symbol the spirit or mind of the artist . . . As human form is not the subject with which it deals, architecture is the mode in which the artistic effort centres, when the thoughts of man concerning himself are still indistinct, when he is still little preoccupied with those harmonies, storms, victories, of the unseen and intellectual world, which, wrought out into the bodily form, give it an interest and significance communicable to it alone. The art of Egypt, with its supreme architectural effects, is, according to Hegel's beautiful comparison, a Memnon waiting for the day, the day of the Greek spirit, the humanistic spirit, with its power of speech. Again, painting, music, and poetry, with their endless power of complexity, are the special arts of the romantic and modern ages. Into these, with the utmost attenuation of detail, may be translated every delicacy of thought and feeling, incidental to a consciousness brooding with delight over itself. Through their gradations of shade, their exquisite intervals, they project in an external form that which is most inward in passion or sentiment. Between architecture and those romantic arts of painting, music, and poetry, comes sculpture, which, unlike architecture, deals immediately with man, while it contrasts with the romantic arts, because it is not self-analytical. It has to do more exclusively than any other art with the human form, itself one entire medium of spiritual expression, trembling, blushing, melting into dew, with inward excitement. That spirituality which only lurks about architecture as a volatile effect, in sculpture takes up the whole given material, and penetrates it with an imaginative motive; and at first sight sculpture, with its solidity of form, seems a thing more real and full than the faint, abstract world of poetry or painting. Still the fact is the reverse. Discourse and action show man as he is, more directly than the play of the muscles and the moulding of the flesh; and over these poetry has command. Painting, by the flushing of colour in the face and dilatation of light in the eye – music, by its subtle range of tones – can refine most delicately upon a single moment of passion, unravelling its subtlest threads. But why should sculpture thus limit itself to pure form? Because, by this limitation, it becomes a perfect medium of expression for one peculiar motive of the imaginative intellect . . . The art of sculpture records the first naïve, unperplexed recognition of man by himself; and it is a proof of the high artistic capacity of the Greeks, that they apprehended and remained true to these exquisite limitations, yet, in spite of them, gave to their creation a mobile, a vital, individuality.[3]

This outline of the development of the arts follows closely Hegel's sequence of architecture, sculpture, painting, music and poetry as marking the process through which the arts mirrored the evolving self-perception of the mind. Equally the division into Classical and Romantic art is retained, which Hegel conceived as the basic categories of Western art since the Middle Ages. But despite the apparent concurrence here, there is one important difference. For Pater, the self-perceiving mind unfolded in the history of art is human and individual. He does not view the self as substance, but as a being ripened by the constant interplay between challenge and response in his dealings with the outside world. Hegel, on the other hand, saw the mind, or spirit, as substance, and the teleological movement of history as the workings of the absolute spirit on its way to self-consciousness. Pater takes over the Hegelian schema of history, but not the notion that gave rise to it. The apparent similarities therefore contain a fundamental difference which becomes even more obvious when one recalls the fact that for Pater art was the ultimate, whereas Hegel wrote: 'For us European art is no longer the highest means in which the actuality of truth is possessed . . . Art in its specific form has ceased to meet the highest requirements of spiritual life.'[4] For in art the absolute spirit achieves a realisation of itself which becomes superfluous when in passing this stage it reaches total self-knowledge. Pater continues to use the Hegelian schema purely in order to examine the human mind in its historical development, and since the mind can only be grasped in so far as it has manifested itself in history, this is for Pater first and foremost the history of art. Self-perception of the mind is made possible through the historically changing art forms by means of which the mind gains access to itself. The subject for Pater is neither a puppet nor 'director of the world spirit', but an *ens realissimum*, which cannot be defined ideally, and so must be understood through the historical process. Thus history provides an inalienable sanction for Pater's conception of art.

As man's inwardness can only be objectified by means of self-expression, the changes in the latter must clearly reflect the changes in the former. The history of the one is the history of the other. With architecture, there is only a rudimentary reflection of inwardness, but with sculpture there is a high degree of individualisation, since it transforms material into the human form. The Romantic arts disturb the balance achieved by sculpture, but in so doing they bring out the complexity of inwardness on the verge of grasping itself. Thus history provides an objective legitimation for style and expression, as advocated by Pater, which together represent the transformation of the world by the human subject. 'Historicism, which was a new mode of understanding not only for the historian but also for human life in general, brought this process of individualisation to an awareness of itself, because it led to comprehending all historical life as the development of individuality, no matter how embedded it was in typical processes and conventions.'[5] In view of Pater's historicism, it was impossible for him to subscribe to Hegel's normative approach, for a priori norms subjugate the individual manifestations which for Pater constitute history itself. Pater saw individualisation not as a logical but as an aesthetic process, communicating inwardness through ever-changing forms, and so it follows that there could be no eschatological fulfilment of history but only an infinity of manifestations lacking any conceivable teleology. Even perfection, such as the Greeks achieved, must sink (though never disappear) into the passing stream.

An essential element of historical development is the fact that it is only possible through polarity, through a never ending tension between opposing trends. Great spiritual movements, when they first arise, establish themselves and dominate life . . . often seem to assume an absolute character, suppressing all opposition, at least for a time.[6]

Pater also took this dialectic view of historical change, for reasons he explained most graphically:

The longer we contemplate that Hellenic ideal, in which man is at unity with himself, with his physical nature, with the outward world, the more we may be inclined to regret that he should ever have passed beyond it, to contend for a perfection that makes the blood turbid, and frets the flesh, and discredits the actual world about us. But if he was to be saved from the *ennui* which ever attaches itself to realisation, even the realisation of the perfect life, it was necessary that a conflict should come, that some sharper note should grieve the existing harmony, and the spirit chafed by it beat out at last only a larger and profounder music.[7]

Here we have two distinct elements of Pater's concept of history, and despite their apparent contradiction, each sheds a good deal of light on the other. One is the unity of the human spirit with itself, and the other is the destruction of perfection. The unity which Pater continually proclaims as the ideal to be striven for[8] is an essential feature of his conception of art. The demand for unity arises out of differences and divisions which come about because the individual finds himself subject to situations from which he wishes to be free. For Pater it is art that achieves this liberation. Expression and style enable the subject to reduce the world to his own dimensions, and by adapting the world to the needs of the mind the self brings about its own unity. The Hellenic ideal was a realisation of this desire. But the mind's unity with itself is not an abstract principle – it is bound up with historical situations, and so whatever harmony is achieved will be temporal and will lose its validity when the respective forms adequate to the self-perception of the mind have to be abandoned in view of changing historical situations. The achieved perfection itself more often than not triggers this process, as its fulfilment spreads the langour of *ennui*, not least because there is no fulfilment of history, and if there were one, it would be of a transhistorical nature which Pater would never have been able to endorse. For him, history is a process divulging the different ways in which the mind has achieved, or at least sought, unity with itself and with the world on its way to unending self-discovery.

History is thus no longer a matter merely of antiquarian curiosity, but is of immediate importance to the mind's quest for self-assurance:

> the proper instinct of self-culture cares not so much to reap all that those various forms of genius can give, as to find in them its own strength. The demand of the intellect is to feel itself alive. It must see into the laws, the operation, the intellectual reward of every divided form of culture; but only that it may measure the relation between itself and them. It struggles with those forms till its secret is won from each, and then lets each fall back into its place, in the supreme, artistic view of life.[9]

Here, then, is the link between history and the present. The various cultures which in their sequence make up the course of history are parallel to 'self-culture' – a fervently advocated and highly acclaimed idea of *fin-de-siècle* aestheticism. The phases of different cultures reflect the subject's own inner development, and this correspondence allows for a growing self-transparency resulting in a grasping of oneself. What is to be obtained from this self-understanding? 'A sense of freedom'[10] is Pater's answer, through which the subject disentangles itself from the enchanted web of necessities in which it has been trapped. Art alone grants these precious moments of freedom, and it reveals to the human mind its capabilities of mastering experiential realities. These are, then, moments of profoundest insight. 'Who, if he saw through all, would fret against the chain of circumstance which endows one at the end with those great experiences?'[11]

Troeltsch once said that the basis of history was the 'category of individual totality',[12] and Pater would have endorsed this, with one modification: that only in art could 'individual totality' come to full fruition. Art records the different phases of the individual's struggle for unity with himself and the world, and so its history is a constant tailoring of the world according to the needs of human self-presentation, turning the world finally into an aesthetic phenomenon. If this history is meant to afford human self-perception, then the meaning of history of art becomes a 're-enactment of past experience'.[13]

Pater's sense of history was guided by the urge to find a frame of reference which would allow him to objectify the function of art as he saw it. History seems to bear out the claim that art is autonomous, and hence ultimate. These qualifications, however, could not be conceptualised in either philosophical or theological terms. For this reason the unending process of history seemed to be the only 'objective correlative'. Its ever-changing sequence of forms and responses provides confirmation, objectifying the aesthetic without ever concretising it or subjecting it to any abstract principle. However, to consider history as a sanction betrays an inherent weakness in the *l'art pour l'art* concept, for whatever is absolute ought to carry its own legitimation within itself. As the claim to art's autonomy could not be sustained, Pater propped it up with history. This, in turn, made his perception of history lopsided. If history is meant to sanction the autonomy of art, it suffers a severe reduction by being confined to the history of art. This shrinkage of history bears witness to the fact that art as the ultimate is a claim that cannot be substantiated but only posited.

Historicity

Pater is in accord with Hegel's new view of history as the setting for a special 'self-revelation' of the spirit.[14] But although this revolutionary concept meets with his approval,[15] the emerging differences cannot be overlooked, as is evident from his reference to the 'facile orthodoxy . . . of Hegel'.[16] Pater takes over Hegel's schematism but, as we have seen, he rejects the ideas within the pattern. Nevertheless, there are passages in Hegel that do seem to correspond to Pater's own ideas, if one disregards their many-layered contextual relations:

> It is essential to note that the movement of the spirit is progressive . . . In this concept there is no determinacy other than that of perfection, which is very indeterminate and leaves behind nothing but changeability; there is no criterion for change, and no criterion for what now exists, to what extent it is right and substantive. There is no principle of exclusion, and no goal, no final purpose is set; it is, rather, change, which constitutes the residue, that alone constitutes determinacy.[17]

Changeableness as the only certainty must have seemed very plausible to Pater, and he found confirmation of this insight in various passages of Hegel's *Philosophy of World History*.

> The entire modern theory of 'development', . . . what is it but old Heracliteanism awake once more in a new world, and grown to full proportions? Πάντα χωρεῖ, πάντα ῥεῖ. – It is the burden of Hegel on the one hand, to whom nature, and art, and polity, and philosophy, aye, and religion too, each in its long historic series, are but so many conscious movements in the secular process of the eternal mind; and on the other hand of Darwin and Darwinism, for which 'type' itself properly *is* not but is only always *becoming*. The bold paradox of Heraclitus is, in effect, repeated on all sides, as the vital persuasion just now of a cautiously reasoned experience, and, in illustration of the very law of change which it asserts, may itself presently be superseded as a commonplace . . . the idea of development (that, too, a thing of growth, developed in the progress of reflexion) is at last invading one by one, as the secret of their explanation, all the products of the mind, the very mind itself, the

abstract reason . . . Gradually we have come to think, or to feel, that primary certitude.[18]

History teaches the certitude of change and is itself a record of change. Here Pater's view would seem to agree with that expressed in the passage from Hegel. But Pater's allusions to Hegel and Darwin ultimately bring out the half-truths told by these witnesses for change. The same applies also to Heraclitus, who described the indefinable power of Logos behind the comings and goings of ever-changing phenomena. Neither Hegel nor Darwin is content merely with the concept of continual development, for each of them attributes a direction to this process. Hegel's philosophy of history is really a theology of history, for in relation to the last step, he sees 'the previous (steps) as inevitably leading to it'.[19] And Darwin also detects an abstract principle at work behind the changes of species and the driving force of evolution: natural selection. For both of them the whole process of development is the expression and realisation of a metahistorical idea. Hegel's eschatology and Darwin's 'struggle for survival' impose a particular form on historical development, but Pater's concept of 'becoming' blocks out such an ideology of progress. The postulation of a fixed meaning in history would place ideas before experience,[20] whereas for Pater history was the ultimate orientation for man's knowledge of himself, and fixed ideas could only limit and so hinder this knowledge. Whenever history is directed towards possible goals, it has one eye on the future, and this is in stark contrast to Pater's view, which remains firmly retrospective.

What Pater expects to gain from history is summed up by the following observation: 'One of the privileges of the larger survey of historical phenomena enjoyed by our own generation, looking back over many unexpected revivals in doctrine and practice, is the assurance that there are no lost causes.'[21] The fact that the past remains reassuringly preserved and may re-emerge in the course of time explains why Pater does not bemoan the transitoriness of perfection. For him, history is neither the sacrificial altar of the world spirit, nor the survival of the fittest; it is the preserver of all that has been. His view of evolution is neither futuristic nor chiliastic; it is historical. The beginning and end of becoming are of no significance beside the actual process of change. Pater's indifference to a philosophy of history is patently clear from the manner in which he lumps Darwin and Hegel together as representatives of modern evolutionary theory without making any distinction between them.

The historical nature of the process of becoming is emphasised in *Plato and Platonism*:

we come into the world, each one of us, 'not in nakedness', but by the natural course of organic development clothed far more completely than even Pythagoras supposed in a vesture of the past, nay, fatally shrouded, it might seem, in those laws

> or tricks of heredity which we mistake for our volitions; in the language which is more than one half of our thoughts; in the moral and mental habits, the customs, the literature, the very houses, which we did not make for ourselves; in the vesture of a past, which is (so science would assure us) not ours, but of the race, the species: that *Zeit-geist*, or abstract secular process, in which, as we could have had no direct consciousness of it, so we can pretend to no future personal interest. It is humanity itself now – abstract humanity – that figures as the transmigrating soul, accumulating into its 'colossal manhood' the experience of ages; making use of, and casting aside in its march, the souls of countless individuals, as Pythagoras supposed the individual soul to cast aside again and again its outworn body.[22]

The perspective of the individual is linked to that of the changing 'Zeitgeist', and the process of development, as far as the individual is concerned, seems harmful rather than beneficial in the sense that he is sacrificed along the road to some future perfection of mankind in the abstract. This vague future perfection, developing through the centuries, is not seen by Pater as a step-by-step ascent to transfigured unity – which was Hegel's view – but as an idea strangely unrelated to our own desires and growing out of the continual destruction of the concrete and the individual. So long as the process of becoming is regarded as a natural process striving towards a future goal, the individual has no value save as a transient sign of an overriding pattern. 'The individual historical appearance became nothing but a means when the idea of development, taken normatively, was overexpanded to the idea of progress. It became a pure end in itself when the idea of individuality focused on it exclusively.'[23] This is the essential difference between a normative and an individual view of evolution. For Pater, as we have seen, history was a means whereby the individual could find reassurance and self-awareness, so that it could never be subservient to any norm. Collingwood brought out the difference in a manner directly applicable to Pater's concept of history:

> Evolution, after all, is a natural process, a process of change; and as such it abolishes one specific form in creating another . . . The past, in a natural process, is a past superseded and dead. Now suppose the historical process of human thought were in this sense an evolutionary process. It would follow that the ways of thinking characteristic of any given historical period are ways in which people must think then, but in which others, cast at different times in a different mental mould, cannot think at all. If that were the case, there would be no such thing as truth . . . The fallacy . . . is the confusion between a natural process, in which the past dies in being replaced by the present, and an historical process, in which the past, so far as it is historically known, survives in the present.[24]

This difference is crucial to Pater. So long as the process of evolution is identified with a normative theory of progress, the past must die, and this is why he describes this process in terms of the 'laws of heredity', which make the individual out to be predetermined. But as he insists at the end of the Winckelmann essay,[25] contact with history should animate the idea of freedom and, furthermore, ensure that 'there are no lost causes'. Such an assurance is in direct contrast to the concept of evolution towards an ultimate purpose, and this is the point at which Pater diverges from Hegel and all other evolutionary theorists. They deny that which is Pater's be-all and end-all: self-assurance through history. This is only possible if the past is alive and present. Evolution seen as the triumph of abstract principles over individual experience is alien to Pater, who prizes individual experience, the accumulation of which always takes precedence over any interpretation of the evolutionary process. Pater's rejection of any philosophy of history has its deepest roots in his concept of time as the background to all events. There is no philosophy of history that does not, in its own way, focus on the *end* of time.

Pater's indifference to beginnings and endings, and his fascination with change, are both evident from the attention he pays to those periods of transition which brought history to life.[26] He considers them intimately related to his own presence, which is equally pervaded by a sense of transition. In Ancient Greece, for example, he found not only the ideal of noble simplicity and quiet grandeur, but also the deep dark depths of the chthonic underworld, the latter being as vital an integrating spiritual factor as the former. Pater expressly points out the fact that Winckelmann failed to notice this darker side of the Greek mind,[27] and he describes the contrast as the Ionic and Doric principle – a concept which Nietzsche called Dionysian and Apollonian. Pater's *Greek Studies* are an attempt to analyse this opposition.[28] The effusive Ionic and the harmonious Doric combine to produce a sculpture that reconciles the opposites. 'In undergoing the action of these two opposing influences, and by harmonising in itself their antagonism, Greek sculpture does but reflect the larger movements of more general Greek history.'[29] Reconciliation in these sculptures arrests this strangely transitional process:

> Greek sculpture deals almost exclusively with youth, where the moulding of the bodily organs is still as if suspended between growth and completion, indicated but not emphasised . . . This colourless, unclassified purity of life, with its blending and interpenetration of intellectual, spiritual, and physical elements, still folded together, pregnant with the possibilities of a whole world closed within it, is the highest expression of the indifference which lies beyond all that is relative or partial. Everywhere there is the effect of an awakening, of a child's sleep just disturbed.[30]

The inbetween-ness of the transition becomes increasingly tangible as suspended movement, as a presentiment of endless possibilities, and as an effect of awakening, but these are not concrete qualities, and can only be conveyed indirectly, and tentatively.

Pater found a similar situation in Late Antiquity, with an equally divided world which he reflects in the experience of Marius. The hero of his novel grows up in an environment that is still under the influence of the magical, mythical cult of fertility.[31] For Marius, the blessing of the fields animates a spiritual world whose traces have burrowed their way deep into his mind. But as he gathers more and more experience and his mind matures, so the old bonds slowly begin to loosen. Central to all his experiences is a massive shift: the hitherto guiding attitudes are now permeated by a sense that the world they had ordered is drawing to an end:

> Such were the commonplaces of this new people, among whom so much of what Marius had valued most in the old world seemed to be under renewal and further promotion. Some transforming spirit was at work to harmonise contrasts, to deepen expression – a spirit which, in its dealing with the elements of ancient life, was guided by a wonderful tact of selection, exclusion, juxtaposition, begetting thereby a unique effect of freshness, a grave yet wholesome beauty, because the world of sense, the whole outward world was understood to set forth the veritable unction and royalty of a certain priesthood and kingship of the soul within, among the prerogatives of which was a delightful sense of freedom.[32]

In his contact with early Christianity, Marius becomes aware of the internalisation of pagan forms of life, and hence of the changeability of things, but this awareness is not a cause of sorrow; the old ways of life are not destroyed by the advance of new ideas, but they are strangely transformed, and so he does not regard Christianity as a break – it is a wondrous metamorphosis which gives him his 'delightful sense of freedom'. Once again we have a blending of opposites, and here the process occurs in such a way that all kinds of completely new variations appear. Marius does not conceive of himself as a Christian, who now might feel obliged to condemn his earlier world, but he incorporates it into the new one, thereby extending both worlds and so extending his discovery of himself.

The Renaissance, too, is for Pater not a break but a blending of Christian and ancient art.[33] And in his own immediate nineteenth-century past, Pater also finds vivid confirmation of his concept of change as a merging of opposites. Here Goethe is the model:

> Goethe illustrates a union of the Romantic spirit, in its adventure, its variety, its profound subjectivity of soul, with Hellenism, in its transparency, its rationality, its desire of beauty – that marriage of Faust and Helena, of which the art of the nineteenth century is the child.[34]

In all these periods of transition, new ideas bring forth hitherto unknown nuances in the old, and the past and future are blended together in a manner that produces mood rather than definition. The process is not seen as abstract, with the present trampling over the dead bones of the past; the present carries the past along with it, and it is only through historical manifestations that the process can be observed, and not through any abstract idea. Pater conceived of this fusion as a model for mediating past and present, which held out the promise that finally the human subject could also be at one with itself and the world. Therefore his view of history was not as disinterested as it sometimes appears; it was imbued with the fervent desire to heal the split between self and world. Although spurred by this intention, Pater was careful not to impose a pattern on history. He was, rather, looking for confirmation that incompatibles can nevertheless be mediated, and this is the reason why he focused so exclusively on periods of transition. What has to be borne in mind, however, is that art for Pater resolved irreconcilabilities and thus became the paradigmatic embodiment of what transition meant to him. The relation of art to periods of transition is thus twofold: as the only genuine representation of the interpenetration of opposites, it nevertheless appears to be dependent on history, which alone provides the backing for such a view. Thus Pater's concept of art received its legitimation from history, which he saw not as a movement towards perfection, but as a continual series of changes in which reality broke up into contrasts, which were then blended together by art. Unlike Hegel, Pater saw no determinate ideal behind this process; change *was* the ultimate law. And the absence of the overriding ideal rendered the process aesthetic, since all these periods of transition invalidated existing norms without replacing them with others. Art, as aesthetic reconciliation, embodied this in-between world and drew its tangibility and its legitimation from history.

'House Beautiful'

We see the majority of mankind going most often to definite ends . . . but the end may never be attained . . . Meantime, to higher or lower ends, they move too often with something of a sad countenance, with hurried and ignoble gait, becoming, unconsciously, something like thorns, in their anxiety to bear grapes; it being possible for people, in the pursuit of even great ends, to become themselves thin and impoverished in spirit and temper, thus diminishing the sum of perfection in the world, at its very sources . . . Justify rather the end by the means . . . whatever may become of the fruit, make sure of the flowers and the leaves . . . To treat life in the spirit of art, is to make life a thing in which means and ends are identified: to encourage such treatment, the true moral significance of art and poetry.[35]

For Pater, the means *are* the end, and any eschatological purpose can only reduce the possibilities and so diminish the 'sum of perfection'. In art, the possibilities of life become an end in themselves, and the restriction of definition gives way to the freedom of variety. Because of its lack of goal, art is sterile – it bears no fruit – but it is precisely this sterility that enables it to be and to preserve itself for its own sake. Through the profusion of its possibilities, the density of its expressiveness, and its powers of evocation, nothing is ever lost 'which has ever interested living men and women'.[36] Art preserves what time destroys, and this preservation is Pater's definition of culture.[37] As art is not orientated by purposes, the link between past and presence is established by memory, and according to W. Ivanov:

> In this sense culture is not only monumental but also initiatory to the spirit. For memory, its sovereign power, allows her true servants to participate in the initiatory rituals of the fathers, and by renewing these rituals inside them, conveys to them the strength of new beginnings and new trends. Memory is a dynamic principle; forgetting is fatigue and interruption of movement.[38]

The grasp of historical change by memory is crystallised by Pater into his concept of the '*House Beautiful*, which the creative minds of all generations – the artists and those who have treated life in the spirit of art – are always building together, for the refreshment of the human spirit'.[39] The 'House Beautiful' is conceived as an almost total identification of art and history. There is no operative principle of selection; instead it blends together all contrasting movements into a totality of life that continues to expand indefinitely. Individual situations and the changeability of history are equally preserved and rendered contemporaneous. Perfection is constantly snatched from the passing stream of time, and accumulative additions result in rearrangements and new cultural configurations.[40] The 'House Beautiful' replaces all abstract principles designed to tackle history, and takes the place which in all philosophies of history is reserved for the respective *telos*. Building the 'House Beautiful' is a process without end, as it is geared to the changeability of history from which it filters out all that is worth preserving. This ever-growing collection should not, in spite of its perpetuity, be mistaken for a mundane reflection of eternity; instead it adumbrates an infinity hidden in human finiteness, allowing man to experience his own unlimited possibilities. In this respect the 'House Beautiful' is similar to that of the 'Imaginary Museum' which according to Malraux represents a modernist view of art.[41] The treasures of the world are brought to this museum and form a realm of blessed detachment which, nevertheless, is in and of this world. In this treasure house, man with all his different historical achievements becomes visible to himself. Culture is 'initiatory memory',[42] and the treasure house is the place in which the past begins to fertilise the present.

The desire implicit in the concept of the 'House Beautiful' is again brought out into the open by Marius:

> he remained, and must always be, of the poetic temper: by which, I mean, among other things, that quite independently of the general habit of that pensive age he lived much, and as it were, by system, in reminiscence . . . there would come, together with that precipitate sinking of things into the past, a desire, after all, to

retain 'what was so transitive'. Could he but arrest, for others also, certain clauses of experience, as the imaginative memory presented them to himself! . . . To create, to live, perhaps, a little while beyond the allotted hours, if it were but in a fragment of perfect expression: – it was thus his longing defined itself for something to hold by amid the perpetual flux.[43]

The 'imaginative memory' is essential to the aesthetic attitude; it is no mere passive registration of events, but actively selects impressions and transforms them. It preserves but at the same time adapts to the requirements of the imagining, remembering individual. It is only through memory thus transformed that the world of the individual is built up, and it is only through memory that he can satisfy his longing to create and live with perfection, or at least with those fragments of perfection that he can rescue from time. Living an aesthetic life means dwelling in the realm of memory which is an earthly paradise tarnished, however, by its pastness. Marius's longing is for that which Pater formulated theoretically with the 'House Beautiful' – the 'imaginary museum' built up by all those minds that 'have treated life in the spirit of art'. This treasure house is neither an idea nor an aesthetic canon;[44] it is the continual extraction of perfection from the process of history.

The 'House Beautiful' emerges out of the perpetual flux of time; it blends art and history into one. History is important in so far as it offers a series of ideal ways in which man can realise himself; art, no longer conceived as mimesis, is a constant transcendence of those conditions to which man appears to be inextricably tied. History finds its meaning in art, and art finds in history the confirmation of its achievements. The inner-worldly transcendence brought about by the work of art manifests itself in an unending variety of thoughts, all of which are borne into the 'House Beautiful' and preserved there by the 'initiatory memory', which is art.

7 The limits of historical legitimation

Plato and Platonism

Pater considered his book on Plato to be the best of all his works.[1] And yet the impact of this book is scarcely to be compared to that of his other writings.[2] Clearly his interpretation of Plato is basic to an understanding of his ideas, and so the book must be regarded more as a personal confession than a critical monograph. It is a collection of lectures, the subject of which is not so much Plato himself as Pater's approach to Plato, and so it would be invidious to accuse him of misinterpreting Plato.[3] Our concern here must be to elucidate Pater's ideas in the light of his treatment of Plato.

Pater's high esteem for this work may be attributed to the fact that it is the clearest embodiment of his concept of history. His perspective is already established at the very beginning of the first essay:

> Dogmatic and eclectic criticism alike have in our own century, under the influence of Hegel and his predominant theory of the ever-changing 'Time-spirit' or *Zeitgeist*, given way to a third method of criticism, the historic method, which bids us replace the doctrine, or the system, we are busy with, or such an ancient monument of philosophic thought as *The Republic*, as far as possible in the group of conditions, intellectual, social, material, amid which it was actually produced, if we would really understand it . . . To put Plato into his natural place, as a result from antecedent and contemporary movements of Greek speculation, of Greek life generally: such is the proper aim of the historic, that is to say, of the really critical study of him.[4]

The reference to *The Republic* is deliberate, for Plato's conception of the state stands at the core of Pater's study. He is at pains to establish the link between historical conditions and Utopian perfection, and as champion of an exclusively historical method, he rejects any metaphysical origins for Platonic philosophy, insisting that Plato is simply the end product of a complex development. The philosophy itself is not new. 'Nothing but the life-giving principle of cohesion is new; the new perspective, the resultant complexion, the expressiveness which familiar thoughts attain by novel juxtaposition. In other words, the *form* is new.'[5] The idea that Plato emerged from historical circumstances and united all pre-Socratic philosophies, merely endowing them with a new form, is basic to Pater's interpretation. Plato was simply a collector reacting to his findings and reshaping them. The only novelty was the perfection of a new shape and therefore it is not surprising that Pater's study of Plato revolved around the latter's aesthetics. It was Pater's aim to show how this perfection grew from interacting historical conditions, for this was the only way in which the aesthetic approach could enable the perfection to be grasped. And this is where he begins to reassess Plato – his starting-point demands a sociological extrapolation of idealistic philosophy from its real conditions. In this way the historic method satisfies a vital need: it explains perfection through historical circumstances. Thus the real world of experience always predominates over philosophical abstraction, and the Platonic concept of idea and copy, in that order of priority, is obliterated. Once more reality triumphs over abstraction, as it did in Pater's concepts of style and beauty.

The individual essays deal with different pre-Socratic philosophies, all of which contribute in a greater or lesser degree to Plato's philosophy. The book begins with Heraclitus, who considered the basic principle of the world to be the eternal flux of things: 'The principle of disintegration, the incoherency of fire or flood . . . are inherent in the primary elements alike of matter and of the soul . . . the principle of lapse, of waste, was, in fact, in one's self.'[6] Heraclitus's monistic concept opened up an insight into the workings of the cosmos which challenged philosophers from Parmenides through to Plato. As the perpetual flux seemed to have its roots in the make-up of man himself, subsequent philosophical endeavours concentrated on damming the endless stream of passing things.

Parmenides, according to Pater, was the first to solve the problem with his principle of the One which is all-encompassing and has not originated out of anything prior to it. 'Motion discredited, motion gone, all was gone that belonged to an outward and concrete experience, thus securing exclusive validity to the sort of knowledge, if knowledge it is to be called, which corresponds to the "Pure Being", that after all is only definable as "Pure Nothing".'[7] Parmenides's abstraction is, in Pater's eyes, a Nothing. Pater cannot accept as real a pure being that exists before all becoming and all experience. He sees Parmenides as an extreme case, whose solution is meaningless because his downgrading of the perpetual flux is not orientated by experience, but on the contrary, arises out of the speculation which negates or at least devalues the real world. Pater accepts Heraclitus's eternal flux, but he rejects any principle that attempts to conquer the flux by way of concepts with a transempirical origin instead of experience itself. His equation of pure being with nothing is only possible because his perspective is totally empirical. Nevertheless, he argues that Plato did take over Parmenides's dualistic concept of the world, but he corrected the empty concept of being by endowing it with a far greater plasticity. For Pater, Plato's ideas are not abstractions, but have the 'firm plastic outlines of the delightful old Greek polytheism' which in this manner, could prevail against 'repellent monotheism'.[8]

'To realise unity in variety, to discover *cosmos* – an order that shall satisfy one's reasonable soul – below and within apparent chaos: is from first to last the continuous purpose of what we call philosophy.'[9] This is the dialectical principle that Pater finds realised for the first time in the work of Pythagoras. For Pater, Pythagoras embodies the great synthesis of early Greek philosophy, for he succeeded in blending the chaotically shifting world of Heraclitus with the abstract substantialist thinking of Parmenides. The latter concept thereby underwent a significant change which was to be given its final form in Plato's theory of ideas. The idea is not a substance independent of and existing before experience but, in Pater's interpretation of Pythagoras, it is a necessity brought about by experience for the ordering of a chaotic reality. Without the ceaseless flux of experience, ideas would be meaningless, since their whole purpose is to impose order on reality – in other words, to act in the service of experience. Thus the idea cannot precede experience. With this argument, Pater is able to remove the unbridgeable divide between abstract idea and sensual experience in order to pinpoint their interplay, in which he discovered the potential for mediation. This is a fundamental theme in the book on Plato. For the 'historic sense' continually roots out these moments in the 'secular process' when contradictions are mediated. As we have seen, Pater's concept of history excluded any eschatological ending, hence mediation was the only purpose of history. Pythagoras was able to mediate between the Heraclitean multifariousness of ever-changing phenomena and the Parminedean rigour of an all-encompassing One – but the principle of mediation remained aesthetic:

> music, which though it is of course much besides, is certainly a formal development of purely numerical laws: that too surely *is* something, independently of ourselves, in the real world without us, like a personal intelligible soul durably resident there for those who bring intelligence of it, of music, with them; to be known on the favourite Platonic principle of like by like.[10]

Music is an aesthetic synthesis of Heraclitus's movement with Parmenides's stasis. It is controlled movement which balances out opposites. The balance is all the more fascinating for Pater in that there are formal laws at work in music that exist independently of man, even though man, if he is particularly sensitive, can feel at one with this objective reality. Music, then, brings man and world together in an ideal unity which represents the objective correspondence to Pater's concept of style. For style assimilates and transforms reality in order to cancel the difference between man and world. This is why Pater sees music as the criterion against which all art must measure itself in the quest for perfection. Mediation is ideally epitomised by music. The untamed mobility of sensual experience and the abstractness of the transcendental idea find common ground in aesthetic qualities in which neither pure experience nor pure abstraction is ultimately triumphant. This is another reason why for Pater the historical process cannot be logical, as it was for Hegel, but must be aesthetic. Instead of purposeful progress, there is only ceaseless mediation, which Pater sees as having first been formulated by Pythagoras's musical principle.

With Socrates, philosophy changed direction. Instead of speculation about the cosmos, he was concerned with man's knowledge of himself. 'Socrates brought philosophy down from heaven to earth.'[11] Self-reflection was dominated by the struggle for assurance,[12] but in spite of this revolution, the same principle is still apparent in Socrates as accompanied the speculations of Pythagoras: 'In the course of his seventy years he has adjusted that thought of the invisible to the general facts and to many of the subtler complexities of man's experience in the world of sight.'[13] In spite of the changed philosophical question, mediation again becomes of paramount concern to Socrates, but unlike Pythagoras's speculative synthesis, he adapts the invisible, abstract reality to man's concrete experience. This leads to insight into correct modes of conduct, but for Pater the insight is not an end in itself. He regards it as 'the first condition of any real power over others'.[14]

The importance of this function for Pater's view of Socrates is evident from his essay on the Sophists, whom he regarded as the ultimate stage leading to Plato: 'sophistry is a reproduction of the Heraclitean flux. The old Heraclitean physical theory presents itself as a natural basis for the moral, the social, dissolution, which the sophistical movement promotes'.[15] The recurrence of the Heraclitean 'all is flowing' in the rhetoric of the Sophists struck Pater as a threat to the achievements of the early Greek philosophers who had sought to impose order on the flux of things. He accuses them of having no controlling principle, such as is necessary to counteract that latent urge for mobility and effusiveness which marks the Greek mind. Instead they devise rules of combination always derived *ad hoc* from commonly shared experiences, thus destroying the delicate balance between experience and ideas.

> With them art began too precipitately, as mere form without matter; a thing of disconnected empiric rules, caught from the mere surface of other people's productions, in congruity with a general method which everywhere ruthlessly severed branch and flower from its natural root – art from one's own vivid sensation or belief.[16]

That which drove the early Greek philosophers to seek a balance is not merely neglected by the Sophists' instruction for achieving success, but is in principle obliterated. The Sophists even divide that which in Nature is combined, as paradigmatically illustrated for Pater by a flower separated from its roots, and therefore they give free rein to Heraclitean changeability, which they consider as man's ultimate experience. 'The essential vice of Sophistry, as Plato conceived it, was that for it no real things existed.'[17] Thus Plato took sophistry for a challenge to which he had to respond.

With the Sophists Pater concludes his discussion of the preconditions that have shaped the philosophy of Plato. Two aspects of this discussion are of special importance. First, Pater sees Plato as the historical product of pre-Socratic aspirations,[18] and he uses the historical method to try to explain how perfection emerged from an accumulation of different philosophical trends. Secondly, and closely connected with this, Pater stresses the basic tendencies of these philosophies, which were to culminate in Plato: namely, the idea of mediation. The fact that he begins the book with Heraclitus is no accident, for Pater shares his basic concept of flux.[19] He then goes on to show how philosophers from Parmenides through to Pythagoras and ultimately to Socrates endeavoured to balance out opposites: Parmenides embodied a direct but one-sided reaction to Heraclitus, bringing about an awareness of order; Pythagoras achieved a balance of the multiple with the single through the aesthetic harmony of music; and finally Socrates discovered in self-reflection the principle of mediation between an invisible world and concrete experience. From this mediation sprang the power to master human life by imposing control on changeability.

The early Greek philosophers achieved this purpose only by hypostatising aspects either of the cosmos or of human life, and Plato's unique achievement was the scope of his synthesis. Pater begins by describing Plato himself, and from the person he then deduces the basic features of his philosophy.

> The lover, who is become a lover of the invisible, but still a lover, and therefore, literally, a seer, of it, carrying an elaborate cultivation of the bodily senses, of eye and ear, their natural force and acquired fineness – . . . into the world of intellectual abstractions; seeing and hearing there too, associating for ever all the imagery of things seen with the conditions of what primarily exists only for the mind, filling that 'hollow land' with delightful colour and form, as if now at last the mind were veritably dealing with living people there, living people who play upon us through the affinities, the repulsion and attraction, of *persons* towards one another, all the magnetism, as we call it, of actual human friendship or love: – There, is the *formula* of Plato's genius, the essential condition of the specially Platonic temper, of Platonism . . . For him, all gifts of sense and intelligence converge in one supreme faculty of theoretic vision . . . the imaginative reason.[20]

What in Platonic philosophy has always been a strict division between idea and copy is seen by Pater as a blending of the two.[21] The abstract realm of ideas is a 'hollow land', which needs contact with concrete experience in order to come to life, and it is only when experience and ideas join together that there is Platonism, according to Pater's interpretation of the term. Instead of division there is interpenetration, which becomes tangible through 'imaginative reason' – a faculty that establishes not only the Platonic order of the world, but also the predominantly aesthetic quality of this order. This is an explicit rejection of the irreconcilable dichotomy in Platonism, for which Pater substitutes the argument that 'Platonism has contributed largely, has been an immense encouragement towards, the redemption of matter, of the world of sense, by art.'[22]

In his interpretation of Plato's doctrine, Pater draws a parallel to this redemption of the senses: 'Generalisation, whatever Platonists, or Plato himself at mistaken moments, may have to say about it, is a method, not of obliterating the concrete phenomenon, but of enriching it, with the joint perspective, the significance of expressiveness, of all other things beside.'[23] The very fact that Platonic ideas are called generalisations is an indication that they have no a priori quality. They are viewed from the standpoint of experience, and are welcome as aids in enriching individual experiences through connections. Nevertheless, Pater's historical sense prevents him from ignoring the a priori quality of ideas, and although he dismisses this as 'mistaken moments', he is thereby compelled to give a more precise definition of what he means by Platonic ideas. They are for him brackets that enclose the complexities brought about by interacting experiences.[24] Ultimately they are 'a passage from all merely relative experience to the "absolute".'[25] Pater leaves no doubt that they are still instruments of cognition, and are nothing but guidelines for grasping the meaning of experience. In the final analysis they represent condensed experiences, and so he can even go so far as to see in them the rebirth of the Homeric gods.[26] For Pater the Platonic idea revives the ancient animist concept of the world, in which all things have a soul.[27] This principle eliminates the distinction between abstraction and experience, and instead fuses them into a pre-intentional unity, again closely resembling a happy mood. The comparison of Platonic ideas to Homer's gods and to archaic animism denotes that the theory of ideas is not to be viewed as dichotomous, but rather as an aesthetic reconciliation – certainly alien to Plato. Nevertheless, the philosophy of Plato is regarded by Pater as being 'to the last rather poetry than metaphysical reasoning'.[28] He maintains that Plato always grasped the abstract in concrete form,[29] and the interpenetration of idea and experience was only brought about because Plato's artistic instinct invented the intelligible world as an enrichment of experience. 'Nothing is more poetic than transitions and heterogeneous mixtures.'[30]

This quietistic harmony requires constant elaboration, as Pater shows in his analysis of Plato's method. He compares the dialectic structure of the dialogues to journeys undertaken towards a specific goal.[31] The implication is that journey and goal are of equal importance. The dialectic mode does not entail step-by-step progress but is an endless dialogue of the mind with itself, blending all voices and all aspects into a notion of the immensity of life. Such a syncretic way of thinking must not block out any experiential facts but must, on the contrary, seek out every alternative in order to fulfil its purpose of an all-embracing synthesis.

> What Plato presents to his readers is then, again, a paradox, or a reconciliation of opposed tendencies: on one side, the largest possible demand for infallible certainty in knowledge . . . yet, on the other side, the utmost possible inexactness, or contingency, in the method by which actually he proposes to attain it.[32]

The certainty of Platonic philosophy is brought about by a method that does not aim for precise results but simply goes on in an endless quest. Thus the Platonic dialectic is 'co-extensive with life itself',[33] for it is directed towards the infinite world of experience. In Pater's eyes, Plato's greatness lay in the fact that by continually observing experience he was able to attain certainty, and so Pater found the embodiment of his own problem in Plato's philosophy. And this is why he says that Western philosophers, from the absolutists through to the sceptics, all invoke Plato,[34] with the former depending exclusively on the eternal certainty of the immutable and absolute character of truth, and the latter on a never-ending dialectic method proceeding parallel to life. What the history of philosophy has revealed as totally different strands, Pater sees as a unification embodied by the figure of Plato.

Plato achieved the longed-for balance in a threefold process: as a poet, he took his worldly experience into the realm of the abstract, thus bringing this realm to life; ideas and experience began to interpenetrate; the idea enriched experience, and experience gave concrete form to the idea. The outcome of this method of constantly confronting experience with idea and vice versa was the attainment of certainty in knowledge. Pater eliminates the fundamental opposites of Platonic philosophy, taking the idea off its pedestal and placing it level and interacting with the replica. It is clear that this reconstruction of Platonism is largely guided by Pater's own conceptions. By establishing a link between earlier Greek philosophers and Plato, Pater was able to explain how perfection could emerge from historical conditions as the achievement of balance.

After elucidating the conditions of this balance, Pater concludes by explaining its function. At the centre of his argument is Plato's aesthetics, which Pater derives from the *Republic*.

> 'The Republic' . . . is the protest of Plato, in enduring stone, in law and custom more imperishable still, against the principle of flamboyancy or fluidity in things, and in

men's thoughts about them . . . those evils of Athens, of Greece, came from an exaggerated assertion of the fluxional, flamboyant, centrifugal Ionian element in the Hellenic character. They could be cured only by a counter-assertion of the centripetal Dorian ideal, as actually seen best at Lacedaemon.[35]

Plato felt the Heraclitean flux and the aimless movement of the Sophists to be a challenge. Pater faced the same challenge in the form of passing experience and the endless movement of time. These had to be mastered, and in his picture of the ideal state, Plato showed how such Utopian mastery might be achieved.

It was art that attained the desired perfection.

Art, as such, as Plato knows, has no purpose but itself, its own perfection. The proper art of the Perfect City is in fact the art of discipline. Music . . . all the various forms of fine art, will be but the instruments of its one overmastering social or political purpose, irresistibly conforming its so imitative subject units to type.[36]

Art as the paradigm of mastery is perfection, and so once again Pater is emphasising how it runs counter to the diffuseness of human experience and conduct. Art enables life to be mastered, but this mastery can only be realised through the state,[37] and so art and state are one. The ideal state is ideal art, and the terms are synonymous. 'Perhaps it can be expressed as follows: the state and power purify the individual and refine his sensitivity . . . making him capable of art. Yes, perhaps that is the right expression; the state makes the individual capable of art.'[38] With this description, Gottfried Benn was outlining the power structure of the Spartan state, but the same principle preoccupied Pater, too.

We are to become – like little pieces in a machine! you may complain. – No, like performers rather, individually, it may be, of more or less importance, but each with a necessary and inalienable part, in a perfect musical exercise . . . or in some sacred liturgy; or like soldiers in an invincible army, invincible because it moves as one man. We are to find, or be put into, and keep, every one his natural place; to cultivate those qualities which will secure mastery over ourselves, the subordination of the parts to the whole, musical proportion.[39]

In order to make this correspondence vivid, Pater juxtaposes a variety of images – music, the liturgy, the army – each of which emphasises the incorporation of the individual into an overall pattern of discipline that binds single units into a whole. Art is harmony, which perfects life to the degree in which it renders life aesthetic. 'And Platonic aesthetics, remember! as such, are ever in close connexion with Plato's ethics. It is life itself . . . he proposes to colour; to get something of that irrepressible conscience of art, that spirit of control, into the general course of life.'[40] Experience transformed by art is the true reality, ideal because life is made controllable by art. It is an idea that we have already observed in Pater's essay on style, but what had there been construed as a demand is here the climax of an historical development – namely, that the world is transformed by art into an aesthetic phenomenon.

Pater can only capture the aesthetic transmutation of the world through the image of Utopia, and his attitude towards Plato's ideal state is somewhat ambivalent. On the one hand he is fully aware of the Utopian elements, but on the other he identifies himself with the citizens of the 'Perfect City'.[41] For him, history means the theoretical assurance of the solution to his problems, and to find this, he must continually twist Plato to suit himself. The search for earthly paradise in experience can only be successful by way of a Utopian fantasy that either negates or overcomes the menaces of reality. But this form of wish-fulfilment, with art transforming reality, must clearly place a limit on the degree of assurance that it can offer, for the world as an 'aesthetic phenomenon' has never occurred in history but has always remained a dream, at best a postulate (Nietzsche). That which is striven for is Utopian, but as history for Pater is not an ideology of progress, it follows that if perfection is to be expected in history, it necessarily fades into Utopianism.

Gaston de Latour

Pater's concept of the 'House Beautiful' and his understanding of Plato's aesthetics are crucial to his interpretation of history. Collected perfection and aesthetic harmony are his goals, but since the collection can never be complete and the world as an aesthetic phenomenon is Utopian, it follows that history could only offer theoretical assurance. The nuances of his personal experiences find very limited confirmation in history, and so in order to justify them, he is forced to re-interpret historical phenomena as is most evident from his treatment of Plato. He must constantly adjust history to his own position, and so as a result facts are invaded by fictions, often designating phenomena as historical which are closer to the realm of fantasy. And where history cannot provide a solid backing for his position, fiction triumphs. This is clearly to be seen in his historical novels, particularly the fragment *Gaston de Latour*, which grow from his endeavour to illuminate particular experiences through historical situations. The novels represent something that cannot be proved by history, which is simply turned into material for the imagination to reshape. Pater's theoretical study of history and his novel-writing are parallel processes, for they both deal with the same material, which is to serve the same purpose. In his study of history, personal requirements and imagination are adapted to the facts; in the novels, the relationship is reversed. Since history cannot supply legitimation for all his needs, he has to find another form to sanction his beliefs, and herein lies the true significance of the novels.

Taken separately from his other writings, they seem elusive and at times insubstantial. Seen against the background of his theoretical work, they illuminate wide areas of his thought.

In his book on Plato, Pater writes:

It might even be said that the trial-task of criticism, in regard to literature and art no less than to philosophy, begins exactly where the estimate of general conditions, of the conditions common to all the products of this or that particular age – of the 'environment' – leaves off, and we touch what is unique in the individual genius which contrived after all, by force of will, to have its own masterful way with that environment.[42]

This is precisely the perspective developed by Pater's novels. While his critical essays seek reassurance through history, his novels seek to portray man's confrontation with the historical environment. How far he succeeds, we shall discuss later. What matters in the present context is the fact that all his fiction concerns the relation between the characters and their historical backgrounds, and in this respect the novels reflect an existential force not to be found in the essays. The very fact that he found it necessary to turn to another genre is an indication of the importance he attached to this force.

Gaston de Latour offers a special insight into Pater's understanding of the relation between man and history. One must, of course, beware of drawing final conclusions from what is, after all, only a fragment, but the narrative mode and the parallels with *Marius* are revealing. Shadwell, who supervised the publication of *Gaston*, remarks in the introduction:

The work, if completed, would have been a parallel study of character to *Marius the Epicurean*; the scene shifted to another age of transition, when the old fabric of belief was breaking up, and when the problem of man's destiny and his relations to the unseen was undergoing a new solution. The interest would have centred round the spiritual development of a refined and cultivated mind, capable of keen enjoyment in the pleasures of the senses and of the intellect, but destined to find its complete satisfaction in that which transcends both.[43]

The time is typical for Pater – the novel is set in the Renaissance, a period of transition which brings about irreconcilable relationships between the character and the world of change with which he is confronted.

In those earlier days of the Renaissance, a whole generation had been exactly in the position in which Gaston now found himself. An older ideal moral and religious, certain theories of man and nature actually in possession, still haunted humanity, at the very moment when it was called, through a full knowledge of the past, to enjoy the present with an unrestricted expansion of its own capacities. – Might one enjoy? Might one eat of all the trees? – Some had already eaten, and needed, retrospectively, a theoretic justification, a sanction of their actual liberties, in some new reading of human nature itself and its relation to the world around it. – Explain to us the propriety, on the full view of things, of this bold course we have taken, or know we shall take![44]

Hidden in these lines is the very core of the novel. Gaston and his generation are still under the spell of an old world view, but their relation to it has become problematical because it hinders them from opening themselves up fully to the present. Gaston's desire for 'unrestricted expansion' shows that the old order is seen as restriction. But he lacks the determination to open himself up to what appears an unbounded present. The biblical metaphor 'eat of all the trees' is a clear indication that such enjoyment is given a negative slant, marring the joy of the new liberty, which required legitimation through a new world view. If the old is a restriction, the new produces insecurity.

In the passage quoted above, there is a characteristic switch of narrative perspective. Pater begins by focusing on Gaston and his time, but by the end there is an extraordinary identification of narrator with character, made all the more striking by the fact that nowhere does Gaston indulge in dialogues with others or with himself. The identification begins at the question marks, and is complete by the end of the passage. The invocation is not addressed to anyone in particular; it simply shows the intensity of the longing for a new justification of what has been discovered, the nature of which is as yet unknown. It is a tug against the reins, vividly symbolising the pressure mounting within. And this is basic to the tone of *Gaston*, which depicts an upheaval that does not know where it is heading.

The 'old' world which Gaston grows up in is a clearly discernible historical reality. Gaston comes from an aristocratic French family whose roots go far back into the past. Right at the start, Pater describes the family seat, the Château of Deux-manoirs, which enables him to bring the past of Gaston's environment into the present.[45] The house itself is a piece of history that imposes an unconscious restraint on Gaston.

A nature, instinctively religious, which would readily discover and give their full value to all such facts of experience as might be conformable thereto! But what would be the relation of this religious sensibility to sensibilities of another kind, now awakening in the young Gaston, as he mused in this dreamy place, surrounded by the books, the furniture, almost the very presence of the past, which had already found tongues to speak of a still living humanity – somewhere, somewhere in the world! – waiting for him in the distance . . . to explain, by its own plenary beauty and power, why wine and roses and the languorous summer afternoons were so delightful.[46]

The latent tension within Gaston is caused by the fact that he is hemmed in by the time-honoured traditions of his environment, which speak to him in a manner different from the yearnings that are beginning to awaken in him. These feelings are directed towards a distant realm, as yet sealed off from access, which is supposed to hold the answers to the growing burden of his immediate and problematic present. His oppressive historical surroundings bar him from penetrating the natural world that increasingly captures his interest. The latent clash between history and Nature is all the more disturbing because, following tradition, he has already decided in boyhood that he will enter the Church. Thus from the very beginning of the book, Gaston is presented in the light of his relation to an historical past grandeur[47] in which he does not feel truly at home.

As a Clerk in Orders, Gaston enters the service of the Bishop of Chartres. The Cathedral becomes the embodiment of historical power, and the boys live in its shadow. But here, too, the other world that Gaston had longed for keeps breaking through. In the midst of all the spiritual and religious discipline, he sees a certain wildness in the faces of the pupils:

> Does not the anthropologist tell us of a heraldry, with a large assortment of heraldic beasts, to be found among savage or half-savage peoples, as the 'survival' of a period when men were nearer than they are or seem to be now, to the irrational world? Throughout the sprightly movement of the lads' daily life it was as if their 'tribal' pets or monsters were with or within them.[48]

The true significance of this wildness lies in its direct contradiction to the strict hierarchic discipline of the Church. It is as if a primordial world were still present and at times resurfacing in this sacred world whose aim was to civilise man. Irrational instinct continues to shine through the superimposed layers of history. What had appeared at the beginning of the novel to be a latent tension between historical and natural forces has now broadened into an explicit clash. The more claims the Church makes on Gaston, the stronger becomes his feeling for the powers of Nature. The old château had made him long to understand the delights of summer afternoons imbued with a particular mood, and now the Cathedral awakens in him a feeling for the elemental and primeval forces still raging in man. Whatever Gaston's historical environment omits arouses his increasing interest and indeed passion.

The path that opens up to Gaston is therefore in the direction of those realities that are not covered by tradition. When the world of the monastery school sinks into the confusion of the religious war, and Gaston is freed from the bonds of his youth, he wonders if the two 'antagonistic ideals . . . in evidence before him'[49] might be reconciled by a third possibility. Significant in this context is the vision he has at the end of the chapter 'Our Lady's Church', where we see Gaston in the service of Chartres. He climbs the tower of Jean de Beauce, which opens up a vast panorama to him.

> At each ascending storey, as the flight of the birds, the scent of the fields, swept past him, till he stood at last amid the unimpeded light and air of the watch-chamber

> above the great bells, some coil of perplexity, of unassimilable thought or fact, fell away from him. He saw the distant paths, and seemed to hear the breeze piping suddenly upon them under the cloudless sky, on its unseen, capricious way through those vast reaches of atmosphere. At this height, the low ring of blue hills was visible, with suggestions of that south-west country of peach-blossom and wine which had sometimes decoyed his thoughts towards the sea, and beyond it to 'that new world of the Indies', which was held to explain a certain softness in the air from that quarter, even in the most vehement weather. Amid those vagrant shadows and shafts of light must be Deux-manoirs, the deserted rooms, the gardens, the graves. In mid-distance, even then a funeral procession was on its way humbly to one of the village churchyards. He seemed almost to hear the words across the stillness.[50]

It is as if Gaston had been lifted out of the narrow confines of his life in Chartres. The higher he climbs, the freer he feels, until finally the 'coil of perplexity' falls away and the irreconcilability of his environment with his longing simply disappears as he gazes on the ever-expanding landscape. Here is something that seems to embrace all opposites. Not even the blue hills on the horizon can close off his view, but indeed paradoxically they seem to open it wider still. The world stretching in front of him points to another world, distant and unseen, but imaginable. The visible landscape awakens longings and ideas that take on a visionary reality – the land of peach-blossom and wine, the sea, and ultimately the new world, which is present not only as an abstract longing but also as a perceivable 'softness in the air'. But the vision does not exclude the past reality – for the mind's eye then returns to Deux-manoirs – or that of the present, since the passage ends with a funeral procession in 'mid-distance'.

Pater employs a technique of juxtaposition in depicting this landscape. The horizon is his equator, simultaneously enclosing the physical country on the near side and pointing to the visionary on the other. Thus what is limited expands into the unbounded, with the Indies, Deux-manoirs and the funeral procession merging into a single experience. Events and imaginings blend together. And over it all lies the promise that divisions and opposites can all be embraced and reconciled. The physical landscape is transfigured into a source of emotions – or, in the words of Amiel, which Pater quotes elsewhere: 'Every landscape . . . is, as it were, a state of the soul.'[51] The passage quoted above portrays such a state; descriptions change into expressiveness, perceptions turn into signs, and the euphoric mood arising out of them is one of anticipation that an inconceivable promise is about to come true. In a word, Gaston's landscape is numinous.[52] He asks at once: 'Would it always survive, amid the indifference of others, amid the verdicts of the world, amid a thousand doubts?'[53]

What Gaston could not find in his historically saturated environment is revealed to him in his contact with Nature. At such precious moments he perceives the union of things, and his longing 'to feel at one with himself again'[54] is fulfilled. At the point where the novel breaks off, almost as a last word, Bruno's pantheism supplies a theoretical basis for Gaston's visionary intuition. The movement towards the unhistorical, natural world is paralleled by the progressive destruction of the old historical one. Gaston's abandonment of his past way of life is facilitated by the sacking of Chartres Cathedral,[55] but the attack on the Church is only one factor in this age of upheaval. It is a period full of violence,[56] 'an age whose very virtues were apt to become insane; an age "guilty and extravagant" in its very justice[57] . . . an age of wild people, of insane impulse, of homicidal mania'.[58] The insanity reaches its climax in the Massacre of St Bartholomew. Against this background, Gaston's vital task is to find some way of encompassing all these conflicting worlds – a quest that is only conceivable 'under the influence of a scene which had for him something of the character of the sea – its changefulness, its infinity, its pathos in the toiling human life that traversed it. Featureless, if you will, it was always under the guidance of its ample sky.'[59] The more destructive the rampant strife of factions turns out to be, the more intense becomes Gaston's yearning for a world which lies buried under the historical one, yet is always ready to erupt through the thinly layered surface of civilisation.

The experience of the transfigured landscape coincides with a change in Gaston's life. He throws off the sacred shackles of his youth and begins his wanderings. The first part of this new life is outlined in the chapter evocatively entitled 'Modernity'. His new path leads away from history and into immediacy, as represented by the poetry of Ronsard.

> Gaston's demand . . . was for a poetry, as veritable, as intimately near, as corporeal, as the new faces of the hour, the flowers of the actual season. The poetry of mere literature, like the dead body, could not bleed, while there was a heart, a poetic heart, in the living world, which beat, bled, spoke with irresistible power.[60]

In the numinous landscape, Gaston had sensed the mighty heartbeat of the natural world. This is what he now demands from poetry. Instead of re-arranging historical facts and literary experiences, it has to bring out the corporeal palpability of natural things, thus making nature and immediacy interchangeable; he deliberately sets them off against the 'mere' literature of Antiquity.[61] 'Modern' poetry must capture scents and colours and all the things of the senses – 'the clangorous passage of the birds at night foretokening rain, the moan of the wind at the door, the wind's self made visible over the yielding corn'.[62] This urgent desire for immediacy is fulfilled by the welter of natural phenomena which his keen sense of observation continually absorbs. The multifariousness of Nature in its eternal presentness is unhistorical – the precise opposite of Gaston's former world, which now cedes its power to the new.

Nay! the most familiar details of nature, its daily routine of light and darkness, beset him now with a kind of troubled and troubling eloquence. The rain, the first streak of dawn, the very sullenness of the sky, had a power, only to be described by saying that they seemed to be *moral* facts.[63]

The 'troubled and troubling eloquence' show clearly that the discovery of immediacy is not the final answer to Gaston's deep-rooted desires. If anything, it sharpens his awareness of the clash between Nature and history. Thus Ronsard's poetry is by no means an invitation to stand and stare – it simply emphasises the importance of the present. The remainder of Gaston's quest concerns the problem of whether this antinomian split can be overcome, and to what extent the immediacy of the here and now is really cut off from an historical past. The task is a disquieting one.[64]

The title of the following chapter, 'Peach-Blossom and Wine', harks back to Gaston's experience of the landscape. This chapter is a bridge between his encounters with Ronsard and with Montaigne, and at its heart is another numinous landscape whose significance is enhanced by its being wedged in between the two encounters. On his way to Montaigne, he reaches the Loire Valley, which once more strikes him with the force of a vision.

Was there light here in the earth itself? It was a landscape, certainly, which did not merely accept the sun, but flashed it back gratefully from the white, gracious, carven houses, that were like a natural part of it. As he passed below, fancy would sometimes credit the outlook from their lofty gables with felicities of combination beyond possibility. What prospects of mountain and sea-shore from those aerial window-seats!

And still, as in some sumptuous tapestry, the architecture, the landscape, were but a setting for the human figures: these palatial abodes, never out of sight, high on the river bank, challenged continual speculation as to their inhabitants – how they moved, read poetry and romance, or wrote the memoirs which were like romance, passed through all the hourly changes of their all-accomplished, intimate life. The Loire was the river pre-eminently of the monarchy, of the court; and the fleeting human interests, fact or fancy, which gave its utmost value to the liveliness of the natural scene, found a centre in the movements of Catherine and her sons, still roving, after the eccentric habit inherited from Francis the First, from one 'house of pleasure' to another, in the pursuit at once of amusement and of that political intrigue which was the serious business of their lives. Like some phantastic company of strolling players amid the hushed excitement of a little town, the royal family, with all its own small rivalries, would be housed for the night under the same roof with some of its greater enemies – Henri de Guise, Condé, 'The Admiral', all alike taken by surprise – but courteously, and therefore ineffectively. And Gaston, come thus by chance so close to them, had the sense not so much of nearness to the springs of great events, as of the likeness of the whole matter to a stage-play with its ingeniously contrived encounters, or the assortments of a game of chance. And in a while the dominant course of the river itself, the animation of its steady, downward flow, even amid the sand-shoals and whispering islets of the dry season, bore his thoughts beyond it, in a sudden irresistible appetite for the sea.[65]

Although this description of the Loire landscape is considerably more detailed, nevertheless it has a good deal in common with Gaston's earlier vision. Once again he moves from the physical reality to its inherent significance, by shading into the visible world another one which cannot be seen. The visible does not disappear in this process, but becomes strangely transmuted. Pater's juxtaposing technique is also in evidence – the light of the sun is reflected by the houses in such a way as to create the illusion of unity, with the houses becoming part of Nature. This impression lures Gaston's fantasy into reaching behind the welter of things to be perceived. But such imaginings are not really pursued, and when their illusory nature becomes apparent to him, his mind's eye returns to the castles, where it conjures up the living drama of human passions, intrigues and destinies. The contrasts are massive – distant prospects, infinite and impersonal, set against the temporal interplay of people pursuing their personal interests. Nature provides the buried background to a determinate, historical pageant.

It is here that Gaston's vision diverges from the earlier one. Previously, distance and proximity, visible and invisible realms, were marked by a striking correspondence which gradually made them merge into one another, whereas now the broad landscape remains in direct contrast to the narrow restrictedness of human life. The two poles certainly act upon one another, but not in a unifying sense. Gaston does not feel that he is close to the 'springs of great events', but that these events are like a play. Historical reality has lost its earnestness, and instead has become a game of chance, narrow, artificial, 'contrived'. This impression is caused purely by the fact that Gaston now views historical life against the background of a Nature which, in its intensity, sets the human world in its proper (and limited) place in the order of things. Now this world seems almost unreal when viewed against the might of Nature, whose never-ending continuity is all the more potent in such a time of historical upheaval.

Gaston's thoughts finally wander away from the castles, on to the river and thence to the sea. The river here takes on a degree of symbolism. It incorporates and links together two distant features: the monarchy, and the flow of life. As the river of the court it stands for historical realities; it is the setting for the tensions and machinations of the real world. But in its constant flow, it also acts as a reminder that nothing stands still. Not even Gaston's thoughts can stand still, for the river takes them and carries them away from the narrow world of historical reality and on to the open sea. It is the dual symbolism of the river that finally unites the opposites. Through it, the 'fleeting human interests' are brought to life with the same vivid intensity as the awareness that their reality is only momentary. This temporality is what endows historical life with its fascination. The flow of the river illuminates the power of time, from whose course all determinate manifestations of existence emerge, only to sink back into it again. But finally, the image of the river also suggests that there is a direction to the flow. It heads towards the open sea. But the contours of this sea remain indeterminate.

The natural scenery of the Loire Valley robs history of its earnestness and dwarfs it to mere play, and the river highlights awareness of life's temporality of which history is nothing but the diversification. Therefore history in its constant changes lacks an inviolable order, and this stimulates Gaston's yearning for permanence, as prefigured in the landscape he perceives. This is the impact of Nature on history. But history in turn influences the observer's view of Nature. Gaston's landscapes exude a mood of expectation – not through the forces of Nature itself, but through the dissatisfaction of man with his own world. The ultimate importance and superiority of Nature arise from the deficiencies of historical reality. Thus the two landscapes mark a significant point of contact between Nature and history. They point to an exit from history rather than a revelation of a new realm of permanence. What they capture is the in-between state that Pater found himself in, and since history could provide no sanction for such a state, he could only convey it through the medium of fiction. The extent to which *Gaston de Latour* focuses on the mood of transition and suspense, as the hero sets out for something beyond history, can be gauged from the final chapters. The ideas evoked by the section on the Loire are cast in more concrete form. The irreality of historical life is dealt with in the chapters entitled 'Suspended Judgement' and 'Shadow of Events', while the last chapter of the unfinished novel, 'Lower Pantheism', offers a concluding survey of the problems previously raised.

Gaston's encounter with Montaigne deepens his insight into the incalculability of human life.[66] The image of the game of chance, which had come to his mind when he was contemplating the Loire, now finds a theoretical base in Montaigne's essays.

> On all sides we are beset by the incalculable: – walled up suddenly, as if by malign trickery, in the open field, or pushed forward senselessly, by the crowd around us, to good-fortune. In art, as in poetry, there are the 'transports' which lift the artist out of, as they are not of, himself.[67]

The visionary observer of the landscape saw historical life as a stage-play, and now, as he considers everyday experience, he sees it as the incalculable. Only art can transcend this incalculability; otherwise there remains only scepticism, which denies all fixed interpretations and conclusions, thus opening up access to existence itself. Through Montaigne, Gaston is able to seize this mode of access:

> In the presence of this indefatigable analyst of act and motive all fixed outlines seemed to vanish away. The healthful pleasure of motion, of thoughts in motion! – Yes! Gaston felt them, the oldest of them, moving, as he listened, under and away from his feet, as if with the ground he stood on.[68]

Gaston's affirmation of movement is only possible because he knows that historical life contains no determinacy solid enough to yield ultimate meaning. Should any claim to ultimacy be raised, the true task of scepticism is to destroy this assumed finality.

But if the ground moves beneath one's feet, what is there left to stand on?

> One's own experience! – that, at least, *was* one's own: low and earthy, it might be; still, the earth was, emphatically, good, good-natured; and he [i.e. Montaigne] loved, emphatically, to recommend the wisdom, amid all doubts, of keeping close to it.[69]

Reassurance through experience means consciously 'keeping close' to the earth, which as the origin of experience reaches beyond historical realities. The 'earthiness' of experience is another way of saying that man's ultimate orientation is through Nature. Thus scepticism cuts across all man's historically inspired definitions and orders of life, and clears the way to a living wisdom of the earth which, as the bed-rock of all experience, will make the latter seem all the richer for its earthiness.

Against this background, the chapter on St Bartholomew's Eve vividly illustrates this particular form of sceptical experience. It is not the wisdom of the earth but the madness of historical forces that triumphs in this chapter, which comes between Montaigne's scepticism and Bruno's pantheism. The old world falls to pieces, but Gaston has already outgrown it, and so the massacre is simply one final and unmistakable confirmation of the insight that he had had in the Loire Valley, that the historical world is a game of chance. In this final phase, the game is revealed to the full extent of its futility.

The final chapter is the only one with a motto, which Pater has drawn from Heine:

> Jetzo, da ich ausgewachsen,
> Viel gelesen, viel gereist,
> Schwillt mein Herz, und ganz von Herzen,
> Glaub' ich an den Heilgen Geist.[70]
>
> [Now that I have grown up,
> Read a lot, travelled a lot,
> My heart swells and with all my heart
> I believe in the Holy Spirit.]

This denotes the end of the wanderings that have brought awareness, and in Gaston's case the insight obtained is embodied in the teachings of Bruno, which confirm retrospectively the expectations aroused earlier by the visionary landscapes. Bruno proclaims the 'coincidentia oppositorum'[71] of things. ' "Nature" becomes for him a sacred term. – "Conform thyself to Nature" '[72] is his demand, which is taken up enthusiastically everywhere. After the internal and external devastation wrought by historical forces, the cry is now for reconciliation, but of a strange kind. 'To unite oneself to the infinite by largeness and lucidity of intellect, to enter, by that admirable faculty, into eternal life – this was the true vocation of the spouse, of the rightly amorous soul.'[73] Gaston now seems close to the fulfilment of his old dream – to be at one with himself and the world. Indeed Bruno promises the unity with 'eternal life', and his pantheism opens up precisely that world which Gaston could not find in his historical environment.

> Nature is not only a thought or meditation in the divine mind; it is also the perpetual energy of that mind, which, ever identical with itself, puts forth and absorbs in turn all the successive forms of life, of thought, of language even.[74]

Gaston's quest culminates in a pantheistically conceived Nature, whose inherent pattern of diversity in unity prefigures the desired goal which the human mind strives for. In Bruno's pantheism a primordial world which lay dormant beneath the surface of history erupts and celebrates its resurrection.[75] Primeval forces now begin once more to shape human life, which turns away from history as the great spectacle of disillusionment.

The invocation of Nature spotlights the inadequacy of the historical sanction through which Pater sought to legitimise his conception of autonomous art. His incomplete novel brings to life the deficiencies of the historical world and – through the landscape images – the manner in which man can break free from it. Longing and expectation meet in these scenes and begin to find fulfilment in a natural, unhistorical existence, the contours of which are finally marked out theoretically by the teachings of Bruno.

The themes of *Gaston de Latour* are given a significant slant by the narrative technique employed, a study of which seems all the more necessary since the fragmentary character of the book precludes any ultimate solution to its problems. Pater's technique also reveals a good deal about his own attitude towards the path he lays down for his hero.

The external structure shows Gaston against a background of historical events. The 'real' world of the novel consists in the religious wars and the encounters with Ronsard, Montaigne and Bruno. The nature of this background is conditioned by Gaston's personal reactions, for reality only serves to awaken desires for another way of life, and is to be glimpsed through the people and experiences he encounters on his way. He does not seek to change historical reality, but only to free himself from it, and in Ronsard, Montaigne and Bruno he senses forms of life that fascinate him without totally satisfying him. And so he wanders on. The historical background is thus relegated to a sort of decor that sets off his dissatisfaction. It seems decorative because Gaston becomes increasingly detached from it, to the extent that at times the description of historical settings obtrudes, as if they were an end in themselves,[76] thus signifying Gaston's growing aloofness from the historical world. The downgrading of elaborate historical panoramas into frozen ornamental tableaux indicates Pater's waning belief in history as a legitimising force of autonomous art, as is clear from its inability to solve Gaston's problems.

This negative function of history raises the question of how Pater presents his hero's break with history. The treatment is revealing in many respects. Gaston's character is hardly described at all, for little is said about his qualities or, in the course of his development, about his intentions; there are no speeches or dialogue with the few other characters. The chapters on Ronsard and, especially, on Montaigne and Bruno, contain no real interaction between them and Gaston, but instead Pater simply sets out the tentative groping of Montaigne's essays and the enthusiastic elation of Bruno's pantheism. In these chapters, mention of Gaston himself is reduced to a minimum. For much of the time, narrative gives way to a critical essay on the respective world pictures of these characters, and just as Pater's imagination often breaks through into his essays, so here, within his novel, he begins to theorise. As a result, Gaston himself seems strangely distant, and when he is in the foreground, his conduct has already been interpreted for us by Pater.

The blurred features and the intermittent disappearance of the hero when Pater interpolates his own reading of scenes and people prevent the development of any distinct plot-line. Gaston does not come to grips with his surroundings, but simply detaches himself from them through a vague feeling of being different. This detachment makes the background merely decorative, since it serves only to point up Gaston's otherness. The absence of meetings and dialogues in turn prevents Gaston's otherness from taking on any form. Ronsard, Montaigne and Bruno become mere possibilities which hold him momentarily without actually giving definition to his quest. Towards the end, Pater tries to find a formula for Gaston's conduct:

> As already in his life there had been the *Shadows of Events*, – the indirect yet fatal influence there of deeds in which he had no part, so now, for a time, he seemed to fall under the spell, the power, of the *Shadows of Ideas*, of Bruno's Ideas; in other words, of those indirect suggestions, which, though no necessary part of, yet inevitably followed upon, his doctrines.[77]

Here Pater is actually telling us what led him to conceive his hero as he did. Gaston under 'the Shadows of Events' could neither comprehend nor direct them. Consequently, there could be no action. Whatever influences him does so indirectly, for at no time is there any direct realisation of the subconscious desires that motivate him. He opens himself up to new possibilities for a certain time, and then turns elsewhere, and so nothing becomes concrete except that from which he wishes to distance himself. And as he has no further connection to it, the historical reality freezes into an ornamental decoration of his life, signifying the disjunction between himself and the world. Gaston is always travelling without ever arriving; he is incapable of making a decision, and so he rushes from one possibility to another, and instead of mastering experience, he is left 'darkling' in the shadow of events. In this manner, the aesthetic attitude is brought to life; its activities spring from dissatisfaction with the empirical world, but this dissatisfaction is a negative force, without the dynamism that might open up new realms. These are only adumbrated by a longing, whose featurelessness makes it impossible to impose a discernible pattern on them.

The consequence of all this is the fact that the power of nature sensed in the landscape scenes and explicitly proclaimed by Bruno cannot develop into a Rousseau-like ideology to be realised through action; instead Pater asks how this longing for nature is to be fulfilled. He finds the answer in chthonic myth.

IV *ART AND MYTH*

8 The ancient gods

Cult and ritual

'How often one feels the urge to go beyond historical consciousness, how often we are tormented by a longing, a homesickness for the primeval forest that lies behind us.'[1] This longing as depicted by Kierkegaard proved to be a hallmark of European aestheticism,[2] the adherents of which delved into ancient myths and primitive rites in order to immerse themselves in the dark sides of an as yet unexplored human life. This holds equally true for Pater, who devoted a substantial portion of his writings to exploring pagan cults and mysteries. If we are to understand this attitude towards chthonic myth, we must first analyse the motives that led him to his preoccupation with the primordial world, and we can do this by studying what he has to say about cult and ritual.

Hitherto, critics have tended to explain Pater's interest in ritual as being due to the aesthetic charm of the ceremonial,[3] which Pater would certainly have appreciated. Oscar Wilde's judgement of *Marius* points in this direction:

> In *Marius the Epicurean* Pater seeks to reconcile the artistic life with the life of religion . . . But Marius is little more than a spectator: an ideal spectator indeed, and to whom it is given 'to contemplate the spectacle of life with appropriate emotions', which Wordsworth defines as the poet's true aim; yet a spectator merely, and perhaps a little too much occupied with the comeliness of the benches of the sanctuary to notice that it is the sanctuary of sorrow that he is gazing at.[4]

This observation occurs in Wilde's *De Profundis*, which reveals his own contact with Christian concepts. It would seem from Wilde's words that only the aesthetic side of the cult is of interest to Marius, but as far as Pater's own fascination is concerned, this is only half the story. He himself stresses the fact that: 'While the ritual remains unchanged, the aesthetic element, only accidentally connected with it, expands with the freedom and mobility of things of the intellect.'[5] Even if the aesthetic element is accidental, and therefore only indirectly connected with the ritual, it bears witness to its dependence on the attitude of the observer, whose fascination by the ritual is articulated aesthetically. The aesthetic pleasure and the significance of the ritual are totally separate things, and Pater makes it quite clear that the aesthetically pleasing element arises out of the impact exercised by the ritual's significance, and hence is not an intrinsic part of it.

In his essay on Winckelmann, Pater describes the meaning of ritual as follows:

Religious progress, like all purely spiritual progress, is confined to a few. This sentiment attaches itself in the earliest times to certain usages of patriarchal life, the kindling of fire, the washing of the body, the slaughter of the flock, the gathering of harvest, holidays and dances. Here are the beginnings of a ritual, at first as occasional and unfixed as the sentiment which it expresses, but destined to become the permanent element of religious life. The usages of patriarchal life change; but this germ of ritual remains, promoted now with a consciously religious motive, losing its domestic character, and therefore becoming more and more inexplicable with each generation. Such pagan worship, in spite of local variations, essentially one, is an element in all religions. It is the anodyne which the religious principle, like one administering opiates to the incurable, has added to the law which makes life sombre for the vast majority of mankind. More definite religious conceptions come from other sources, and fix themselves upon this ritual in various ways, changing it, and giving it new meanings. In Greece they were derived from mythology, itself not due to a religious source at all, but developing in the course of time into a body of religious conceptions, entirely human in form and character.[6]

Ritual, then, precedes religious experience, which only gradually links up with it as patriarchal usages change and the original meaning is forgotten. And myth, too, despite all its complexities, has its roots in human conduct and not in religious revelation. Ritual anticipates myth and religion, both of which merely elevate patriarchal usages on which they remain dependent. Religious worship springs from this consecration, and it is this anthropological interpretation that makes Pater's conception of ritual so revealing – an interpretation that becomes all the more distinctive if viewed against the results of modern research into myth and ritual.

According to Walter F. Otto, cult and ritual often presuppose a myth, although myth and cult frequently mirror each other.[7] Cult and ritual are solidified forms by means of which the epiphanies of myth are to be eternalised. The language of worship inscribed into the cult

shows the numinous to be so near that man, by offering his own person, must himself turn into an expressive gestalt of it, which those other more distant languages were called upon to create through the medium of stones, colours, sounds and words.[8]

All forms of cult are determined by the nearness of the divinity, and it was this original contact that gave rise to the ritual whose splendour indicated the presence of the god. Jung and Kerényi maintain that all 'ceremony is putting mythological matter into action'.[9] The gods of myth are 'so "primordial" that with a new god, there is always the birth of a new "world": a new age or a new world view'.[10] Whatever may be the individual connections between myth and ritual, an epiphany of the god remains the decisive experience to be preserved in the ceremonial actions of the ritual.

It is obvious that this view is quite different from Pater's. For him, the myths of ancient gods were subservient to the function of consecrating archaic rhythms and forms of human life. This anthropological explanation, current in the nineteenth century, conceived of myths and cults as translations of basic human needs. It reduced all phenomena that claimed to be supernatural or religious to their human origins, as exemplified by Feuerbach's anthropological reduction of Christianity. There is, however, one vital shift that sets Pater apart from his contemporaries, and that is his emphasis on glorification, which he believes to be the distinctive mark of ritual[11] that freezes the transfigurations of human life. This glorification is not due to any supernatural revelation, but is the result of man himself becoming the object of worship, so that whatever elements of human life have been separated by history appear, in the light of cultic ceremony, to be still in unison with each other.

This concept of ritual is not due in any way to an antiquarian interest in the conditions of prehistoric times; on the contrary, Pater considers it to be an existential necessity.

> Complex and subtle interests, which the mind spins for itself may occupy art and poetry or our own spirit for a time; but sooner or later they come back with a sharp rebound to the simple elementary passions – anger, desire, regret, pity, and fear: and what corresponds to them in the sensuous world – bare, abstract fire, water, air, tears, sleep, silence.[12]

Evidently the complexities of later civilisation cannot hold human interest for any length of time. Sooner or later a secret longing to turn back to the primordial forms of existence re-asserts itself. Pater's abandonment of the sophistications of modern civilisation is not motivated by a desire to leave the world for a promised transcendental redemption; instead he wants to fathom what lies underneath the glittering surface. When the perception of telluric forces captures the imagination, emotions which seemed to have been forgotten long ago will be stirred and released. The mind's discontent with the present results in the re-animation of the distant past. For Pater the archetypal is far more important than the transcendental. It is therefore clear that his concept of ritual is not attributable solely to the psychological views of his time; it sprang, rather, from a need to consecrate the archetypes of primeval times. In this struggle to revive primitivistic forms of life, Max Picard rightly – if somewhat polemically – observed that:

It was the multifarious meaning of primitive expression that attracted these neo-impressionists: with the primitives, who said nothing determinate and allowed everything to be sensed, the neoimpressionists felt comforted. They no longer felt that they lacked conviction or the ethos without which form cannot be regarded as necessary. The neoimpressionists created the world as it had been in the beginning, so that everything could emerge from this beginning, including the ethos that they needed . . . one forgets completely that this primitiveness is only there as a source for the development of infinite possibilities in the hope that one day final certainty might be obtainable.[13]

'Primitiveness' here means primordial form, and is not meant pejoratively. Picard has picked on an essential feature of the 'primitive' movement – namely, the aesthetic element. Through this approach to the archetypes, which Pater saw as being embodied in ritual, the attractive illusion looms large that a totality of human experience can be regained. This idea is aesthetic, because it does not demand any decision regarding conduct in actual life. Instead it takes care to permeate human life with its primeval images, thereby elevating and glorifying it.

Pater found this idea realised in Wordsworth's poetry. There he perceived 'the first characteristic power of the nineteenth century'.[14]

And it was through nature, thus ennobled by a semblance of passion and thought, that he approached the spectacle of human life. Human life, indeed, is for him, at first, only an additional, accidental grace on an expressive landscape. When he thought of man, it was of man as in the presence and under the influence of these effective natural objects, and linked to them by many associations. The closest connexion of man with natural objects, the habitual association of his thoughts and feelings with a particular spot of earth, has sometimes seemed to degrade those who are subject to its influence, as if it did but reinforce that physical connexion of our nature with the actual lime and clay of the soil, which is always drawing us nearer to our end. But for Wordsworth, these influences tended to the dignity of human nature, because they tended to tranquillise it. By raising nature to the level of human thought he gives it power and expression: he subdues man to the level of nature, and gives him thereby a certain breadth and coolness and so solemnity.[15]

In Wordsworth, man and Nature interact, thus bringing about the ancient *hieros gamos*, the unification of separate forces. Man comes closer to his own destiny, the closer he comes to Nature. He animates Nature, which in turn elevates and ennobles him, freeing him from his isolation, restoring his inner balance, and placing him in a setting that is superior to his own existence.[16] He loses his predominance and becomes an ornament in the 'expressive landscape', which in fact takes on its expressiveness through him. This flight to Nature confirms that man's existence is totally permeated by civilisation, and yet the resulting alienation of man's historical existence belongs to his own human nature.[17]

It is therefore natural that man should escape into the richness of prehistoric life. In seeking to define himself through Nature he loses his importance, but he gains intensity. In the words of Klages: 'for the homeless superiority of an unworldly intellectuality' man substitutes 'entanglement in the polymorphic diversity and inexhaustible richness of life'.[18]

The unity that Pater found in Wordsworth was what he himself continued to long for, and from this grew his preoccupation with ancient cults and myths. In these primordial forms of existence he hoped to ascertain what created that totality which could no longer be found in the historical world. The telluric, chthonic, primitivistic beliefs of the ancient past, with the primal realities of earth and birth, blood and death,[19] promised him the wholeness that he sought.

'The myth of Demeter and Persephone'

> Modern science explains the changes of the natural world by the hypothesis of certain unconscious forces; and the sum of these forces . . . constitutes the scientific conception of nature. But, side by side with the growth of this more mechanical conception, an older and more spiritual, Platonic, philosophy has always maintained itself, a philosophy more of instinct than of the understanding, the mental starting-point of which is not an observed sequence of outward phenomena, but some such feelings as most of us have on the first warmer days in spring, when we seem to feel the genial processes of nature actually at work; as if just below the mould, and in the hard wood of the trees, there were really circulating some spirit of life, akin to that which makes its energies felt within ourselves. Starting with a hundred instincts such as this, that older unmechanical, spiritual, or Platonic, philosophy envisages nature rather as the unity of a living spirit or person, revealing itself in various degrees to the kindred spirit of the observer, than as a system of mechanical forces. Such a philosophy is a systematised form of that sort of poetry . . . which also has its fancies of a spirit of the earth, or of the sky, – a personal intelligence abiding in them, the existence of which is assumed in every suggestion such poetry makes to us of a sympathy between the ways and aspects of outward nature and the moods of men.[20]

These words, in the introduction to Pater's essay on Demeter and Persephone, set the scene for his approach to myth. Mythical Nature is seen as a counter to the contemporary mechanistic world he lives in,[21] and the very contrast endows the mythical world with its plasticity. Pater's interest in reviving this ancient lore is – as has already been observed – by no means antiquarian, for in the old concept of Nature he discovers the same life forces that present-day man senses in the rhythm of the seasons. It is as if this feeling of interlinkage between man and Nature were an echo of a past wholeness that has been lost. The unity, however, is not left in the abstract, but takes on concrete form through images: the forces of Nature are personified, thus signifying the identity of man and Nature. In the earlier, unconscious world the two had not yet been separated, and poetry, by means of its images, connects up with this earlier world and enables us to merge with the 'spirit of life'. Mythical Nature unfolds a dazzling interplay of primeval instincts which are not governed by reason, and it is this link with instinct that constitutes the fascination of myth for Pater. Instinct embodies man's original communion with Nature[22] – it is his own natural being, which can only restore its original wholeness through myth. His intellectual understanding of himself is to be found in history, but his instinctive awareness of himself is to be found in myth. Again and again Pater is drawn to the pre-Homeric world of the gods, where 'outward nature' and the 'moods of men' are one. 'Myth allows that which is internal to happen externally.'[23] In all mythology man steps back into his own origins,[24] for the 'primeval [is] the most alive'.[25] Thus Pater claims that 'old mythology seemed as full of untried, unexpressed motives and interest as human life itself'.[26] The closeness of the link that Pater saw between myth and human life is clear from his comments at the start of his Demeter study. This myth is 'in itself full of interest and suggestion, to all for whom the ideas of the Greek religion have any real meaning in the modern world'.[27] It follows that the ancient myths raise and cover certain problems that modern man finds difficult to solve. The questions that history could not answer might be answered by myth, for in the words of Jung and Kerényi, everything 'that man ought to [have] in a positive or negative sense, but cannot yet [have], lives as mythological form and anticipation beside his consciousness'.[28]

Pater notes three distinct phases in the myth of Demeter and Persephone, each of which brings out a different aspect.

> There is first its half-conscious, instinctive, or mystical, phase, in which, under the form of an unwritten legend, living from mouth to mouth, and with details changing as it passes from place to place, there lie certain primitive impressions of the phenomena of the natural world. We may trace it next in its conscious, poetical, or literary, phase, in which the poets become the depositaries of the vague instinctive product of the popular imagination, and handle it with a purely literary interest, fixing its outlines, and simplifying or developing its situations. Thirdly, the myth passes into the ethical phase, in which the persons and the incidents of the poetical narrative are realised as abstract symbols, because intensely characteristic examples, of moral or spiritual conditions.[29]

It is evident that Pater's main interest here lies in the poetic presentation of the myth – the actual forms through which men take possession of what is revealed. He is in no way concerned with elucidating any supernatural origins, for myth to him is a poetic rendering of the human world. Therefore only poets and sculptors are able to preserve, by means of narrative and expression, what myth represents. As a self-explication of man, still deeply rooted in his instincts, myth – according to this latter-day aestheticism – cuts out the distinction between poetry and life. Consequently the wholeness itself is poetic, as can be seen from the continuous transformation of myth represented by the different phases. These phases are not peculiar to the Demeter story, but they are a natural order, 'based on the necessary conditions of human apprehension'.[30] For Pater, mythology grows from human truths, embodying no epiphany, but only man's poetic understanding of the world.

The first phase of the Demeter myth 'appears as the peculiar creation of a country-people of a high impressibility, dreaming over their work in spring or autumn, half consciously touched by a sense of its sacredness, and a sort of mystery about it'.[31] In this phase, Demeter is 'the goddess of dark caves . . . of the fertility of the earth in its wildness . . . She is the most definite embodiment of all those fluctuating mystical instincts, of which Gaia, the mother of the earth's gloomier offspring, is a vaguer and mistier one.'[32] Demeter embodies the chthonic origin of things, and as such she is an ambiguous figure, both frightening and holy. In this early age, Pater sees her as the projection of country folks' imagination,[33] objectifying the rhythms of Nature in the goddess. Such a personification of the earth is a way of identifying man with Nature, but at the same time the country folk see their conception of the world as being elevated and consecrated by the goddess. In this phase of the myth, Demeter the chthonic goddess stands dominant in the foreground, although the daughter, originally almost interchangeably connected with the mother, gradually becomes detached and individualised by going down into and returning from the earth, thus signalling the rhythm of the seasons.[34]

In the second phase, there is a significant change: the relationship between Demeter and Persephone becomes the focal point. The divine mother of the earth appears as the 'weary woman . . . our Lady of Sorrows, the *mater dolorosa* of the ancient world, but with a certain latent reference, all through, to the mystical person of the earth'.[35] The levels of meaning overlap here, but they remain connected: Demeter does not lose her chthonic character in this new development, it merely gives way to other aspects. It is the loss of her daughter that comes to the fore in the dramatic development of the second phase. 'Demeter cannot but seem the type of divine grief.'[36] Of chthonic origin, of unlimited life-giving power, and yet also boundless in her grief, Demeter attracts the poets from Homer to Ovid.[37]

> The fluidity of the primal mythical state presupposes unity with the world, a complete assimilation of all its aspects. On the basis of Arcadian mythology we might say that one may realise the most general idea of the living being by entering into the figure of Demeter – i.e. persecuted and robbed, for indeed there is robbery, not understanding but raging and grieving, and yet finally restored and reborn.[38]

While the first phase of the myth objectified human life as a natural rhythm, the second phase denotes grief as the undercurrent of the world, represented by the earth goddess. Pater ascribes greater consciousness to this stage,[39] because it is no longer human life but a basic aspect of human conduct that is here mythologised.

This links up with the third phase, in which the focal point is the return of Persephone. 'Persephone is the goddess of death, yet with a promise of life to come.'[40] In this 'ethical' phase, Demeter becomes an image of reconciliation:[41]

> she is not without a certain pensiveness, having seen the seed fall into the ground and die, many times. Persephone is returned to her . . . the image of Persephone may be regarded as the result of many efforts to lift the old Chthonian gloom, still lingering on in heavier souls, concerning the grave, to connect it with impressions of dignity and beauty, and a certain sweetness even; it is meant to make men in love, or at least at peace, with death.[42]

> The daughter separated from the mother, and the cut corn are two symbols of something indescribably painful that is contained within the Demeter aspect of the world; but also of something very comforting . . . The totality of the Demeter idea is restricted neither to purely human forms and relations nor to the great world reality of grain. But it is more comprehensive in the forms of this non-human reality than in the purely human. The corn figure is one of origin and result, of mother and daughter, and so it points beyond the individual occurrence to the general and eternal. It is always the 'grain' that sinks into the earth and returns, that is cut down in its golden prime and yet remains intact as full and healthy corn, mother and daughter in one.[43]

The magic, elemental unity of man and earth, loss, and finally resuscitation are the three dominant themes that Pater finds in the different phases of the Demeter myth. Their ultimate importance depends on their interaction. They do not embody separate aspects of the world, but in their succession they elucidate a basic rhythm of life, an archetypal human experience. For all their contradictions, it is the inseparable interlinkage of loss and return that endows the unalterable sequence with meaning. This is why Pater is at pains right from the start to convey 'a total impression'[44] of myth. It is through the interconnectedness of the three phases that there emerges what Pater is seeking – namely, the secret promise.

It is typical of Pater that he should devote the largest part of his essay to Demeter's grief. Against the background of chthonic forces, which are embodied in Demeter, this takes on an exemplary elevation. Even so, loss is only the transition to return, and as such it is a necessary phase in the rhythmic movement of the world. It ceases to be meaningless since it becomes a part of the whole, whose effect is all the more sublime because it is born out of grief.

> With such experience, the individual is meaningfully incorporated into the life of the generations, so that all unnecessary obstacles are removed from the stream of life which is to flow through the individual. But in addition he is released from his

isolation and restored to his wholeness. Every cultic engagement with archetypes in the last analysis has this purpose and this success.[45]

At the end of his essay, Pater writes:

The myth of Demeter and Persephone, then, illustrates the power of the Greek religion as a religion of pure ideas – of conceptions, which having no link on historical fact, yet, because they arose naturally out of the spirit of man, and embodied, in adequate symbols, his deepest thoughts concerning the conditions of his physical and spiritual life, maintained their hold through many changes, and are still not without a solemnising power even for the modern mind, which has once admitted them as recognised and habitual inhabitants; and, abiding thus for the elevation and purifying of our sentiments, long after the earlier and simpler races of their worshippers have passed away, they may be a pledge to us of the place in our culture, at once legitimate and possible, of the associations, the conceptions, the imagery, of Greek religious poetry in general, of the poetry of all religions.[46]

Herein lies the decisive reason for Pater's preoccupation with myth. It is a prehistoric region in which man could still view the world as a whole. History merely records the aimless changeability of things, whereas in myth all changes relate to a perceivable totality. History unfolds itself in temporary mediation of opposites, whereas in myth the opposing forces converge into an overarching meaning, as typified by the return of Persephone and the return of the grain. Such an experience elevates and purifies the emotions, and so has a healing effect on the modern mind entangled in confusions and contradictions. Myth fulfils Pater's longing to view the whole – a longing which for him could not be fulfilled by history, as this would have demanded action and commitment, inconceivable for the quietism inherent in the aesthetic attitude. Myth, however, corresponds to this disposition: it is poetry, requiring no more than aesthetic contemplation, without the need for ethical decision.

The poetic character of the Demeter myth links up with another important aspect of Pater's study. All three phases of the myth 'embodied themselves gradually in the Greek imagination'.[47] The aesthetic faculty of the imagination is considered to be the origin of the myth. Thus the country folk of the first phase 'dream' about their daily tasks, and from their 'dreams' arise the images of the chthonic Demeter.[48] This is why Pater talks of the 'poet-people',[49] who embody the 'abstract spirit of poetry'[50] in their activities.

The second phase, describing Demeter's grief, is the work of the poets.

The 'worship of sorrow', as Goethe called it, is sometimes supposed to have had almost no place in the religion of the Greeks. Their religion has been represented as a religion of mere cheerfulness, the worship by an untroubled, unreflecting humanity, conscious of no deeper needs . . . But this familiar view of Greek religion . . . involves a misconception, akin to that which underestimates the influence of the

> romantic spirit generally, in Greek poetry and art; as if Greek art had dealt exclusively with human nature in its sanity, suppressing all motives of strangeness, all the beauty which is born of difficulty, permitting nothing but an Olympian, though perhaps somewhat wearisome calm. In effect, such a conception of Greek art and poetry leaves in the central expressions of Greek culture none but negative qualities; and the legend of Demeter and Persephone, perhaps the most popular of all Greek legends, is sufficient to show that the 'worship of sorrow' was not without its function in Greek religion; their legend is a legend made by and for sorrowful, wistful, anxious people; while the most important artistic monuments of that legend sufficiently prove that the Romantic spirit was really at work in the minds of Greek artists, extracting by a kind of subtle alchemy, a beauty, not without the elements of tranquillity, of dignity and order, out of a matter, at first sight painful and strange.[51]

With this insight, Pater ranks among the true discoverers of Greek Romanticism, reaching beyond the classical, Olympian world and perceiving the authenticity of Greek culture in the chthonic cults, mysteries and tragedies. The Demeter myth typifies the tragic experience which Pater regarded as the core of Greek art. The myth of grief became the birth of art. This art, however, inspired by suffering, communicates not only grief but also its transfiguration. As the 'worship of sorrow' it consecrates grief, thus taking out the sting by making it sublime – as Pater had already pointed out in the 'Conclusion' of *The Renaissance*.[52] Myth was the legitimation of his concept of art, and the second phase of the Demeter myth provided the perfect illustration of art as the transfiguration of man's primal suffering. The work of the poets and sculptors consisted in 'many efforts to lift the old Chthonian gloom, still lingering on in heavier souls'.[53]

The third phase of the Demeter myth is also a product of art. Sculptors create statues depicting reconciliation, and a statue in Attica, the 'stone of sorrow', shows Demeter 'represented in her later state of reconciliation, enthroned as the glorified mother of all things'.[54]

Pater's aesthetic conception of myth contains the same three all-important definitions of art that he developed in his critical writings. In its original state, art brings about unity between man and world. In the imagination of the 'poet-people' that which is separate in the historical process is present as a totality. Man is Nature, and Nature finds its expression in man. Secondly, as the transfiguration of suffering, art provides the objective fulfilment of Pater's longing to transcend the burdensome character of experience. And finally, the image of reconciliation embodies the aim of all art, which is to bind opposites together. Myth becomes the 'objective correlative' of Pater's aesthetic creed. But it is not only these individual features of unity, transfiguration and reconciliation as basic attributes of art that Pater finds objectified in myth; these attributes in turn highlight the fact that art alone is self-produced perfection. As we have already seen, 'art for art's sake' means that art cannot be subordinate to any reality outside itself. It follows that if art is absolute and autonomous, the world must be an invention of art. This claim must appear problematical in the light of experience, but myth seems to reaffirm its validity. For in myth, the world presents itself as the invention of artistic imagination, and this is why Pater took no interest in the epiphanies of gods as the origin of myth, let alone in myth's stages of reception, which are nothing but explanations of beginnings. Myth for him signifies the birth of the world out of the spirit of art. The realities of this world are therefore not determinate experiences; rather they merge into one another. It is a world of 'indefiniteness', and as such it appears as 'a theology with no central authority, no link on historic time, liable from the first to an unobserved transformation'.[55] Thus myth becomes an aesthetic religion, whose character is manifested in its fluidity. In myth, art and religion melt into a totality that is absent from historical periods. In the historical world, art's claim to autonomy rests solely on defamiliarising the given or on transformation of the existing world, whereas myth offers exemplary justification of the claim. Art invents the world and constantly transforms it by achieving the unification of opposites.

'A study of Dionysus'

Pater's study of Dionysus both complements and supplements his interpretation of the Demeter myth. The perspective is the same. Looking back on his Dionysus essay, Pater writes:

> So far, I have endeavoured to present, with something of the concrete character of a picture, Dionysus, the old Greek god, as we may discern him through a multitude of stray hints in art and poetry and religious custom, through modern speculation on the tendencies of early thought, through traits and touches in our own actual states of mind, which may seem sympathetic with those tendencies.[56]

Modern speculation and a spiritual affinity underlie his interpretation, and so it is evident that what he is seeking is not scholarship but the forces immanent in the myth. Such a search must inevitably result in a remoulding of the myth, as Dowden pointed out:

> Pater recognises in classical art and classical literature a considerable element of romance . . . and to re-fashion the myths of Dionysus and even Apollo in the romantic spirit is an experiment in which there is more than mere phantasy.[57]

What is 'more than mere phantasy' arises because Pater's quest was for more than an imaginative objectification of his basic beliefs.

Despite a certain structural disunity in this essay, which we shall discuss later, the figure of Dionysus is moved into focus according to the same schema which guided Pater's interpretation of the Demeter myth: 'Dionysus and his circle, a little Olympus outside the greater, covered the whole of life, and was a complete religion, a sacred representation or interpretation of the whole human experience.'[58] Dionysus is distinct from the other gods in that he quite independently embodies this totality. Thus he is in himself a hierarchy of world order outside that of Olympus, where each of the gods gives presence to diversified aspects of the cosmos. Pater's particular interest in this all-embracing representative of human life can be gauged from the fact that he also occurs in Pater's fiction.[59]

Like Demeter, whose mythical range often intersects that of Dionysus,[60] the wine god embodies an unfathomable interplay of forces in the chthonic world. Originally the cult of Dionysus was linked to tree-worship,[61] and gradually from cults of vegetation and fertility emerged 'the hierarchy of the creatures of water and sunlight in many degrees'.[62] This hierarchy radiates out to all elemental symbols, and they and their opposites come together in the figure of Dionysus. He is the symbol of growth, and 'the whole productive power of the earth is in him'.[63] While he encompasses the chthonic aspect of Demeter, he also overlaps with Apollo.

> Dionysus inspires and rules over all the music of the reed, the water-plant, in which the ideas of water and of vegetable life are brought close together, natural property, therefore, of the spirit of life in the green sap.[64]

The age-old connection between moisture and vegetation is symbolised by the reed as the instrument of a cultic music, and wine and music together endow the chthonic myth of Dionysus with its sublimity. They exalt and transform human life as well as signifying the god's tangible power over it. Dionysus

> explains the phenomena of enthusiasm . . . the secrets of possession by a higher and more energetic spirit than one's own, the gift of self-revelation, of passing out of oneself through words, tones, gestures . . . It is in this loosening of the lips and heart, strictly, that Dionysus is the Deliverer.[65]

The familiar world of man is shattered by the appearance of the god, and yet the destruction of all individualisation is experienced as deliverance. Ecstasy splits the self asunder, and makes the world of facts evaporate; the Dionysian frenzy wipes out the individual's alienation from Nature, and it is in this sense that the god becomes a deliverer. This idea brings Pater close to Nietzsche:

> Add to this awe the blissful ecstasy which rises from the innermost depths of man, ay, of nature, at this same collapse of the *principium individuationis*, and we shall gain an insight into the being of the *Dionysian*, . . . Under the charm of the Dionysian not only is the covenant between man and man again established, but

> also estranged, hostile or subjugated nature again celebrates her reconciliation with her lost son, man.[66]

This removal of divisions, with the return of man to his earthy origins, constitutes the first aspect of Dionysus for Pater. Music and wine, both fruits of the earth, arouse the enthusiasm in man that reunites him with Nature. The individual self that has separated him from Nature is seen by Pater as the result of historical experience, as illustrated in 'Emerald Uthwart' and 'Child in the House'. But what these stories reveal to be incompatible is obliterated through the Dionysian ecstasy – man throws off the individuality imprinted on him through historical experience, and suddenly seems close to his goal of achieving unity with himself and the world. What Pater was unable to achieve, the Dionysian myth featured as fulfilment: an exit from historically conditioned individualisation into shapeless plenitude.

The second aspect that interests Pater is the extraordinary contrasts that the god encompasses. Dionysus is 'a dual god of both summer and winter'.[67] This duality again overlaps with the range of Demeter, but in Dionysus it is not confined to the alternating seasons; it extends to all the basic discords of human life and cosmic being. He incorporates the whole of human experience, which includes the realms of Demeter and of Persephone (through his connection with Hades).[68] Intensified life and death flow together in him, and in his ecstasy, one realm will always simultaneously evoke its counter-realm. Thus the epiphany of the god gives presence to an ineluctable doubleness: summer and winter, life and death, ecstasy and grief,[69] hunter and hunted,[70] pain and pleasure,[71] which dwarf all human systems,[72] for the god floods them with his abundance and submerges them to the depths of oblivion.

> But the god himself is not touched and seized merely by the ghostly breath emanating from the depths. He is himself the monster that dwells in those depths. Through a mask the monster gazes on men and shocks them through the doubleness of near and far, life and death in one. His spirit holds the opposites together. For he is the spirit of excitement and savagery, and everything live that bubbles over and glows rises above the division from its opposite and has already absorbed it into the ardour of its pleasure. Thus all earthly powers are one in him: generating, nursing, intoxicating ecstasy, life-giving inexhaustibility, heart-rending grief, deathly pallor, the silent night of whatever has been. It is the rapture that whirls round wherever there is creation and birth, its wildness ever ready to march on to death and destruction. It is life that in overflowing becomes frantic, and, in its deepest lust, is akin to death . . . Thus its storm rips humanity out of all custom and middle-class morality, hurling it into life intoxicated by death, where it glows most brightly . . . There the most distant is near, the past is present, and all times are mirrored in the moment that is now.[73]

Constantly splitting the god up into his various opposing aspects denotes a completely different world order from the modern one. Pater saw time as being the ultimate background of things, as he indicated in his 'Conclusion'; against this background, life and death are utterly distinct and oppressively certain. Within time, the opposites are irreconcilable, and so it was in art that Pater found the balance and mediation he sought. In the dualism of Dionysus, where the opposites are both distinct and coincident, Pater sees a power which removes the differences brought about by time.[74] The removal of contradictions means the annihilation of time, and opens up vistas on totalities which had been lost sight of through man's imprisonment in the temporality of his developing consciousness. In cancelling out both time and consciousness, Dionysus is for Pater the answer to the individual's entanglement in the modern world. Dionysus incorporates destruction and plenitude simultaneously, and their vivid presence indicates that life is not subjected to any principles, but is palpable in a ceaseless interplay of what is mutually exclusive. And for the objectification of this process, Pater turns not to any transcendental theory – for no idea *could* objectify such a process – but to the dynamism of myth.

Dionysus, then, represents a totality that invalidates yet embraces all systems orientated by time, and Pater emphasises this in his analysis of the third aspect of the god. Dionysus

> has . . . a peculiar message for a certain number of refined minds . . . A type of second birth, from first to last, he opens, in his series of annual changes, for minds on the look-out for it, the hope of a possible analogy, between the resurrection of nature, and something else, as yet unrealised, reserved for human souls; and the beautiful, weeping creature, vexed by the wind, suffering, torn to pieces, and rejuvenescent again at last, like a tender shoot of living green out of the hardness and stony darkness of the earth, becomes an emblem or ideal of chastening and purification, and of final victory through suffering.[75]

Dionysian time is a circle with a rhythmic renewal of all that time destroys.[76] The promise for human souls remains vague, but Pater's metaphor refers to growth emerging from darkness, and victory from suffering. The dismemberment of the god is an inalienable sign of his resurrection; thus destruction, instead of indicating loss, generates hope. Recurrence as an eternal process takes the sting out of time and eliminates its menacing character.

> For the circle, in its self-contained completeness, symbolises time that is also self-contained and complete, and no longer points to a future beyond itself. In this respect the circle symbolises real, self-contained eternity that no longer runs on into infinity.[77]

Thus the finiteness of life seems to be annulled, and Dionysus symbolises the eternity of life, thereby objectifying Pater's vague expectation.

The idea of return is the all-embracing aspect of Dionysus, encompassing as it does both the ecstatic aspect and that of interpenetrating dualities. It is therefore the return that provides the dominant subject-matter of the essay and is already hinted at in the subtitle, which refers to the double birth of the god. For Pater he is 'The Spiritual Form of Fire and Dew'.[78]

> The fire of which he was born would destroy him in his turn, as it withered up his mother; a second danger comes; from this the plant is protected by the influence of the cooling cloud, the lower part of his father the sky, in which it is wrapped and hidden, and of which it is born again, its second mother being, in some versions of the legend, Hyé – the Dew.[79]

This double birth indicates Dionysus's human and divine origin. Semele, his mother, wanted to see her lover, and so Zeus appeared to her as lightning and fire, which consumed her. Zeus carried the child in his thigh until he was born again, ringed with water and dew. For Pater the opposing attributes of fire and dew represent the divinity and humanity out of which Dionysus has arisen.

This duality underlies all features of Dionysus, whose ultimate importance Pater saw in the decisive impetus he gave to Greek art. The Greek imagination created its sculpture out of these countervailing aspects of the god.

> The office of the imagination, then, in Greek sculpture, in its handling of divine persons, is thus to condense the impressions of natural things into human form; to retain that early mystical sense of water, or wind, or light, in the moulding of eye and brow; to arrest it, or rather, perhaps, to set it free, there, as human expression . . . With such habitual impressions concerning the body, the physical nature of man, the Greek sculptor, in his later day, still free in imagination, through the lingering influence of those early dreams, may have more easily infused into human form the sense of sun, or lightning, or cloud, to which it was so closely akin, the spiritual flesh allying itself happily to mystical meanings, and readily expressing seemingly unspeakable qualities.[80]

What sculpture achieved Pater can only describe with oxymora. The magical powers of the earth are linked to the human figure, and disparate qualities are forced together in art, which lives in a continual tension 'between the palpable and limited human form, and the floating essence it is to contain'.[81] In the historical world, art becomes the legitimate continuation of myth, preserving its tensions by relating the opposites to one another. The forces of myth are also present in art – earth, Nature, magic and elemental powers gain shape in the human form. Thus for Pater Dionysus was a 'spiritual form; form with hands, and lips, and opened eyelids – spiritual, as conveying to us, in that, the soul of rain, or of a Greek river, or of swiftness, or purity'.[82]

The 'spiritual form' compresses what had been separated into the three basic aspects – that interplay between form and forces which makes ecstatic madness into deliverance. The mythical unity entails the sacrifice of individuality, which turns man into the embodiment of natural powers. For Nature remains silent until she is given a form. The unity of the myth solidifies as man loses his individuality and Nature begins to speak through tangible forms. The term 'spiritual form' is Pater's objectification of this process, out of which art arises, binding opposites together in an elevated communion. Art bears witness to the reality of myth in an historical world. Indeed, in art the historical world discovers a new myth. The old gods have faded away, but the foundations of their myth are preserved in art, which thus provides the historical world with the perfection it yearns for.

We mentioned earlier that Pater's study of Dionysus appears somewhat disjointed, and this is because he sought to uncover the connections between art and myth, which constituted a major problem for him. The unity of the myth is aesthetic, for it is immanent and not brought about by an abstract idea. Art becomes a mythical reality by preserving in the historical world a unity that cannot be deduced from human experience. And if myth incorporates the totality of prehistoric human experience, as Pater maintains, then art represents the absolute in history. Art, then, objectifies myth, while myth in turn is the objective legitimation of art.

9 The limits of mythical legitimation

'Apollo in Picardy'

The full significance of pagan myth for Pater can be gauged from his fictional treatment of the ancient gods. As Harrison rightly pointed out, Pater's 'was a mind not content with the fruits of pure research; his learning fed his imagination and feelings quite as much as his mind'.[1] The Dionysus essay culminated in the idea of the return, which in his fictional writings is set in such a light that what he regarded as the limits of mythical legitimation becomes strikingly clear. Where myth is regarded as a refuge, the focal point of hope is the return of the ancient gods, but this is not the advent of the longed-for millennium. The gods do not return to their ancient homes in a blaze of glory; they wander as pariahs through a world that is now foreign to them. This is brought out most vividly in the story 'Apollo in Picardy', which describes Apollo's return in mediaeval Christian times. The pagan powers undergo a very revealing transformation which obviously requires fiction if it is to be fully explored. Critics have pointed out that Pater borrows extensively from Heine,[2] whose short story 'Die Götter im Exil' depicts the gods as emigrants forced to take up a trade in the bourgeois world they have come back to. 'Under such circumstances many whose sacred groves had been confiscated were forced to earn their daily bread as woodcutters here with us in Germany, and to drink beer instead of nectar.'[3] Although Pater's Apollo is presented as a shepherd,[4] the difference in the treatment of the theme is unmistakable. Heine's presentation of the gods' return is bathed in subtle irony, which is nowhere to be found in Pater. Heine's gods are caricatured, as is the bourgeois world they find themselves in, but Pater has no such satirical intention. He is interested only in the decline of mythical powers when they return to the historical world. His tale is serious, and so in direct contrast to Heine's ironic treatment. Against the background of his preoccupation with and interpretation of ancient myths the earnest tone is scarcely surprising – a man who finds the promise of totality in the return of Dionysus is hardly likely to regard the arrival of the ancient gods as a subject for comedy.

'Apollo in Picardy' describes the situation and consequences of Apollo's re-appearance in the Middle Ages. Following Heine he is cast as a shepherd living near a monastery. The juxtaposition of ancient god and monastery – particularly with the Prior Saint-Jean – already points to the subject-matter, which is the clash of opposing forces. Through the god the vast elemental power of Nature and earth comes to life again. 'He and his fascinations, his music, himself, might at least be taken for an embodiment of all those genial influences of earth and sky . . . the Prior and his companion, were come in contact for the first time in their lives with the power of untutored natural impulse of natural inspiration.'[5] This is the hyperborean Apollo,[6] and the allusions to his seasonal migration towards the north[7] show that Pater wishes to present the 'Romantic' Apollo who incorporates the chthonic element of an all-embracing Nature. It is a concept that reveals not only the importance for Pater of chthonic myth and the ancient gods, but also his fascination with a possible return of the primal undividedness of all things.

Prior Saint-Jean, the pagan god's adversary, is – despite his asceticism – extremely sensitive to the plenitude of Nature. Shortly before taking his post as prior of the monastery near which the strange shepherd lives, he has a last look at the countryside from the tower of his present abode:

> you saw . . . the green breadth of Normandy and Picardy, this way and that; felt on your face the free air of a still wider realm beyond what was seen. The reviving scent of it, the mere sight of the flowers brought thence, of the country produce at the convent gate, stirred the ordinary monkish soul with desires, sometimes with efforts, to be sent on duty there. Prior Saint-Jean, on the other hand, shuddered at the view, at the thoughts it suggested to him; thoughts of unhallowed wild places, where the old heathen had worshipped 'stocks and stones,' and where their wickedness might still survive them in something worse than mischievous tricks of nature.[8]

The feeling for Nature in this passage is ambivalent. On the one hand, the green, the air, the flowers create a longing akin to that of Gaston, whose yearnings were also intermingled with the beauty of Nature spread out before him; on the other, what Gaston's vision had grasped as a vague promise of unending expansion and undividedness makes the prior shudder with horror. What he sees is not the all-embracing totality of things, but the pagan origins of Nature. The 'wickedness' of Nature-worship is in direct contrast to the gentle longing of the 'ordinary monkish soul'.

This contrast lies at the heart of the tale. The prior goes to Picardy and there meets the shepherd, who leads him to destruction. That farewell look at the countryside, which had linked longing to apprehension, had set the scene for the clash between heathen Nature and Christian faith.

Despite the title 'Apollo in Picardy', alluding to the classical god of light, the god in the story is called Apollyon. This change is symptomatic of the radical reshaping of the old myth, with emphasis now being placed on what Heine called the 'Verteufelung'[9] (diabolising) of the god. In the Christian world, mythical powers appear as demons. They embody the forces hostile to the Christian order, and from time to time they are a threat to it, as the prior is to find out for himself. Apollo becomes Apollyon, who is driven out of his old realm and into a Christian one, where he is transformed into a devil. Since Phineas Fletcher[10] and Bunyan,[11] Apollyon has been equated with Lucifer and the 'foul Fiend'.[12] Pater's Apollo serves Satan, and there is a tangible effect on the mind of the prior. The devil's ambience surrounds the harmless-looking shepherd, and his hidden power throws monastic life into confusion. While the classical Apollo combined insight, self-knowledge, moderation and order,[13] Apollyon does 'Devilry, devil's work'.[14] While Apollo cleared away all the evil to create security,[15] Apollyon fills the countryside with the horror of the daemonic.[16] As the ancient god of healing, Apollo cleansed the stain from the guilty,[17] whereas Apollyon brings suspicion down on the innocent.[18] Instead of enlightenment he brings frenzied confusion, and instead of radiance he creates 'a veritable "solar storm" '.[19] When the prior is writing the last book of his 'summa', Apollonian light suddenly floods the room, the logical character of his work begins to fall apart, and in ecstatic visions he gazes on blasphemous truths.[20] He sees the earth revolving round the sun, perceives the cohesion of the Copernican system and hears Pythagoras's music of the spheres. He tries to capture these visions, but if

> he set hand to the page, the firm halo, here a moment since, was gone, had flitted capriciously to the wall; passed next through the window, to the wall of the garden; was dancing back in another moment upon the innermost walls of one's own miserable brain, to swell there – that astounding white light! – rising steadily in the cup, the mental receptacle, till it overflowed, and he lay faint and drowning in it. Or he rose above it, as above a great liquid surface, and hung giddily over it – light, simple and absolute – ere he fell. Or there was a battle between light and darkness around him, with no way of escape from the baffling strokes, the lightning flashes; flashes of blindness one might rather call them.[21]

The Apollonian light is transformed into 'hell-fire',[22] which brings neither knowledge nor insight but blots out all moderation and order.

> Prior Saint-Jean . . . lay sometimes in a trance . . . from which he would spring up suddenly to crowd, against time, as much as he could into his book with pen or brush; winged flowers, or stars with human limbs and faces, still intruding themselves, or mere notes of light and darkness from the actual horizon.[23]

The prior's strange encounter with Apollyon illuminates the relationship between two conflicting worlds. Saint-Jean's life's work is devoted to explaining the Christian cosmos. The contact with Apollyon seems to bring the longed-for enlightenment, with everything suddenly being made clear to him. He is inspired, even if the visions confront him with unexpected experiences. But he cannot capture the richness of what he perceives; the vista now opened up on the cosmos overwhelms him. He drowns in the light of this illumination, which paradoxically begins to darken his mind, so that what he puts down on paper is nothing but images of confusion – winged flowers etc. These are grotesque symbols of a distorted vision denoting the failure to grasp what in actual fact he thought he could see. What Apollyon has revealed to him, exceeds his faculties of comprehension. And so the light of illumination increasingly blacks out cognition, and sight changes to blindness. From now on, the prior's work is called 'Prior Saint-Jean's folly'.[24]

Clearly the return of the ancient gods created insoluble problems for Pater. Their resurrection results in a disturbance of the Christian order, and indeed it is only through such a disturbance that the impact of their reappearance can be felt. But this, in turn, has repercussions on the gods themselves; the Christian order inscribes itself into their character by inverting their own basic attributes – the god of light is now tarnished by the devilish attributes of Lucifer. Thus, instead of Apollyon enhancing and transfiguring the reality to which he returns, he neutralises all efforts to explain and comprehend the order of life, leaving disrupted realities in his wake. All that the prior is able to perceive is an unresolved battle between the forces of light and darkness.[25]

In the Christian world, primal, instinctive Nature is anathema,[26] as indicated by the 'diabolising' of the ancient god. But the return of the gods does not mean that the historical reality of Christianity must suddenly give way to a resurrected Nature; instead, the two worlds overlap and neutralise life. Pagan Nature can do no more than disturb the Christian order, it cannot replace it. And so the return of the gods symbolises for Pater an ominous clash between antagonistic forces, with pagan Nature and Christian faith cancelling each other out. The prior experiences hitherto inconceivable vistas of the cosmos, opened up by his encounter with Apollyon, only as a darkening of his mind. In the end, he is found guilty of murder committed after he has been overcome by insanity,[27] while Apollo becomes a pariah and finally a devil within the Christian world.

The reciprocal derangement of the two worlds is paralleled by Apollyon's Satanic fits. While Hyacinthus, the prior's young companion, and Apollyon are quietly playing with the animals near the monastery, Apollyon suddenly breaks into extraordinary violence: 'Tired, surfeited, he destroys them when his game with them is at an end; breaks the toy; deftly snaps asunder the fragile back.'[28] His magic powers had attracted the creatures to him, and the birds especially had flown to him, only to meet their death. But it is not only surfeit that gives rise to Apollyon's cruelty – sometimes it springs from hidden impulses, totally impenetrable even to him. The doves in the monastery garden are fondled and cherished by 'gentle monastic hands'.[29] One morning they are all found dead.

Who then, what hawk, or wild-cat, or other savage beast, had ravaged it so wantonly, so very cruelly destroyed the bright creatures in a single night – broken backs, rent away limbs, pierced the wings? And what was that object there below? The silver harp surely, lying broken likewise on the sanded floor, soaking in the pale milky blood and torn plumage. Apollyon sobbed and wept audibly as he went about his ordinary doings next day, for once fully, though very sadly, awake in it; and towards evening, when the villagers came to the Prior to confess themselves, the Feast of the Nativity being now at hand, he too came along with them in his place meekly, like any other penitent, touched the lustral water devoutly, knew all the ways, seemed to desire absolution from some guilt of blood heavier than the slaughter of beast or bird.[30]

His own destructive savagery makes Apollyon weep: some incalculable instinct has driven him to destroy those very creatures which, as an embodiment of Nature,[31] he should in fact protect. The harp, stained with the blood of birds, is broken too, symbolising the destruction of harmony wrought by his frenzy. His penitence shows the extent to which this outburst of cruelty runs counter to his true nature, and his desire for absolution seems to indicate some heavier guilt than that of bloodshed. His Satanism has made him act against that which originally he was meant to represent, and so he seems now to be broken – he is a divided god. It follows that the return of mythical Nature to a Christian world must bring division and ultimately perversion of both realms. Apollyon's frenzied cruelty comes about because in the Christian world he is an alien, diabolical god, though this contradicts his original status. The Satanism results from and at the same time indicates the deep equivocalness of untamed Nature, which is released from control by pagan myth when it reappears in the Christian world.[32] 'Apollyon [is] actually a part of . . . that irredeemable natural world.'[33] Because it is irredeemable, Nature, when set within a Christian world, can only become a demonic power whose frenzied destructiveness gives full weight to the forces of chaos.

The return of the gods, then, is not an answer to the problems by which *fin-de-siècle* aestheticism was beset. By breaking into an historical world totally alien to them, pagan Nature and Christian faith exclude each other. As representative of the Christian world, the prior is driven to confusion and madness by his encounter with the god, unable to grasp the plenitude revealed to him, and plunged from light to darkness. Apollyon, as representative of pagan Nature, finds himself changed from god to devil; in having to turn against himself, he gives presence to a deranged Nature which becomes tangible in an unrestrained Satanism.

Against historical realities, the return of the gods is no longer desirable, and Pater has shown the link between myth and faith to be illusory. It is here that the mythical legitimation of art reaches its boundary, and it was in order to draw this boundary that Pater had to resort to a fictional presentation of the gods. In his critical writings he objectified those aspects of the gods that were relevant to his longing for unity; his fictional presentation is dominated by the insight that the mythical world is now past. Time has left it behind, and the only way that it can now manifest itself in history is as a force of destruction.

Pater and Nietzsche

A few critics have pointed out certain similarities between Pater and Nietzsche.[34] On the surface their concepts of myth do indeed have something in common – for instance, the discovery of the tragic myth,[35] the mythical origins of tragedy,[36] the interrelation between Apollonian and Dionysian,[37] and the attack on Euripides.[38] Beneath the surface, however, their concepts are very different. In *The Birth of Tragedy* Nietzsche argued:

> Without myth, however, every culture loses its healthy creative natural power: it is only a horizon encompassed with myths which rounds off to unity a social movement. It is only by myth that all the powers of the imagination and of the Apollonian dream are freed from their random rovings. The mythical figures have to be the invisibly omnipresent genii, under the care of which the young soul grows to maturity, by the signs of which the man gives a meaning to his life and struggles: and the state itself knows no more powerful unwritten law than the mythical foundation which vouches for its connection with religion and its growth from mythical ideas.[39]

The dissimilarity to Pater's concept is clear. Pater did not seek to explain modern life through myths, but simply wanted to objectify a longing that could not be fulfilled in the historical world. This purely personal quest made him indifferent to the dynamic element inherent in Nietzsche's rediscovery of myth, and in no way did he ever contemplate activating the primal forces of mythical existence in order to redefine culture. While Nietzsche used the myth of Dionysus to construct his theory of the eternal return,[40] Pater's study of Apollo shows the impossibility of activating these mythical forces in the historical world. Nietzsche believed that myth could renew man and the world, but Pater's gods, when they return to the historical world, bring chaotic confusion and division. For Nietzsche myth was a moral power; for Pater it was an aesthetic phenomenon. And indeed for Pater this was its fascination, for it imposed no obligations and yet, in its magnanimity, offered edifying experiences that time-bound man could enjoy. In the elevated images of myth, Pater could fulfil his desire for a wholeness that modern man had lost.

This is why Pater speaks of 'sympathetic . . . tendencies'[41] between the modern mind and the mythical world, and what he expects from myth is 'elevation and purifying of our sentiments'.[42] Such a secular edification is purely aesthetic, and therefore sterile – a sterility made abundantly clear in the return of Apollo. The contrast with Nietzsche's moral concept is all the more striking in that Pater saw myth as a legitimation for autonomous art. He regarded myth as poetry through which man shaped and ordered the world. It was the model realisation of his concept of art, and confirmed that the totality of the world originated in art. In the immemorial beginning, art and theology and religion were all one. In myth artistic man created an image of the world that exorcised the sinister powers by giving them tangible form.

History showed art to be a power of reconciliation, and myth reflected the world that was born of art. But the harmony of art turned out to be Utopian in history, and the primal totality of myth belonged irrevocably to the past. Thus the limits of Pater's concept of history and myth as the legitimation for autonomous art are obvious. The boundaries which *Gaston de Latour* and 'Apollo in Picardy' had made discernible bring us now to the final problem of how the aesthete is to act in view of his awareness that the reassurance he sought from history and myth is undermined by the limits of the sanction he has found. It is this problem that gave birth to Pater's most important works of fiction: *Marius the Epicurean* and *Imaginary Portraits*.

V *THE AESTHETIC EXISTENCE*

10 *Marius the Epicurean*

The form

The very form of Pater's *Marius* is symptomatic of the peculiar problem he intended to tackle. This is of such paramount importance that at times the novel is taken over by theoretical discussion which evidently cannot be coped with by the narrative. The reader has the strange impression that topic and narrative mode seem to fall apart, in consequence of which the narrative is punctured by an apparent inability to capture the dimension of the problem to be communicated. Thus the novel is hard to categorise, as strikingly borne out by Lubbock, who had difficulties in subsuming it under the types of narrative he had devised as a model for criticism. He writes that

> in *Marius* probably, if it is to be called a novel, the art of drama is renounced as thoroughly as it has ever occurred to a novelist to dispense with it. I scarcely think that Marius ever speaks or is spoken to audibly in the whole course of the book; such at least is the impression that it leaves. The scenes of the story reach the reader by refraction, as it were, through the medium of Pater's harmonious murmur.[1]

David Cecil, in a short essay on Pater, sums up his reaction as follows:

> The impression left in the memory by Marius, and the rest of them, is that of tableaux, in which in front of an elaborate and beautifully painted background are posed figures beautifully and elaborately clothed, but who are faceless, speechless and incapable of motion.[2]

These two judgements accurately reflect Pater's technique. The lack of drama mentioned by Lubbock comes about because there are no real confrontations, which is perhaps a little surprising in view of the fact that Pater uses 'showing', which Lubbock places next to 'telling' as a basic category of the novel. *Marius* does indeed consist of a series of scenes, but their order and relationship is such that all dramatic elements are suppressed and the actions that there are seem strangely subdued. Hence the static impression described by David Cecil – the characters do not establish themselves as real people, but instead gain their outline by being thrown into relief against a luxuriously elaborated background.

Furthermore, Pater's narrative technique deviates from established patterns. Although the proceedings are described from an omniscient point of view, comprising Marius's life-span from birth to death,[3] we are told little of the hero's actual life. Concrete events are kept to a bare minimum, and turning-points are often mentioned only incidentally: 'The emperor Marcus Aurelius, to whose service Marius had now been called, was himself, more or less openly, a "lecturer".'[4] This new development is conveyed quite indirectly, simply tucked away in a subordinate clause. The relegation of decisive events in Marius's life to a mere mention indicates a shift of importance away from actions to something else. Actions are reduced to a bare minimum, serving only to provide links for situations devoted to the portrayal of Marius's inner life. These situations, however, which are arranged in the scenic mode of showing, deviate from showing in so far as they are totally without drama. Undramatic showing spotlights the hero's reluctance to come to grips with the world, as he wants to indulge rather in his sensations and ideas, as indicated by the subtitle of the novel. The setting within which Marius moves functions almost exclusively as a stimulant for his feelings and ideas; the Roman world is present only through the hero's impressions. Again an in-between quality comes to the fore. The panoramic strategy of narration reduces action, and the scenic one eliminates dramatic tension. Telling and showing in their mutual interference present all the evolving conflicts in a state of frozen neutralisation, which allows the aesthetic existence to be conveyed in a kind of slow motion.

This lay-out of narrative makes the story dwindle to insignificance. Yet, according to E. M. Forster, 'we want to know what happens next. That is universal and that is why the backbone of a novel has to be a story.'[5] Forster defines the story as 'a narrative of events arranged in time sequence',[6] and although Pater adheres to the time sequence, the uneventful life of Marius does not consolidate into a story. As the backbone, a story gains shape by the outcome of events, whereas in *Marius* all events remain inconclusive.

Since the hero has no life through action – borne out by inverting the strategy inherent in both telling and showing – the focal point of Pater's interest is clearly the relationship between self and world, depicted through the way in which the world is reflected in Marius's impressions: 'he learned that the object, the experience, as it will be known to memory, is really from first to last the chief point for consideration in the conduct of life'.[7] He feels 'the impulse to surrender himself . . . to anything that . . . attracted or impressed him strongly.'[8] Clearly his conduct, then, is purely passive, and this is already hinted at during his youth in the Temple of Aesculapius, where he becomes aware of a way of life that is to prove central to his attitude: 'a diligent promotion of the capacity of the eye, inasmuch as in the eye would lie for him the determining influence of life.'[9] If reality is conceived as an optical phenomenon, it can be encountered from a distance, and Marius as a keen observer need not participate in it, but has only to open himself up to it. As seeing and observing are uppermost in his mind, he must avoid all commitments which will distract him from the contemplative attitude to be adopted. Marius is pure receptivity, and his only task is to train the eye. He is involved in no action – or if action *is* required of him, it will only be in a negative sense, when the demands made on his perceptions are too great and he must therefore turn away. An example of this is during the slaughter of the animals in the amphitheatre: 'the humble follower of the bodily eye . . . was aware of a crisis in life'.[10] He distances himself from what he sees, and such crises arise from sensitivity and not from action.

It is this optical relationship between the hero and his world that structures the novel as a series of selected scenes. The world is present only through the individual images which Marius perceives, and since he sees it in passive wonderment from a distance, reality appears as a dazzling pageant, devoid of action and so devoid of tension. Instead of these, we are given the elaborate background which compensates for what has been debarred: the story and the interaction between hero and reality. But herein lies a paradox. Reality in this novel is only present in the form of the hero's perception, but the hero in turn lives only through his perceptions, so that the view we get of him depends on what is perceived. The world and the hero are thus interdependent and indeed indivisible. From this fusion arises the strangely subdued and dreamlike mood of the novel, giving the impression of what David Cecil described as tableaux of motionless figures posed against an artificially elaborated background. There is no clash between hero and world; instead Pater's interweaving of the two replaces tension with mood.

It follows that Marius also deviates from categories according to which characters are fashioned – in E. M. Forster's terms he is neither 'flat' nor 'round'.[11] Flat characters serve to illustrate norms, values or meanings, and although Marius is called the Epicurean, there is no real effect of demonstration in the sense indicated by Forster and Muir.[12] He is not subordinated to an idea, and indeed he is continually drawing away from all such systems as Epicureanism, Stoicism and Christianity. All that he does demonstrate is that no idea can give permanent satisfaction, and this very negativity precludes the uniformity inherent in the 'flat character', which according to Forster may be summed up in a single sentence.[13] Flat characters draw their existence from unifying ideas underlying the novel's 'story', but Marius draws his existence from his constant abandonment of all unifying ideas. On the other hand, he is not – in spite of a self-imposed isolation – a 'round character' either, for he cannot master his own fate through action.[14] He is open to experience, and is therefore led by experience and not by his own determinacy. The fact that he exists only through his reflections of experience might make him into an allegorical figure, but even this category falls by the wayside, for he does not personify any idea – he only denotes the empty space which ideas might fill. He is an intermediate being, and his indeterminacy demonstrates nothing but a sort of melancholy helplessness.

This is well illustrated by a passage in which Marius begins to address the reader directly. This is in the chapter entitled 'Sunt Lacrimae Rerum', a quotation from Virgil that refers to a theme developed in Marius's diary.

> It was become a habit with Marius – one of his modernisms – to keep a register of the movements of his own private thoughts and humours; not continuously indeed, yet sometimes for lengthy intervals, during which it was no idle self-indulgence, but a necessity of his intellectual life, to 'confess himself', with an intimacy, seemingly rare among the ancients.[15]

The theme of this confession is man's experience of suffering.[16] This occurs mainly when man's centre lies outside himself because of a dependence that he is aware of but cannot change.[17] This corresponds to Marius's optical relation with the world. But in the confession there seems to be a strange disproportion between inside and outside, between man and world, and with his awareness of this opposition, Marius can get no satisfaction merely through optical perception. Indeed his perceptions seem to release feelings that crystallise into a contradiction of what he sees. Then his confession constitutes an aesthetic attempt to bridge the differences. The very fact that he feels impelled to 'confess' is an indication that he has another side to his character that reaches beyond the perceiving self, and this potential being results in certain incipient actions which begin to endow Marius with some individuality. For in the process of perceiving, Marius distances himself from those impressions that do not correspond to his potential self. This gives rise to what movement there is in the novel, though it never develops into a story, because the potential qualities are never activated. The confession is the nearest that Marius comes to individualisation. The perceivable world is shown to be an experience of suffering, and so Marius draws life from the inadequacy of a merely optical contact with reality. What is demonstrated here is a clear contradiction: on the one hand, Marius is completely committed to this optical relation, but on the other he experiences a longing to go beyond what he perceives.

This contradiction is what motivates the intense self-preoccupation that is the novel's theme. It renders all the minor characters quite unimportant, for they become mere ciphers, serving only as pretexts to allow rhetorical expositions – as is the case, for instance, with Cornelius Fronto, Lucian and Hermotimus.[18] There is no character in the novel correlated to Marius, let alone of equal standing – Flavius and Cornelius are just shadowy companions adumbrating Marius's longings and with hardly any existence outside his. Their subordination is symptomatic of the hero's self-absorption and the lack of any developing story. Marius remains suspended between his optical way of living and his dissatisfaction with it. He only gains in distinctness through the clash between the two, but since a resolution demands a developing action, and no such action ever takes place, the novel remains static and the hero remains undefined.

The curious form both of the novel and of its hero is mirrored by an equally curious attitude on Pater's part towards his fiction. The novel is set in late Roman times, during the reign of Marcus Aurelius, and yet there are several passages in which Pater alludes to historical events that took place much later. Pater himself is fully aware of the liberties he is taking by violating the illusion, for he occasionally apologises to the reader:

> That age and our own have much in common – many difficulties and hopes. Let the reader pardon me if here and there I seem to be passing from Marius to his modern representatives – from Rome, to Paris or London.[19]

The relevance of past to present gives Pater the occasion to reach out beyond the world of his novel, and of course the novel itself is Pater's way of objectifying a present problem through an historical situation. For history offers closed cases of human experience, and so for his purposes he needs only to extract the nuances embodied in Marius's feelings. Had he made the present his scene of action, he would have needed an overall view of that present in order to establish his fictional reality, but since it is precisely the overall view that is excluded from all his concepts, he could only take for his background a world that had already solidified into a finalised shape. This is why almost all Pater's fictions have an historical background. He chose periods that were particularly relevant to his present, so that he could extrapolate what he wanted without being forced into any theory that might impose an order on the present.

It is not only the present that intrudes on Pater's fiction; he also alludes to events in the Middle Ages and the Renaissance. For instance, when Marcus Aurelius returns from his military campaign against the Teutons, Pater interrupts his description of the triumphal procession to discuss the work of Andrea Mantegna, whose paintings depicted similar scenes.[20] Such diversions always occur when what is to be presented cannot be realised in terms of action but only through short reports or allusions. Demonstration replaces action, in precisely the same way as the hero is conceived in terms of thoughts and not deeds. In order to communicate such a way of life, Pater is forced to bring into his narrative events and descriptions in which his themes have been objectified. The technique is already apparent at the beginning of the novel, when Pater describes

Marius participating in the celebration of the cult of Numa, and alludes to Wordsworth in order to capture the feelings of the young Roman.[21] The less action there is, the more necessary it becomes to seek points of comparison elsewhere. These allusions to other realities also mirror Marius's lack of commitment to his own world, and the manner in which Pater intrudes upon his fiction serves to underline the absence of consequences in the fictional world he creates. This is in direct contrast to what the realistic novel was meant to achieve: the realisation of a certain purpose by means of a diversified action. The string of flickering impressions, however, does not suffice to communicate the inner workings of the hero's mind,[22] and therefore Pater has to resort to images, events, allusions, quotations and historical situations outside his fictional realm in order to compensate for what his truncated narrative leaves open. Where action ceases, the illusionary world of the narrative must be punctured. It is a technique which has become increasingly potent in the modern novel.

This leads to a final observation regarding the form of the novel, whose loosely connected scenes make the lack of an overarching purpose all too obvious. A component part of narration has been faded out: there is no plot-line, and hence no organising principle by means of which events may be bracketed together. The plot-line need not necessarily impose a causal relationship on the narrative sequence, but it has to do more than just arrange coincidental and at best associative connections between what happens. Plot is turned into a minus-function, and its omission allows for a portrayal of the hero as drifting from one possibility to another until his very end. The multiplicity of possibilities is therefore the only thread running through Marius's life, and he has to open himself up to them all, as each of them might be one of those precious moments he keeps longing for. As plot cuts down on possibilities in favour of a purpose to be made apparent, the subversion of plot becomes a strategy of communication.

Furthermore, plot signals a hidden optimism in so far as it conceives of reality as potentially capable of being mastered. As a passive observer, however, Marius is not set on mastering reality but, if anything, on refining his sensibilities, and so plot gives way to a disconnected succession of choice moments. In this respect Pater might be called a precursor of Virginia Woolf. Although superficially the form of his novel harks back to the old *Bildungsroman*, his hero does not embrace any single concept of life but remains suspended among all the possibilities that experience offers him. As none of these can fulfil him, he can only go on from one experience to another, a process of extension that in turn is only possible *because* he rejects every concept and so retains his freedom.

The future will be with those who have most of it; while for the present, as I persuade myself, those who have much of it, have something to hold by, even in the dissolution of a world, or in that dissolution of self, which is, for every one, no less than the dissolution of the world it represents for him.[23]

The problem

The narrative mode of Pater's novel is often little more than a pretext to enable him to discuss questions that are clearly of more interest to him than plot or character. Indeed the demands of narrative and the demands of discussion are sometimes so far apart from one another that the thoughts of the hero are frequently conveyed in the form of essays instead of through direct action.[24] Clearly Pater's aims required this strange mixture of essay and fiction, and it is a mixture that is to be found in all his narrative texts. This hybrid form corresponds exactly to the in-between world whose territory Pater wanted to chart.

At the beginning of the novel, Marius attends a celebration of the Religion of Numa. His feelings during the rites set him apart from the other persons present.[25] While they experience the ceremony as conventional observance, it rouses him to 'much speculative activity'[26] – an activity that is to play a central role in his life. Whenever he is confronted by a specific reality, he always feels a difference that separates him from things and people, and the resultant detachment enables him to reshape his impressions according to his own ideas. The activity is speculative in that it imposes a subjective pattern on the distantly perceived world. The result is a certain duality in the character of Marius: in perceiving the world he becomes aware of his singularity, and this in turn strives to adapt the perceived material to form a world suited to itself. This duality becomes problematical when Marius's detachment cannot bring about a new and suitable reality.

Marius himself seems to sense the difficulty right from the start, for his growing indifference to all religions – especially to that of his childhood – intensifies his longing 'towards . . . some great occasion of self-devotion . . . that should consecrate his life'.[27] The opportunity does present itself at the end of the novel, but Marius is unable to seize it.

The unconscious feelings of childhood first become concrete when Marius leaves home.

> A singularly virile consciousness of the realities of life pronounced itself in him; still however as in the main a poetic apprehension, though united already with something of personal ambition and the instinct of self-assertion.[28]

In this context, personal ambition and self-assertion are linked not to a conflict with or a conquest of reality but to an aesthetic attitude towards it, while 'poetic apprehension' denotes the transformational perception of things. The two are inevitably bound together, for only by transforming reality can Marius reduce it to meet his own requirements. The aesthetic attitude encompasses both detachment from and transformation of reality, and this is the keynote of Marius's early days. The first opportunity he has to orientate his quest comes about through his meeting with Flavian.

Flavian, a classmate of Marius's, is a literary mannerist.[29] He introduces Marius to the mannerist literature of Late Antiquity, especially the *Golden Book*.[30] His own interest lies exclusively in the magic of language as an instrument of power.[31] As the son of a slave, he has none of the traditional ties that bind Marius – who has grown up under the spell of the old religion[32] – and he 'believed only in himself'.[33] Hence his interest in the power of the word, which alone can ensure that he, as the ultimate reality, can achieve the effects he desires. 'To Marius, at a later time, he counted for as it were an epitome of the whole pagan world, the depth of its corruption, and its perfection of form.'[34] It is the 'perfection of form' that fascinates Marius in Flavian's manipulation of language, and when he comes to evaluate his contact with Flavian, Pater says:

> He was acquiring what it is the chief function of all higher education to impart, the art, namely, of so relieving the ideal or poetic traits, the elements of distinction, in our everyday life . . . that the unadorned remainder of it, the mere drift or *débris* of our days, comes to be as though it were not.[35]

Flavian has appealed to that side of Marius which is set on poeticising reality; for a poetic reality is one that can be mastered, since it is formed by the desires of the individual; 'ideal moments' may be extracted and preserved in such a way that the everyday 'débris' is cast aside, and herein lies the transforming power of the word. Against such a background, it is easy to understand why Marius seeks distance from reality, for not only will this permit mastery, but it will also hold off the pain of the real world.[36] This process permeates the whole novel. Whenever Marius is confronted by a reality that suits him, poetic impressions are set forth which, for the most part, conceal the harsh truths that might undermine the artificially created harmony. Training in the use of the *mot juste* is just the first stage in Marius's education to a poetic apprehension of the world. Pater's essay on style deals with the same problem, except that what is there developed as an overriding concept is here just one of several themes. Style in *Marius* relates only to man's mastery of life.

Flavian's death suddenly confronts Marius with dimensions of existence that cannot be poeticised.[37] Death, after all, is a reality from which one cannot be detached, and its inevitability denotes the limits to which reality can be mastered. What Pater had conceptualised in his essay on style is put to the test by being translated into the fictional biography of his artist-hero. This shows that his critical notions always had existential implications, the unfolding of which were a decisive propellant for his fiction. As abstractions the concepts were unable to bring out the potential diversifications of that which they designated, and therefore art itself was the only medium through which he could capture and convey what they entailed. This holds true even if failure looms large, as indicated by the boundaries drawn round the power of words. This new experience ends the first part of *Marius*, laying bare his basic situation and the problem of adequate orientation. There are limits to the extent to which experience may be poeticised by means of detachment from reality, and so Marius must now begin: 'Sich im Denken zu orientiren – to determine his bearings, as by compass, in the world of thought.'[38]

'Animula Vagula' is the heading of the chapter in which Marius tries to orientate himself afresh. It is typical of Pater's own way of thinking that once Marius has lost his childhood faith, he turns to the Heraclitean 'flux' as the ultimate reality of this world. When world pictures have lost their validity, ever-changing experience becomes the crux of existence.

> The negative doctrine, then, that the objects of our ordinary experience, fixed as they seem, are really in perpetual change, had been . . . but the preliminary step towards a large positive system of almost religious philosophy.[39]

Out of this basic experience of human life, Marius must now use the transformative power of his imagination to extract reliable guidelines of behaviour.

> He was become aware of the possibility of a large dissidence between an inward and somewhat exclusive world of vivid personal apprehension, and the unimproved, unheightened reality of the life of those about him.[40]

The vague feeling he had during the Numa ceremony has now become a certainty. He now knows that he stands apart from current reality and from other people's conception of that reality. All he can do is activate his own singularity and make himself the standard,[41] but this gives rise to a new problem. His singularity is known to him only through the negativity of his detachment from given reality; as a consequence, he becomes insecure and inactive as soon as he is called upon to conceive his otherness in positive terms.

Marius therefore turns to the 'ancient Greek masters', to see which of them might hold the answer to his problem. At first he thinks he may have found it in Aristippus.[42] It is characteristic of Pater's own intellectual uncertainty that his characters do not develop orientation out of themselves but depend on the findings of others. There is a latent contradiction here which in fact is what sets in motion the restricted movement that is to be found in the novel. On the one hand, Marius's singularity is his ultimate standard, but conversely he relies on other people's ideas in order to reveal himself to himself. The result of this contradiction is that he can never find satisfaction, since no one else's ideas can ever correspond entirely to his singularity.

Through the school of Cyrene, Marius learns that truth is to be found in sensual impression.[43] This discovery is reassuring,[44] in so far as it gives man the upper hand in his relations with the world: his impression is his grasp of the world, which must therefore submit to his individuality.

> And so the abstract apprehension that the little point of this present moment alone really is, between a past which has just ceased to be and a future which may never come, became practical with Marius, under the form of a resolve, as far as possible, to exclude regret and desire, and yield himself to the improvement of the present with an absolutely disengaged mind.[45]

The moment brings together both the 'perpetual flux'[46] of things and the singularity of self, and from now on it is to orientate Marius's life. But his openness to the experience of the moment can lead no further than the enjoyment of it, for there can be no consequences – he must always be ready for the next moment. Thus his receptivity remains totally passive, and since the present consists only of this endless series of unconnected moments, it follows that the present can never contain its own destination. Consequently Pater must separate it from the past, which has gone forever, and from a future which 'may never come', and so the moment is like a single atom within and subordinate to the flow of time. It cannot be defined in terms of its own reality, it races past and is difficult to grasp, and none but the 'absolutely disengaged mind' can salvage anything from its transience. If the mind is engaged on anything else, it will fail to exploit the moment, and so passivity and enjoyment are the only suitable modes of conduct. The transience even prevents any processing of what has been perceived, and so the moment remains abstract, and its richness as fleeting as its duration.

In this respect, Pater's concept of the moment is very different from Virginia Woolf's.[47] In her novels, it gives a kaleidoscopic form to the way in which experience is mirrored in human consciousness, whereas for Pater the moment does not even have a potential power to give form to anything. It is impossible to describe Pater's concept of the moment in any positive terms – he himself could only delineate it negatively. His moment remains embedded in the flow of time, whereas Virginia Woolf lifts it out of time, or rather she sees it as cutting across the sequence of past, present and future to which Pater adheres so rigidly. For her it is a mode through which time-transcending forms of human consciousness may be captured, while for Pater it remains an atom that can only be perceived in the abstract. The sole consequence that Marius can draw from his 'abstract apprehension' is that: 'He too must maintain a harmony with that soul of motion in things, by constantly renewed mobility of character.'[48] This mobility is an abstract quality that can only become concrete when particular ways of life are to be renounced. Thus it makes time itself a determining factor for Marius, and even he cannot escape the negative consequences of such an orientation.

What drew him to the Cyrenaic school of thought was the idea that, by way of the moment, fleeting experience could be transformed – even if only temporarily – to pleasure. The particular needs of the individual determine which 'atoms' in the endless flow of time are best suited to this purpose. The indeterminacy of time itself is such that the individual does not need to set himself any goals or to make any decisions; the only response required of him is an uncommitted enjoyment – and this attitude highlights the aesthetic mode of conduct. Pater's 'Conclusion' suggested the same approach, but what was there offered in a theoretical context is here translated into terms of real life. As always, concepts assume their significance for Pater in the light of their practical consequences, and therefore Marius is meant to answer the question of what living is like according to the maxim: 'To burn always with that hard, gemlike flame.'[49] But accompanying his Aristippian mobility there are feelings that threaten to undermine the whole philosophy. 'It was intelligible that this "aesthetic" philosophy might find itself . . . weighing the claims of that eager, concentrated, impassioned realisation of experience against those of the received morality.'[50] And indeed the one is in direct conflict with the other, since the philosophy of the moment must by definition reject any overall system that would relate the moment to a wider context from which it has to be marked off in order to gain significance. If Marius were content with the pleasure of the moment, then all would be well, but it transpires that he is actually searching for something:

> Really, to the phase of reflection through which Marius was then passing, the charge of 'hedonism', whatever its true weight might be, was not properly applicable at all. Not pleasure, but fulness of life, and 'insight' as conducting to that fulness – energy, variety, and choice of experience . . . whatever form of human life . . . might be heroic, impassioned, ideal.[51]

It is this desire that launches Marius into the existential crisis of his life. On the one hand he is committed to a sequence of unclassifiable moments, but on the other he longs for an ideal form of life. The clash between the philosophy of the moment and existing forms of life now breaks out within Marius himself.

The initial consequence of this conflict is that

> there would come, together with that precipitate sinking of things into the past, a desire, after all, to retain 'what was so transitive' . . . To create, to live, perhaps, a

little while beyond the allotted hours, if it were but in a fragment of perfect expression: – it was thus his longing defined itself for something to hold by amid the 'perpetual flux'.[52]

The transitoriness of the moment, demanding mobility of character, fails to satisfy that side of Marius that longs for some vague ideal. Even when the ideal does arise, it is soon gone again, and so he yearns for something constant and lasting. And yet, this craving for permanence is highly derivative and would never have arisen had the fleeting moment culminated in that plenitude it seemed to promise. For this reason permanence remains an empty notion, only meant to compensate for what the cherished moments have been unable to yield.

Hence Marius's yearning is for the arresting of transience, which should result in a preservation of perfection. The *im*perfection, however, which permeates his life, marked by a continual disappearance of pleasurable moments, causes in him an experience of growing anxiety. When he sets out for the emperor's court in Rome, as a 'modern romantic traveller',[53] a fall of rocks and the rustling of trees arouse a strange terror in him.

That was sufficient, just then, to rouse out of its hiding-place his old vague fear of evil – of one's 'enemies' – a distress, so much a matter of constitution with him, that at times it would seem that the best pleasures of life could but be snatched, as it were hastily, in one moment's forgetfulness of its dark, besetting influence. A sudden suspicion of hatred against him, of the nearness of 'enemies', seemed all at once to alter the visible form of things . . . His elaborate philosophy had not put beneath his feet the terror of mere bodily evil; much less of 'inexorable fate, and the noise of greedy Acheron'.[54]

Marius is not afraid of something concrete – his anxiety is a deep-rooted insecurity, and the 'enemies' are not human but metaphorical. We are never told the origins of this inexplicable anxiety, but it is so intense that it mars his basic form of existence: to make the most of the moments as they pass. Kierkegaard's definition of anxiety is not inapposite in this context:

Anxiety is a matter of reflection, for we are afraid 'of something', and therefore we separate the anxiety from its object, and in our anxiety relate the object to ourselves. Furthermore, anxiety includes reflection on time: I cannot be afraid of something present, only something past or future. But the present alone can directly determine the individual; the past and future can only do so through reflection.[55]

Marius has cut the past and future out of his aesthetic philosophy, and lives only in the direct present. But the present moment is harnessed to past and future, and these resist his efforts to exclude them, so that his own life consequently eludes his control. His longing for an ideal is accompanied by the desire to snatch something permanent from the flow of time. His anxiety, on the other hand, is an experience of helplessness that is so great as to eclipse the pleasure of the moment. In both cases, the moment reveals itself in all its deficiencies; longing and anxiety indicate what the philosophy of the moment excludes: past and future, whose obtrusion on the moment exposes the futility of this philosophy. In this respect Pater's novel brings to life a decisive feature missing or perhaps even deliberately omitted from the 'Conclusion'. There he had put forward the aesthetic moment as a theoretical guideline for conceiving human life, whereas in *Marius* he spotlights the spiritual problems arising from such an aesthetic conceptualisation of life by revealing the moment as the genesis of longing and anxiety. Both are moods into which Marius is plunged, as longing is devoid of a definable aim and anxiety of a tangible object, so that in the final analysis they are indicative of the failure built into the aesthetic attitude. Interestingly enough, nearly all Pater's narrative fictions are designed as an existential test of concepts outlined in his critical writings; he wanted to find out to what extent the aesthetic attitude could be sustained in life, and this is an indication of his admirable integrity.

So far Marius has felt the inadequacy of the aesthetic approach only as a mood of uneasiness. His Cyrenaic philosophy has been drawn mainly from theory, and he has not yet experienced any real 'moments'. But now in Rome he is confronted for the first time with an approach to life whose certainty is derived from incontrovertible principles. From the very moment of his arrival in the city, he undergoes two different levels of experience: there are real 'moments'[56] such as the spectacle of Marcus Aurelius's return from his military campaigns; but there is also the philosopher-king himself, whose self-contained and balanced approach to life is *not* orientated by the moment. The novel alternates between the colourful show, offering pleasure without commitment, and the thought and philosophy of Marcus Aurelius and his circle. For all the fascination of the Roman spectacle, Marius is drawn more to the person of the emperor. For the pageant of the procession and of Roman life generally still fails to supply the vision Marius longs for. Immediately after his return from his first campaign, Marcus Aurelius makes a philosophical speech in the Senate, and Marius is present. 'Marius could but contrast all that with his own Cyrenaic eagerness, just then, to taste and see and touch; reflecting on the opposite issues deducible from the same text.'[57] The new experience for Marius is the fact that life – 'the same text' – can evidently be interpreted from totally opposite viewpoints. Therefore the philosophy of the moment is not identical to life, but is merely one way of looking at it, and an inadequate way to boot. Having hitherto orientated himself only by moments, he now hears the emperor condemning such an approach. Marcus Aurelius describes the transience of things:

This hasteth to be; that other to have been: of that which now cometh to be, even now somewhat hath been extinguished. And wilt thou make thy treasure of any one of these things? It were as if one set his love upon the swallow, as it passeth out of sight through the air![58]

And yet until now Marius has built his life on precisely such passing swallows. The emperor recognises the flux of things, just as Marius does: 'The world, within me and without, flows away like a river.'[59] But he draws a totally different conclusion from this. Now, for the first time since his childhood, Marius is confronted, in the emperor's Stoicism, by a coherent world view which as a closed concept in fact negates his own ideas. The confrontation is all the more startling through the fact that Marcus Aurelius is at home amid all the aesthetic splendour of Roman life and yet reacts negatively to it. Pater describes Marius's response as that of a strange awakening:

It was, in truth, the air of one who, entering vividly into life, and relishing to the full the delicacies of its intercourse, yet feels all the while, from the point of view of an ideal philosophy, that he is but conceding reality to suppositions, choosing of his own will to walk in a day-dream, of the illusiveness of which he at least is aware.[60]

What had earlier been felt only as a mood now ripens into an awareness that perhaps he has hitherto seen only the shadows of things. His way of life so far has been constricted, and although he does not accept the emperor's philosophy unreservedly, he now realises that the philosophy of the moment cannot encompass the vastness of reality.

Marius's enhanced self-awareness in his new surroundings comes to a peak during the episode in the amphitheatre. Here he witnesses the crowd's fanatic lust for blood, while the emperor sits unmoved in their midst. Instead of exploiting the richness of this extraordinary moment, Marius feels 'the loyal conscience within him'.[61]

He at least, the humble follower of the bodily eye, was aware of a crisis in life, in this brief, obscure existence, a fierce opposition of real good and real evil around him, the issues of which he must by no means compromise or confuse; of the antagonisms of which the 'wise' Marcus Aurelius was unaware.[62]

Suddenly the principle of the uncommitted experience, free from the restraints of responsibility and decision, begins to be undermined by an awareness of moral opposites. Marius's conscience offers itself as a guide to the selection of impressions. And this experience leads to a crisis because the real world has thrown up unmistakable moral alternatives which impose an inescapable obligation that cannot be resolved through compromise or reconciliation. The crisis is due to the fact that what Marius perceives is a direct contrast to the ideal he longs for, and so the world of experience to which he had opened himself unconditionally not only fails to satisfy him, but actually moves counter to his expectations. In his awareness of the crisis dawns the potential presence of an ideal, whose realisation, however, would require action, and action in turn would require a knowledge of the form which the potential ideal might take; this growing awareness of an impending change is again conceivable for Marius only in negative terms. He sets himself off from Marcus Aurelius, whose Stoic imperturbability amid the carnage they are witnessing makes him conscious of his own otherness. 'There was something in a tolerance such as this, in the bare fact that he could sit patiently through a scene like this, which seemed to Marius to mark Aurelius as his inferior now and for ever on the question of righteousness.'[63] The emperor's abstract philosophical principles do not tally with the demands of reality. Marius feels the urgency of these demands, and is plunged into a crisis because they put pressure on him to make decisions which he is unable to take.

It is typical of Marius that he only grasps his own singularity through his negative responses to events and ideas around him. It is this trait that justifies the degree of historical detail offered by the novel, for the hero can only get to know himself, and hence the path he must follow, by being exposed to a variety of possible forms of life. These must be historical because only history contains frozen forms of life against which the blurred features of an aesthetic attitude could best be offset and thus objectified; it is simultaneously revealed that this very attitude is unable to constitute a world of its own. By always distancing himself from all the historical forms of life he encounters, Marius becomes the embodiment of a difference that animates the aesthetic existence. He seeks the fullness of life[64] by never committing himself. But the moment a decision is demanded of him, as in the amphitheatre, the aesthetic self is plunged into a crisis. If Marius were to decide in favour of a moral principle, he would cut himself off from the welter of fleeting impressions, and subordinate experience to an ethical code. 'Anyone who wishes to determine the task of his life ethically will generally not have a very large choice of possibilities; in fact the act of choosing will mean all the more to him.'[65] Marius does not want to sacrifice the potentially unlimited range of choices, for in the abundance of possibilities he hopes at last to find his ideal.

The anxiety and the longing of the youthful Marius, together with his crisis in the amphitheatre, have demonstrated the inadequacy of the philosophy of the moment.

> His conscience still vibrating painfully under the shock of that scene in the amphitheatre, and full of the ethical charm of Cornelius, he was questioning himself with much impatience as to the possibility of an adjustment between his own elaborately thought-out intellectual scheme and the 'old morality'.[66]

The resultant self-reflection leads once more to a re-orientation. He realises that the philosophy of Cyrene was one to be embraced by youth – 'ardent, but narrow in its survey – sincere, but apt to become one-sided, or even fanatical'.[67] In this awareness – brought to full fruition by Marius's encounter with Marcus Aurelius – Pater voices reservations about the concept he has developed in his 'Conclusion'. This shift in attitude is all the more remarkable as it comes about when Pater himself translates his elaborate notions into the actuality of life. His concepts stand corrected when viewed from that situation for which they were meant to provide guidance. Although he sensed this disparity when he tried to legitimise his ideas by linking them to history and myth, it is now in his fiction that the disparity itself becomes the actual subject-matter. The philosophy of the moment

> had been a theory, avowedly, of loss and gain (so to call it) of an economy. If, therefore, it missed something in the commerce of life, which some other theory of practice was able to include, if it made a needless sacrifice, then it must be, in a manner, inconsistent with itself, and lack theoretic completeness.[68]

This passage from the chapter entitled 'Second Thoughts' uses economic terms to describe the philosophy of the moment, and in terms of profit and loss, one might say that the pleasure of the moment is the profit, and the unfulfilled longing is the loss. Time, as the be-all and end-all, does not allow the temporality of the moment to be ignored. Marius now finds himself confronted with the problem of whether to leave the aesthetic sphere of the moment for the ethical sphere of continuity. If he chooses the latter sphere, he will reduce the multiple possibilities of life's moments to a moral framework that will endow his life with an unmistakable direction. The life of moments will yield the profit of pleasure and the loss of potential ideals; the life of a realised ideal will attain moral coherence, thus liberating it from its contingent temporality. Since Marius's ideals remain undefined, making themselves felt only through his drive to differentiate himself from the world around him, there can be no question of him taking a decision – which in Kierkegaardian terms would have to be qualified as a leap – and so he remains trapped amid his crises of longing and anxiety.

The way out of the trap is to broaden the philosophy of the moment in such a way that it can also embrace moral moments.

> In the apprehension of that, just then, Marius seemed to have joined company once more with his own old self; to have overtaken on the road the pilgrim who had come to Rome, with absolute sincerity, on the search for perfection. It defined not so much a change of practice, as of sympathy – a new departure, an expansion, of sympathy.[69]

'Must not all that remained of life be but a search for the equivalent of that Ideal, among so-called actual things – a gathering together of every trace or token of it, which his actual experience might present?'[70] The shock of the amphitheatre scene has not altered Marius's basic attitude; it has simply shifted the emphasis away from immersion in the pleasurable moment to a more discriminating search for what perfection might be. As he does not know the nature of the ideal, he hopes that it will one day emerge from his experiences, but since experience comes and goes with time, it follows that the ideal must also be subject to time. If it were ever to become concrete, it would fade like everything else. As a transient phenomenon it therefore cannot change the temporality of human experience, and so even with his new selectivity, through which he concentrates on those moments that vaguely promise perfection, Marius still contemplates the possibility of moral conduct as an aesthetic phenomenon.

If the shift of emphasis in Marius's philosophy of the moment were truly to come to life, it would require at least the beginnings of an action. And if the philosophy of the moment were to give way entirely to an ethical continuity, it would require a genuine plot, linking events in an order of cause and effect. But what development there is in this novel comes about because of Marius's restlessness – a state that signifies a lack of moral continuity and of the security that such continuity would bring.

Of these sections of *Marius* Hugo von Hofmannsthal remarked: 'The third book, "Marius the Epicurean", shows a basic inadequacy whenever one tries to build one's whole way of life on the aesthetic view of the world. The book is immensely clever, but its effect is arid, without greatness, and without true humanity.'[71] Hofmannsthal's judgement points, however indirectly, to what the novel was meant to demonstrate, for Pater did not set out to depict 'true humanity', but the consequences of the aesthetic life which remains the basis of his world view.

The third book, which unfolds the ethical problem, culminates in the dawning of a vision. Marius comes increasingly to feel his singularity as loneliness. This is inevitable, since he can only grasp his individuality by distancing himself from other people and their attitudes. But now that he is seeking in experience the equivalent of his ideal, he suddenly feels during a ride through the Roman countryside that ideality may lie in community.[72] He realises the extent to which his spiritual and physical being is encompassed by Nature, but as a tangible expression of this awareness he longs for 'an unfailing companion'.[73]

> The purely material world, that close, impassable prison-wall, seemed just then the unreal thing, to be actually dissolving away all around him: and he felt a quiet hope, a quiet joy dawning faintly, in the dawning of this doctrine upon him as a really credible opinion. It was like the break of day over some vast prospect with the 'new city', as it were some celestial New Rome, in the midst of it. That divine companion figured no longer as but an occasional wayfarer beside him; but rather

as the unfailing 'assistant', without whose inspiration and concurrence he could not breathe or see, instrumenting his bodily senses, rounding, supporting his imperfect thoughts.[74]

This occurs during the chapter 'The Will as Vision', and it is Marius's desire for the ideal that conjures up his vision of the divine companion. It is a projection of his longing, and at the same time a counterpart to his actual experience. Since Marius is only groping towards something beyond the here and now, the companion remains featureless, though fashioned by the desire to provide completion for indefinable thoughts and feelings arising out of what the temporality of human existence denies. The companion is figured as someone who might overcome the transience of moments through his 'boundless power of memory'.[75] He is an incarnation of the 'House Beautiful'. He preserves perfection which Marius cannot do himself owing to his absorption in the flux of time. The companion therefore promises continuity, and points the way to some all-embracing order which alone appears to be able to endow life with meaning. He is 'the necessary exponent of our own and the world's life, that reasonable Ideal to which the Old Testament gives the name of *Creator*, which for the philosophers of Greece is the *Eternal Reason*, and in the New Testament the *Father of Men*'.[76] Religion is necessary as an idealisation and healing of human experience, and in the last book of the novel, Cornelius, Marius's friend, will open the way to the early Christian world.

The construction of the last book is antithetical, with the individual chapters alternating between pagan and Christian ideas. It is typical of Pater that these two different world views are defined only in relation to each other. This is so because they are not presented for their own sakes but as possible solutions to the hero's problem as he searches for hope and security. He has to weigh the one view against the other in order to gauge which of them comes closer to his ideal. The contrast between paganism and Christianity is strikingly illuminated at the beginning of the book, in the chapter entitled 'Two Curious Houses'. Among a select company of famous Roman men of letters, Marius meets the idol of his youth, Apuleius.[77] In a conversation about gods and their power, Apuleius admits to an ultimate lack of certainty in this world. Marius wonders whether there might not be a world that is 'wider, perhaps, in its possibilities than all possible fancies concerning it'.[78] 'For himself, it was clear, he must still hold by what his eyes really saw.'[79] In Cecilia's house he seems to find a realisation of the ideal that Apuleius had excluded. Through Cornelius he makes his first contact with a Christian community, and attends a Christian mass for the dead. As he enters the precincts of the church close to Cecilia's house, the narrator asks tentatively: 'Was he willing to look upon that, the seeing of which might define – yes! define the critical turning-point in his days?'[80] Confronted by religion, the aesthetic attitude finds its lack of commitment decisively challenged. The Christian mass which Marius witnesses kindles within him a totally new feeling of hope.

> Clearly, these people, concurring in this with the special sympathies of Marius himself, had adopted the practice of burial from some peculiar feeling of hope they entertained concerning the body; a feeling which, in no irreverent curiosity, he would fain have penetrated.[81]

This feeling is intense, because Marius's philosophy of the moment had been unable to cope with the reality of death, and so until now his 'hope' had been no more than a vague longing, whereas he senses unmistakably that for the Christians it is something real.

In the two 'Curious Houses' Marius encounters two concepts that are directly relevant to his situation: pagan uncertainty about the finality of human knowledge dissolves into speculation; Christian certainty gives solid form to hope. The two views of life are presented through paradigmatic situations – the first in a celebration for the living, and the second in a ceremony for the dead. The pagan feast is in accord with Marius's guiding principle of exploiting experience to the full; yet the Christian mass appeals equally to him, for it is proof of hope in the face of death. Each of them strikes a particular chord in him, but he simultaneously knows that the gap between them can only be bridged if he changes his life drastically.

The radical change, however, does not take place. Marius's reaction to Christianity is 'a singular novelty of feeling, like the dawning of a fresh order of experiences upon him'.[82] The ideality which he eagerly embraces is conceived as an opportunity to obtain hitherto unsuspected effects from his basic commitment to experience. This, however, is not a break with his former way of life so much as an extension of it. The Christian attitude gives his life 'a more effective sanction and motive than it had ever possessed before'.[83] 'It was Christianity in its humanity, or even its humanism, in its generous hopes for man, its common sense and alacrity of cheerful service, its sympathy with all creatures, its appreciation of beauty and daylight.'[84] His apprehension of Christianity is aesthetic.

It is characteristic of the structure of the novel that in the chapter 'Conversation not Imaginary' aesthetic Christianity now gives way to an ironic appraisal of pagan philosophers, whose claims to the authenticity of their respective doctrines are dissolved. Lucian and Hermotimus discuss the truth that the latter believes he has found in Stoicism.[85] The dialogue ends with the conclusion that certainty of truth can only be hypothetical, and that all philosophy – unless it is marked by sceptical wisdom – is deduced from positions which in themselves are questionable and impossible to prove.[86] Marius's Christian experience is framed by his encounters with Apuleius and Hermotimus. The former knows the uncertainty of knowledge; Hermotimus's supposed certainty gives way to the same insight during his conversation with Lucian. The contrast with the Christian experience is thereby emphasised. But it is Marius's own wishes that dictate which aspects of Christianity are of significance here, and since it was death, the last reality, that Marius's aesthetic approach could not cope with or avoid, he sees Christianity as primarily a cult of death; there is no mention of dogma or of eschatology.

From early youth right through to the episode in Cecilia's house, Marius has striven to get away from the given conditions of his life. Experience seems to push him into a succession of alternatives. The death of Flavian, the moral shock in the amphitheatre, and the Christian hope have all shown him the narrowness of the world that revolves around the aesthetic moment. Each new possibility carries him further away from his starting-point, but at no time does he ever subject his life to any order, be it ethical or religious. He remains in a constant state of transition, wanting to transcend time and finiteness, but never committing himself to any ethical or religious code. His secular experiences make him long for fulfilment, but this must happen by means of experience itself. Ethics and religion are not new levels of existence for him, but are simply idealised projections of inadequate experience, as is evident from the balancing operation they must perform: the 'unfailing companion' and Christian hope are both means of compensating for time's denial of continuity and fulfilment. This craving for compensations highlights the deficiencies inherent in the temporality of the aesthetic moment. Instead of pulling himself away from the recognised imperfections, Marius wants to wipe out the agonising differences between the aesthetic, the ethical and the religious spheres of human life, so that the aesthetic – propped up by the other two – may play its desired role of earthly fulfilment. 'The aesthetic sphere is that of immediacy; the ethical is that of demand . . . the religious is that of fulfilment.'[87] But for Marius, the demand and fulfilment only exist in order to enrich immediacy. The consequences of this in-between state are apparent from the conclusion of the novel.

> Throughout that elaborate and lifelong education of his receptive powers, he had ever kept in view the purpose of preparing himself towards possible further revelation some day – towards some ampler vision, which should take up into itself and explain this world's delightful shows, as the scattered fragments of a poetry, till then but half-understood, might be taken up into the text of a lost epic, recovered at last.[88]

This distant goal underlines the duality of Marius's attitude. On the one hand he wishes to orientate himself by the moments that race by completely out of his control, but on the other he seeks something quite specific in this passing stream: an ideal of totality. So long as he lives only by experience, he remains passive and receptive, but his desire to find wholeness requires action. The only action he can perform, though, is to move from one set of ideas to another: the philosophy of the moment, ethics, religion. He is for ever halfway – distancing himself from the secular experience, hoping to find totality, unable to commit himself. The image of the poetic fragments belonging to a lost epic is both striking and apposite: Marius's experiences have no inner cohesion, therefore barring him from any insight into them, but he hopes that one day they might link up and reveal the meaning of life. Experience can only give him sections, but some vision must bring them together. The epic, though, is a literary form, and thus the simile makes him believe that the goal he is striving for is just a matter of composition. Again this attitude reveals itself as purely aesthetic – out of the combination of the given and the endlessly experienced must suddenly emerge the great oneness of things. But the epic is 'lost', that is, the totality belongs to the past, and the present has only been able to preserve fragments of it. Furthermore, the epic is literature, a fiction, and so Marius's quest is cast in terms dissociating it from the troublesome path which cuts through reality. And indeed it is only literature, with its absence of obligation, that can express a desire brought about by the inadequacy of real experience. The ideal itself can never be real. Marius wants to free himself from conditions around him, but he can never take the decisions necessary to step out of his growing dissatisfaction. His life is simply a series of reactions against what is, so that his experiences lead to a change of attitude but never to a final goal. If the aesthetic attitude feels itself to be superior to reality, it is a feeling based on illusion, and since the ideal can never be realised, the aesthetic attitude must eventually meet its own disillusionment.

In the chapter entitled 'Sunt Lacrimae Rerum' Marius sees life as suffering. 'We are constructed for suffering! What proofs of it does but one day afford, if we care to note them, as we go – a whole long chaplet of sorrowful mysteries!'[89] It is a lament that he confides to his diary, and is the only passage in the novel where we begin to hear Marius's own voice. Just for a moment he escapes from the guiding hand of his author, and the very fact that Pater allows him to express himself only in relation to suffering is evidence enough of the importance of this emotion. Marius speaks of the pain and the burden of experience.

> I wonder, sometimes, in what way man has cajoled himself into the bearing of his burden thus far, seeing how every step in the capacity of apprehension his labour has won for him, from age to age, must needs increase his dejection. It is as if the increase of knowledge were but an increasing revelation of the radical hopelessness

of his position: and I would that there were one even as I, behind this vain show of things![90]

Here we have the motivating force behind Marius's quest. The real world is a 'vain show of things', and man's journey can lead only to a growing certainty of 'radical hopelessness'. This awareness, coming after his encounter with religion, shows clearly that the Christian ideas served only to enrich his immediate experience, and not to alter his basic mode of behaviour. Had he become a Christian, then he would certainly have reported in his diary the joy of his new way of life.[91] But what he says here about suffering indicates that Christianity remains no more than an ideal sublimation, for it does not change the basic situation. From Marius's profound disillusionment, it is apparent that religion can only offer him a temporary idealisation of experience, but the here and now can never offer a lasting definition of life. There are isolated moments that are like oases amid the waste, but they are rare exceptions, and whoever tries to build his life on them will suffer increasing disillusionment. Suffering, according to Marius, is the 'principle in things'.[92]

The conflict in Marius had already been outlined very early on in the novel:

And while he learned that the object, the experience, as it will be known to memory, is really from first to last the chief point for consideration in the conduct of life, these things were feeding also the idealism constitutional with him – his innate and habitual longing for a world altogether fairer than that he saw.[93]

It is experience, then, that arouses in Marius the desire to go beyond experience. As long as he is animated by this impulse, he abides in an illusion; mere distance from the flux of time is not enough to make illusion real, and since the aesthetic observer can only react and never act, the 'fairer world' must remain an illusion. It is the detachment from real objects and situations that endows the novel with its dreamlike atmosphere, but the detachment – and so the dream – are always exposed to the danger of suffering, and thus throughout the novel there is a continual shattering of the illusion into which Marius had fled. Right up until Marius's death, this alternation remains the basis of the novel's development.

In the end, Marius and his Christian friend Cornelius are taken prisoner. The Roman legionnaires assume that Marius is also a Christian,[94] but by bribing some soldiers, he is able to get Cornelius freed so that he can prepare the trial to which as Roman citizens they are entitled.[95] When Cornelius has gone, Marius is overcome by a feeling of total desolation. For the first time in his life he finds himself trapped in a situation from which he cannot escape.

We wait for the great crisis which is to try what is in us: we can hardly bear up the pressure of our hearts, as we think of it: the lonely wrestler, or victim, which imagination foreshadows to us, can hardly be one's self; it seems an outrage of our destiny that we should be led along so gently and imperceptibly, to so terrible a leaping-place in the dark, for more perhaps than life or death . . . Another motion of the clock, and our fatal line – the 'great climacteric point' – has been passed, which changes ourselves or our lives.[96]

Evidently Pater saw this crisis as embodying the fate not only of Marius but of man in general, as is indicated by the first person plural pronoun. For Marius himself, the inner conflict that had been present all through his life now reaches its climax – he is forced to make a decision, for if he is to change a situation he must act. And yet the very thought of making a choice seems to render him unrecognisable to himself. In the past he had occasionally experienced a hint of the pain of decision, as with his shock in the amphitheatre or his encounter with the Christian community, but now the point that he has reached seems to him an 'outrage' of destiny. What had not been realised in his encounter with the ethical and religious spheres seems now to have been forced on him by fate. He knows that this leap in the dark will change his life radically, and in his isolation the pressure of the choice seems unbearable. Lonely wrestler or victim – the image is only comprehensible if one considers his lifelong avoidance of choice. It is anathema to everything he has believed in. Now it is as if he must break away completely from the form of life that has always been second nature to him. The realm he must leap into is dark because he has hitherto lived only for the immediate moment, and all his experiences were linked to this immediacy. Now he must leave all that had remained to him of his security, and even the transcendent realm seems dark to him, because it represents not a new promise, but a threat to the life he is used to. Thus he is both wrestler *and* victim, for he is in a fight which he cannot win.

Marius's constant in-between position makes him totally unsuited for this final decision. Throughout his life he has wanted to transcend finite experience, but at the same time he has rejected all overarching systems as codes of orientation. His dissatisfaction with reality and his scepticism towards the absolute have achieved a balance by means of illusion, since illusion makes life appear to be temporarily controllable. But now, in the 'great crisis', he is finally exposed to the reality of the choice, and the task proves impossible. He does not make the decision. He dies in the awareness of a vague hope:

Surely, the aim of a true philosophy must lie, not in futile efforts towards the complete accommodation of man to the circumstances in which he chances to find himself, but in the maintenance of a kind of candid discontent, in the face of the very highest achievement; the unclouded and receptive soul quitting the world finally, with the same fresh wonder with which it had entered the world still unimpaired, and going on its blind way at last with the consciousness of some profound enigma in things, as but a pledge of something further to come.[97]

Aesthetic conduct is discontented with human experience and achievement, rejects all fixed systems, and journeys through an endless sequence of new possibilities towards not a meaning, but a 'profound enigma', which Marius interprets as a promise. There is no ultimate certainty, and so there is no obligation but, at the same time, there *is* hope.

Thus Marius's life has no coherent story or shape; he is made to move but never to act, and however different his experiences may be, their form is constant – he is attracted to phenomena, which he then abandons in favour of new ones. It is a 'devil's ride'[98] of possibilities that leads through suffering which can only be ended by death. The basic mood of the final chapter is one of weariness. Marius's aesthetic conduct, his halfway position between reality and the transcendent world, can only be indicated by changing moods in which he finds himself enshrouded. Such a condition poses problems for a narrative text, for normally protagonists become conceivable to the extent to which they realise themselves in the course of action. A mood, however, more often than not eludes embodiment, let alone impersonation. Furthermore, it has only a short-lived duration and then either changes or dissolves again. If the hero serves as a means of depicting moods, his contours both shift and fade continually; he moves like a flickering shadow through the turn of events. Simultaneously the narrative falls apart into a sequence of disconnected situations, testifying to the hero's inability to cope with what he encounters. Reality is inadequate, the ideal is unattainable, and so the hero dies as he had lived, suspended between the two. Thus the novel unfolds a sophisticated spectacle, acting out the foundering of the aesthetic existence.

11 *Imaginary Portraits*

The form

The short stories which Pater assembled in the volume *Imaginary Portraits* tie in with a problem of *Marius*; there is, however, a marked shift in focus. The paradoxical nature of the novel showed itself in that the suggested development of the hero never took place. Instead the chain of events presented itself in a more or less static sequence of extraordinary situations which bore a close resemblance to one another. This is equally true of their structural pattern. Even if Marius's experiences did intensify his 'will . . . of vision',[1] their form remained the same, and so did their result, which was to leave the hero in a mood of discontent, ready to seek consolation in the next experience which, in turn, evaporated into another mood. And as mood lacks intentionality, its momentariness became a basic form of life for Marius, which manifested itself in a continuous cancellation of any overriding purpose that began to emerge. For such a depiction, the form of *Imaginary Portraits* is far more suitable. Each short story is a self-contained 'moment', dissociated from any overarching reference, and hence with no obligation to establish and shape an overall concatenation, as is the case with the novel.[2] Indeed *Marius* itself might at times be conceived in terms of imaginary portraits rather than as a novel, so little evidence is there of a structured cohesiveness, but here with the explicit form of the portrait, Pater is able to focus exclusively on a single situation. With *Marius* in mind it can be assumed that each one deals with an exemplary moment whose individual truth and intention inevitably reflect Pater's own preoccupations; the exposition of the extraordinary moment, static and disconnected from any purpose outside itself, is ideally epitomised by the form Pater has chosen for his *Imaginary Portraits*.

The form of the novel has imposed on Pater the necessity of a final outcome. The novella – which is what we might call each of these portraits – imposes no such obligation. F. T. Vischer defines the genre in the following terms:

The novella in relation to the novel is like a single ray in relation to a mass of light. It does not give an overall picture of what the world is like, but only an extract from it, which with intensive, momentary power trains the perspective onto the greater whole; it gives not the complete development of a personality, but a fragment of human life in a state of tension and crisis, and by sharply accentuating a twist of fate or of feeling shows us what human life actually is. It has been simply and rightly called a situation, as distinct from the novel's development through a sequence of situations.[3]

The focus on a single situation in a moment of crisis is the predominant feature of *Imaginary Portraits*. The crisis and the self-contained situation elucidate one another; the crisis is the offshoot of a situation which stands dissociated from any frame of reference, so that its resolution would demand a reintegration of the situation into something beyond itself. In all four portraits, however, the protagonists die young, indicating their failure to relate to the world from which they are cut off. Each story features a variant of a crisis-ridden moment, and in this respect the youthful protagonists are quite distinct from Marius, who moved from one critical situation to another, seeking to find compensation for what was missing from the current moment. It was this quest that conditioned the form of *Marius*, since he had to remove the threat by discovering new possibilities. Any balance he did achieve was purely temporary, and so he wandered on through a sequence that could only be ended by death, signifying ultimate exhaustion. The characters in *Imaginary Portraits*, however, are placed right in the heart of a crisis which destroys them, and their death indicates that the resultant dislocation of man and world cannot be set right even temporarily.

If 'portrait' denotes a picture of a person, 'imaginary' makes it clear that the picture does not aim at likeness, but is fashioned by an overmastering fantasy, which is bound to reveal a good deal about the 'artist' himself. This is all the more remarkable as Watteau, Dionysus and an eighteenth-century duke are historical figures and not purely invented characters. Since these are portrayed to the dictates of Pater's imagination, the moment of crisis into which all of them are plunged must be seen as a paradigm of the aesthetic existence. The outcome of this crisis may be one of two possibilities: either life is experienced as suffering – in which case the account will lay bare the nature of suffering – or there will be an attempt to act by leaping into the dark in order to gain what suffering denies. Both tendencies are discernible in *Imaginary Portraits*. As suffering, however, prevails, failure inscribes itself into the aesthetic attitude. Yet failure, in turn, has to be given expression, and it is here that Pater's fantasy finally triumphs, not by making the characters fall short of what they had envisioned as the ideal, but through the ensuing mood of deep melancholy. A mood – whatever its colouring – indicates that the split between subject and object is obliterated, opposites have interpenetrated and are thus dissolved. For once the subject can be at one with itself. Pater, however, leaves no doubt about the price to be paid if the aesthetic attitude is sustained; it finds its paradoxical fulfilment in continual failure.

'A Prince of Court Painters'

The first portrait is of Watteau. We follow his life from his native Valenciennes to his rise in Paris and his death in Nogent-sur-Marne,[4] but the presentation is strikingly condensed in the form of a diary kept by a selfless and loving lady-friend from Valenciennes. It is not a daily record, but concentrates only on major events, the selection of which lays emphasis on those features of Watteau that interest Pater. Thanks to the diary form, no overall 'plot' is required, and the painter's life is simply set down in snatches which are like static impressions with everything seen as it were from a distance. The events are strangely deadened by the impersonality of the descriptions and by the apparent randomness of the entries. There are often long gaps between these, as if to stress that only the most vital incidents have been recorded and the trivia have been omitted. The resultant feeling of restraint permeates the whole book and sets the scene for the real subject-matter for which the painter's life is simply the pretext: melancholy. The diary breaks Watteau's life up into a sequence of impressions that mirror the basic sadness which underlay that life. By selecting individual moments, the diary does not need to establish a unity or a meaning – it is selectively true to reality, copies faithfully, but does not impose meaning or development. Thus the form captures the passiveness of the mood which permeates Pater's Watteau, and the pictures of melancholy encompass the basic experience of the painter's life.

> I seem to have heard of a writer who likened man's life to a bird passing just once only, on some winter night, from window to window, across a cheerfully-lighted hall. The bird, taken captive by the ill-luck of the moment, re-tracing its issueless circle till it expires . . . human life may be like that bird too.[5]

The image foreshadows the course of Watteau's life. The bird is caught in an alien world which restricts its movements. It tries to escape, but the effort exhausts it. Chance and senselessness characterise the tension between man and world, and the desperate search for a solution culminates in death from exhaustion.

This abstract sketch of human life gains added complexity from the fact that Watteau as an artist ought to be able to cope with the world. And indeed at first he appears to act his given part in the 'garden comedy of life'.[6] But the diarist observes that: 'Those coquetries, those vain and perishable graces, can be rendered so perfectly, only through an intimate understanding of them. For him, to understand must be to despise them . . . Hence that discontent with himself, which keeps pace with his fame.'[7] The equation of understanding with despising shows that Watteau is not at one with the world, and so through his art he tries to bridge the gap and at the same time to distance himself from reality. The idea of art being a means of detaching oneself from suffering is central to Pater's philosophy. The detachment is achieved by poeticising the world – a process in which the *Peintre des Fêtes Galantes* scarcely had any equal. Poeticising entails adapting the world to the needs of man, so that man can master it. This is possible because of the 'magical exhilaration of his dream – his dream of a better world than the real one'.[8] Thanks to this dream, the importance and oppressiveness of the real world is diminished, and because he despises it, Watteau is able to distance himself from it and to reduce it to a sort of sophisticated charm.

Here Pater's Watteau differs from the diarist's brother, Jean-Baptiste, who comes to study under Watteau and one day finds himself dismissed. His pictures show 'more truth to life, and therefore less distinction'.[9] He lacks the dream of a better world which art can bring to life. He clings to the given reality and in reproducing it fails to bring out that which makes it special. Watteau did not seek to copy, but to transcend. The wellspring of his art was not conformity but opposition to reality.

Up till now this concept of the 'prince of court painters' corresponds to Pater's basic concept of art. However, the portrait goes beyond mere exposition and offers an illuminating interpretation. By poeticising the world, Watteau becomes famous, but his fame does not assuage his discontent. Indeed he dismisses Jean-Baptiste because the latter admires his art too much.

> Can it be that, after all, he despises and is no true lover of his own art, and is but chilled by an enthusiasm for it in another, such as that of Jean-Baptiste? as if Jean-Baptiste over-valued it, or as if some ignobleness or blunder, some sign that he has really missed his aim, started into sight from his work at the sound of praise – as if such praise could hardly be altogether sincere.[10]

Watteau's attitude towards his art is ambivalent – he even seems to despise it, and his fame makes him suspicious, as if it signified that he had failed in his purpose. He dreamed of a better world, which his art was to express, but the real world – which he lives in, despises, and wishes to escape from – applauds him. If his art can only lead to praise from the world he despises, then he must have failed to transform that world into an illusion. This knowledge inhibits him in his work. 'It is pleasanter to him to sketch and plan than to paint and finish; and he is often out of humour with himself because he cannot project into a picture the life and spirit of his first thought with the *crayon*.'[11] This inability has its source in Watteau's profound melancholy: 'I find, throughout his course of life, something of the essential melancholy of the comedian . . . He died with all the sentiments of religion. He has been a sick man all his life. He was always a seeker after something in the world that is there in no satisfying measure, or not at all.'[12] He longed for a perfection he could not find, and he took admiration of his work to be a sign of his artistic failure. The melancholy, which initially he was able to control by means of his art, gradually took over. His pictures remained fragments as the sadness weighed down on his talents, and he dismissed his admirer for the same reason as he mistrusted his own work: it could not lift the shadow of melancholy. The greater his fame, the greater his dissatisfaction. He died without ever finding what he was looking for.

What is most striking in Pater's portrait of Watteau is the fact that art cannot remove the melancholy of a man living in a world he despises. In his 'Conclusion' Pater had argued that art was man's ultimate consolation, enabling him to endure life.[13] Without doubt Watteau was one of what Pater called the 'wisest . . . children of this world',[14] who in the midst of passing life seek fulfilment through art, but in practice it now transpires that even if art may take on new qualities of expressiveness through melancholy, it cannot conquer melancholy. The deficiencies of the aesthetic attitude, of living life according to what art has to offer, become unmistakably apparent. Poeticising the given world is not enough to create a better world, and melancholy is an indication of this, with the absolute presenting itself in the trappings of time. It denotes the boundaries beyond which an art-orientated life cannot step. Art ends with a poetic transcendence of reality, while melancholy longs to replace reality with a totally different world. Pater's Watteau was unhappy because his transformation of reality still remained bound to the old world, which he despised; what he wanted was a new and unattainable world. Although it was unattainable, in accordance with Pater's scepticism, the ensuing failure is nevertheless marked by a Pyrrhic victory, as the aesthetic attitude sustains its equidistance from both worlds. This attitude comes about by withdrawing from pedestrian realities, and it would vanish if fulfilment were possible. The in-between state resulting from it leads to a self-consuming exhaustion, and thus makes death appear a natural end.

'Denys l'Auxerrois'

The theme of the second tale is the return of Dionysus in medieval Christian times. For the people of Auxerre, the return of the god lies at the heart of the legend of a golden age. Such legends, says Pater,

> will hardly be forgotten, however prosaic the world may become, while man himself remains the aspiring, never quite contented being he is. And yet in truth, since we are no longer children, we might well question the advantage of the return to us of a condition of life in which, by the nature of the case, the values of things would, so to speak, lie wholly on their surfaces, unless we could regain also the childish consciousness, or rather unconsciousness, in ourselves.[15]

These legends of return exercise an enduring fascination, because they are, according to Pater, always indicative of man's perpetual dissatisfaction with the real world. The legends are projections of human longing, to which they give a concrete form – in Pater's case, the longing for fulfilment beyond the confines of experience. But it is always characteristic of such earthly paradise that it is past, not merely in time – as the distant golden age – but also, and more importantly, in man's attitude. The fulfilment contained in the legends reflects the naïveté that belonged to a preconscious view of the world. When consciousness, however, provides the guidelines for action, these old tales turn into symbols of wish-fulfilment, which depends for its reality on a childhood level of consciousness.

The golden age can only be seen as an unreality, and so any effects it may have on human life are bound to be of doubtful value. Either man is forced to return to his preconscious beginnings, or he will view the intrusion of the supernatural powers as a threat to his existing concept of life. This dual situation lies at the basis of Pater's tale. The equivocalness surrounding the god's return is indicative of the fact that the realisation of the longing is by no means identical to the re-establishment of an earthly paradise.

Pater's technique in this tale seems to detach author from narrative. The first-person narrator is a wanderer who comes to the town of Auxerre.[16] In describing the town, he concentrates on certain details that are directly relevant to the strange legend.[17] But then the process of detachment begins: he goes to an antique dealer and comes across a remarkable piece of glass which provides the first link with the legend.[18] The dealer tells him about it, and now he sets out to follow the tracks of the legend. A priest provides him with a good deal of information,[19] and gradually he is able to fit together the different accounts and findings into a complete picture of Denys. The fragmentary presentation of the character arouses a curiosity that demands to be satisfied, and it is here that the author's hidden link with his narrative becomes apparent. He does not share the preconscious and childlike experience the townsmen of yore must have had, and so this jigsaw technique is necessary to bring to light the significance of the bizarre legend that so excited the people of Auxerre.

Since the subject-matter of this tale overlaps with that of 'Apollo in Picardy', which we have already discussed in some detail, we shall only deal here with those elements that elucidate the basic problem underlying the *Imaginary Portraits*. Denys embodies nearly all aspects of Dionysus,[20] and he is transformed only in so far as he now makes his appearance in the world of the Middle Ages. Outwardly he is in the same situation as Pater's Apollo, who wandered the countryside as a shepherd. There is also something rustic about Denys,[21] though this is merely the cover for his Dionysian powers, and generally it may be said that this novella is another variation of the typical Paterian theme of the gods in exile. 'Apollo in

Picardy' ends with Apollyon leaving to go North, but Denys suffers a very different fate. His re-appearance is enshrouded in an uncanny atmosphere and leads to an extraordinary intensification of life, which makes the people of Auxerre believe that the golden age has returned.[22] This is quite unlike the demonic conflict created by Apollyon. And whereas the latter simply disappears at the end – which Dionysus might easily have done as well, given the rhythm of the seasons that he incorporates[23] – Denys is torn to pieces by a frenzied mob.

Denys's arrival in the medieval atmosphere of a provincial French town brings about a revolution 'in the temper and manner of individuals'.[24] He throws an unfathomable spell over man and Nature, raising both to a kind of ecstasy: the countryside bursts into flower and fruits, while man and beast are rejuvenated wherever he goes.

> And the new spirit repaired even to church to take part in the novel offices of the Feast of Fools. Heads flung back in ecstasy – the morning sleep among the vines, when the fatigue of the night was over – dew-drenched garments – the serf lying at his ease at last: the artists, then so numerous at the place, caught what they could, something, at least, of the richness, the flexibility of the visible aspects of life, from all this.[25]

This ecstasy revolutionises human feelings and the social order, with the old world fading away, to be replaced by a total freedom from all ties. But the joy of this transformation is short-lived; the new life collapses under the pressure of its own intensity.

> A kind of degeneration, of coarseness – the coarseness of satiety, and shapeless, battered-out appetite – with an almost savage taste for carnivorous diet, had come over the company. A rumour went abroad of certain women who had drowned, in mere wantonness, their newborn babes. A girl with child was found hanged by her own act in a dark cellar.[26]

There are several murders, and the presence of corpses in vineyards unmistakably denotes the hand of Denys. The god of ecstasy becomes Zagreus, and the mythical unifier of opposites now brings to the historical world a disastrous separation and alternation of those opposites. Denys 'was like a double creature, of two natures, difficult or impossible to harmonise'.[27] The impossibility can only lead to destruction, and so the legend of the return becomes increasingly questionable. The world's transformation will only last for moments, and must therefore end in a cruel awakening. Reality had seemed to undergo a radical change through the ecstasy of the god, but as he breaks into an historical world, the transformations wrought cannot be channelled into continuity, and simultaneously the mythical duality of Dionysus is disrupted. Denys now has to hide, as the people of Auxerre seek their revenge.[28] He flees to a monastery, where he is purged of his demoniacal possession,[29] but the loss of his metaphomorphic power entails the loss of his ecstatic happiness. 'He was left a subdued, silent, melancholy creature. Turning now, with an odd revulsion of feeling, to gloomy objects.'[30] His death is a fitting climax to the gloom – he is torn apart by a maenadic mob,[31] and in contrast to the ancient myth does not come back to life.

In keeping with the basic theme of the *Imaginary Portraits*, the longing for a new world ends in failure, made all the more dramatic by the death of the main character. Death here means not merely the end of a life but, even more significantly, the failure of a quest. The plenitude of life conjured up by Denys was unable to transform the world in such a way that all previous experience of man was invalidated. Pater's ideal of 'fulness of life'[32] can only be glimpsed in moments, and when these have passed, the return to the sober world one has left becomes a matter of pain and suffering. Death is the final triumph of the world that was to have been changed. The earthly paradise is past, and if it returns, the end result can only be confusion and defeat. Denys's death goes a step further than 'Apollo in Picardy' in destroying the legend of the return. Apollyon had appeared as a kind of devil–god, working his evil and then withdrawing. But Denys changes reality only to learn that the historical world splits his own nature, which is then unable to give permanence to the changes he has wrought. First melancholy[33] and then death symbolise the impossibility of establishing a permanent paradise on earth.

'Sebastian van Storck'

This tale is set in seventeenth-century Holland. It is the only one in the collection with a fictional hero, although there are certain links with the philosophy of Spinoza. As Sebastian is neither mythical nor historical, Pater has far greater latitude for his own ideas, and we may assume that he devised the character in order to illuminate particular aspects of the problem he was concerned with. The narrative is built on striking contrasts between the hero and his surroundings. Pater describes in some detail the warmth and comfort of Sebastian's world,[34] emphasising the artistically decorated middle-class Dutch home, the colours of the landscape, and the bright and lively society, all of which serve to set off the strange behaviour of Sebastian himself.

> The contrast was a strange one between the careful, the almost petty fineness of his personal surrounding – all the elegant conventionalities of life, in that rising Dutch family – and the mortal coldness of a temperament, the intellectual tendencies of which seemed to necessitate straightforward flight from all that was positive. He seemed, if one may say so, in love with death; preferring winter to summer; finding only a tranquillising influence in the thought of the earth beneath our feet cooling

down for ever from its old cosmic heat; watching pleasurably how their colours fled out of things.[35]

The story develops from this irreconcilable difference between Sebastian and his world, with the hero's attitude always being one of rejection in relation to what Pater calls his 'positive' surroundings. The wealth and security of the family, and the vivacity and colour of Dutch society ought to fill Sebastian with joy and not revulsion, and Pater's poetic descriptions of life and of the paintings that capture that life suggest a high degree of aesthetic perfection.[36] Even Sebastian occasionally feels 'something of poetry in all that',[37] but would rather die than take any active part in such a world. He wants the colours to fade, the warmth to cool and the possessions to disappear, and his longing can only be fulfilled by the destruction of the world he lives in. If this is 'positive', then Sebastian's quest is a passion for negativity, or a 'passion for distance'.[38] He sees the world as an illusion[39] that must not be confused with what he considers to be reality. 'The one alone is: and all things beside are but its passing affections, which have no necessary or proper right to be.'[40] 'The one' – which precedes all evolution and development – makes the natural world of things fade into mere shadows, the lure of which must be avoided. This leaning towards philosophical abstraction ultimately demands the obliteration of all man's links to concrete experience.

Detachment: to hasten hence: to fold up one's whole self, as a vesture put aside: to anticipate, by such individual force as he could find in him, the slow disintegration by which nature herself is levelling the eternal hills . . . To restore tabula rasa, then, by a continual effort at self-effacement.[41]

This is the only way in which 'the one' can be approached, for only by blotting out all contours can man and world merge into their abstract origin. Pater sees two possibilities for philosophy.[42] One of them is subservient to the human need to have experience explained and new aspects of reality uncovered. Pater had already made this demand elsewhere,[43] when disputing philosophy's claim to exclusiveness; for him philosophy is only an instrument to enrich experience and to engage man in reality. Sebastian rejects this possibility.[44] Pater explains the rejection as being due to 'some inherited satiety or fatigue in his nature'.[45] This shows clearly that he is not seeking any new ideal through philosophy. On the contrary, such feelings are indicative of a state of quiescence that Sebastian desires, and his aim therefore is not to enrich experience but to use philosophy – and herein lies the second possibility – in order to extinguish experience by means of abstraction. Such a radical purpose is evident from his desire to efface the self, ultimately through death.

For him, that one abstract being was as the pallid Arctic sun, disclosing itself over the dead level of a glacial, a barren and absolutely lonely sea. The lively purpose of

> life had been frozen out of it. What he must admire, and love if he could, was 'equilibrium,' the void, the *tabula rasa*, into which, through all those apparent energies of man and nature, that in truth are but forces of disintegration, the world was really settling.[46]

The relapse of things into a featureless void shows the extent to which this philosophical concept depends on human experience. Only against the background of a busy Dutch society does Sebastian's quest for annihilation have any meaning. Philosophical abstraction serves to disengage him from all aspects of humanity, including himself, for the self supplies the most binding links to humanity.

Spinoza's philosophy, parts of which Sebastian adopts,[47] illustrates a process that is vital to him: the process of detachment. Spinoza's pantheism is irrelevant for him. His aesthetic detachment is accentuated by the fact that, as Pater points out several times, he has hidden practical and artistic leanings.[48] The distance he seeks to establish is not only from the world, but also from his own gifts, as there would be a danger that the practical and artistic elements of his character might reconcile him to the world he lives in. The threatened coastline of Holland[49] and the diversified activities of an artistically orientated upper-middle-class society offer ideal conditions for man to be at one with the world and himself – a demand which Pater is always making and which reverberates throughout the nineteenth century. But Sebastian asks: 'Why add, by a forced and artificial production, to the monotonous tide of competing, fleeting existence?'[50] It is this penetrating insight that explains his struggle for detachment, 'carrying us, as on wide wings of space itself, far out of one's actual surrounding'.[51] Art for him is no adequate means of transcending the basic experience of life, which is transience, and this is the reason for his at first incomprehensible rejection of the poetic world he lives in. He does not believe in the transforming power of art, because it does not enable him to forget the passing of time. This can only be done by disengagement, and so Sebastian embodies Pater's own quest for distance, which he saw as a vital factor in countering the flux of experience.[52] Here, though, the quest is radicalised, since it grows from the disillusioning fact that even a poeticised world cannot conceal the transience of things. Thus for Sebastian it is not a matter simply of withdrawing from the oppression of a given experience, but of actually blotting out all features of given realities in order to destroy altogether the significance of experience for man. Since Dutch life is so rich, his avowed aim is a void. And the fatigue that leads to this extinction by abstraction of everything around him runs counter to the Paterian maxim that one must make the most of what experience has to offer and: 'To burn always with this hard, gemlike flame.'[53] Such intensity may in fact burn out the aesthetic self, and so the hectic watchfulness gives way to an exhaustion that finally covets a state of quiescence.

Sebastian embodies a consequence of Pater's aesthetic approach, and it speaks volumes for Pater's integrity and awareness that he should have recognised the negative side of his philosophy. Poeticising the world will not change man's basic experience. For Sebastian the only solution is to detach himself, but this in itself is a negative reaction to the world, depending on the very situation it seeks to escape from, and so detachment cannot generate a new ideal. Theoretically the void may be the ideal, since the reaction is one against what Pater calls 'fulness', but a void is absence, not presence, and life is presence.

Sebastian does indeed try to make his detachment radical and real. But the story ends when a dike is breached on the Dutch coast, and Sebastian sacrifices his life saving a child.[54] He dies, therefore, in action. It is a death that demonstrates the failure of his quest for fulfilment through detachment, which in the end proves to be no more than a melancholy luxury that offers no guarantee at all that life may be mastered. At the same time, however, the fact that he dies while acting testifies to Pater's conviction that a practical deed could not be the answer to the challenge of his avowed aestheticism. Sebastian's death is a sign that neither total detachment nor a switch to action can be considered as a solution; instead it freezes the in-between state of the aesthetic attitude in all its splendid artificiality.

'Duke Carl of Rosenmold'

The last story in *Imaginary Portraits* begins with a strange situation. One day, during a period of stormy weather, the bones of two people are found beneath an uprooted tree on a lonely heath.[55] A link is established between this mysterious find and the disappearance of Duke Carl, who has been missing since the war at the beginning of the eighteenth century.[56] The discovery shows the reader that the duke must have met an unnatural death. The theme of the tale, however, is hope for renewal of the human spirit, and so this beginning automatically provides a permanently sceptical perspective through which we view the duke's enthusiastic quest. His violent death acts as a continual contrast to his search, and the reader is always aware of the ultimate failure. This narrative device robs the tale of any temporal tension which might build up during the narration and be resolved only by its outcome. Instead of such an 'Ob-überhaupt-Spannung' (i.e. whether the conflict will find a resolution at the end of the time-sequence) as Lugowski described it, the reader's attention is focused on the possibilities by means of which the duke hopes to change reality. These, of course, remain in the shadow of the scepticism aroused by his death, and thus Pater's technique gives the reader an in-between position from which to view the duke's actions.

'To bring Apollo with his lyre to Germany'[57] is the duke's avowed aim.

'There was something in the sanguine, floridly handsome youth, with his alertness of mind turned wholly, amid the vexing preoccupations of an age of war, upon embellishment and the softer things of life.'[58] The duke believes that this embellishment is to be found in art. He devotes all his energies to re-awakening the sleepy old town of Rosenmold. This aesthetic longing for change, however, does not take on the form of a specific ideal, for his is a receptive but not a creative nature. His discontent with the war-torn life of the present, and his desire to enhance experience through art, are the only realities for him. What sort of art this is to be, though, he does not know. At first he opens himself up to all the influences, especially that of the new French literature.[59] But this willingness to absorb all that is offered to him does not satisfy his inner longing. He becomes an active seeker and embarks on a vagrant life.[60] He wants to see European art, especially that of the ancients, in its original setting, so that he can take some of its glory back to what Pater calls his 'candle-lit people'.[61] His journey into history shows how impossible it is for him to set up an aesthetic ideal of his own: through the history of art he strives to give some kind of shape to his vague notions.

The duke exemplifies a vital aspect of Pater's ideas: art can only be defined through the sequence of its historical forms and manifestations.

> To understand, would be the indispensable first step towards the enlargement of the great past, of one's little present, by criticism, by imagination. Then, the imprisoned souls of nature would speak as of old . . . The spirits of distant Hellas would reawake in the men and women of little German towns. Distant times, the most alien thoughts, would come near together, as elements in a great historic symphony . . . Surely, past ages, could one get at the historic soul of them, were not dead but living, rich in company, for the entertainment, the expansion, of the present.[62]

This is precisely Pater's concept of the 'House Beautiful',[63] and lies at the very heart of his concern with history. It is not an abstract ideal but the many different forms that constitute the essence of art which the duke is seeking. And it is these forms that legitimise his aesthetic struggle to make the past fertilise the present.

> Duke Carl was still without suspicion of the cynic afterthought that such historic soul was but an arbitrary substitution, a generous loan of one's self. The mystic soul of Nature laid hold on him next, saying, 'Come! understand, interpret me!'[64]

For the duke as for Pater, history is not sought for its own sake but as a means whereby man might understand himself. The soul 'borrows' historical concepts and refashions them in the belief that they will thus give objective confirmation of the subjective self. But what Pater regarded as self-evident, the duke at this stage of his development has not yet realised – this awareness will only come to him at the end. Since history offers only restricted possibilities of self-understanding which are readily exhausted, it is now to Nature that the duke turns, just as Pater himself did, in order to ascertain that side of man which eludes objectification through history. Once more Pater struggles with the problem of legitimising art,[65] and for the duke it is history and Nature that objectify the vague longing for aesthetic transformation. 'Straight through life, straight through nature and man, with one's own self-knowledge as a light thereon, not by way of the geographical Italy or Greece, lay the road to the new Hellas, to be realised now as the outcome of home-born German genius.'[66] The self-understanding gained from history and Nature makes it possible to re-invoke the forces of the past in such a way that they will awaken the present. The duke ends his wanderings in order to put this knowledge to effect.

It is at this point that the story moves beyond Pater's earlier theoretical discussion of the problem. The duke has been appointed governing prince of Rosenmold,[67] and so now is the time for him to demonstrate how his desire is to become reality. But hardly has he returned home when he decides to marry a 'beggar-maid',[68] and while the couple are waiting for the priest in a hut on a lonely heath, the place is overrun by an enemy army; the discovery of their bones a century later suggests that they were killed by the enemy soldiers. Thus the hope of a new dawn of art is brutally shattered, and Pater then feels impelled to break through his own fiction to announce that the duke was a precursor of those aspirations that were to be fulfilled by Goethe and his contemporaries: 'It is their aspirations I have tried to embody in the portrait of Carl . . . there had been a thousand others, looking forward to a new era in German literature . . . to the permanent reality of a poetic ideal in human life.'[69] The significance of this story, however, lies not so much in the fact that Goethe was to fulfil the duke's aspirations as in the sudden destruction of hope for an aesthetic transformation just at the moment when the duke was in a position to act. This chance death releases Pater from the obligation to give concrete form to the 'poetic ideal in human life'. He could only present this as a hope, and the aesthetic life remains as it were suspended in anticipation of action. This state of suspense, of in-betweenness, characterises the aesthetic, for it is always manifested as dissatisfaction with existing experience, without ever being able to change it and fashion a new and real ideal. In other words, the longing and the aesthetic way of life are one and the same thing. If the longing is embodied by living characters, these must fail at the moment when they are called upon to act. It was the chaos of war that drove the duke to seek an enhancement of life through a new form of art; when he is to put his ideas into practice, he falls victim to that same chaos of war.

There are several possible conclusions that may be drawn from this. The duke's death could mean that the need for an aesthetic transformation of the world is even more urgent than the duke had made it seem. It could also be ironic, in that his death demonstrates the futility of his quest. If it is not ironic, then it is tragic, for it thwarts the duke's hopes at the very moment of their possible fulfilment. Pater cannot have meant any one of these interpretations to be exclusively valid, or he would have directed the reader more precisely, and indeed he must have been aware of these different possibilities, since he added his coda softening the death-blow with the information that others achieved what the duke could not. But the very fact that the duke did not realise his dream is consistent with the aesthetic conduct of Pater's other characters; the aesthetic subject remains suspended in his expectations. The significance of death is then twofold: it endows the expectations with a kind of solemnity, and at the same time it shows that the ultimate meaning of an aesthetic life is expectation, and anyone who wishes to take a step further and to act is doomed to failure. For every action is the realisation of a possibility, and thus excludes all other possibilities. But the aesthetic subject lives through the multiplicity of possibilities.[70] Action restricts and orientates life, thus destroying the liberty and unlimited receptiveness of the aesthetic way of life.

Conclusion

The characters in the *Imaginary Portraits* draw life from a state of disharmony with the world, and thus they embody Pater's own concept of reality. There are subtle differences between the four heroes, but in the poeticising of the world, the richness of life, detachment and hope lie four possible ways in which Pater sought to counteract the inadequacy of reality. The problem and the various solutions provide the basis for his critical writings as well. But where the fiction departs from the theory is in the fact that the characters are given the chance to act, and in all cases are unable to fulfil their longings: action becomes synonymous with failure. The stories show just how conscious Pater was of the problems associated with the aesthetic sphere. Through action the characters would depart from it and would enter the moral sphere, whereas living aesthetically means living without obligation and commitment, but ultimately without fulfilment. It is a sphere suspended halfway between dissatisfaction with human experience and the moral resolve to change reality. The outstanding product of this indeterminate in-between situation is mood – and although the moods vary with the characters, whenever they crystallise into a channelled feeling or a readiness for action, the character dies. The end of the mood coincides with the end of the person. And in this respect there arises the paradox that they are fulfilled through their death, for if they did not die, they would have to act and so leave the aesthetic sphere. For them, as for Marius, death is a meaningful conclusion to that which they all embody. But as death is also the event that Pater dreaded most, it is a fulfilment that asks more questions than it answers.

It is therefore no coincidence that Pater's last object of study before his own death was the work of Pascal. His essay on Pascal is only a fragment, but even that fact might be regarded as the typical end to an aesthetic existence. Notwithstanding this, Pater's approach to Pascal is revealing: 'In his scruples, his suspicions of visible beauty, he interests us as precisely an inversion of what is called the aesthetic life'.[1] This being so, it may perhaps seem strange that Pater should wish to study an attitude diametrically opposed to his own. The key, however, lies in the fact that the young man-of-the-world and author of *Letters to a Provincial by one of his Friends*[2] had been a pupil of Montaigne. This gave Pater a feeling of kinship, despite the totally different conclusions that Pascal drew from the 'earthly prospect of poor loveable humanity'.[3] What Montaigne had perceived as man's inexplicable activity, Pascal removes from its uncommitted scepticism and transplants into another context marked by an inexorable alternative: 'In this world of abysmal dilemmas, he is ready to push all things to their extremes. All or nothing; for him real morality will be nothing short of sanctity.'[4] This 'All or nothing' demand is regarded by Pascal as liberation from man's vertiginous existence which hangs halfway between nothingness and sanctity. If every manifestation of life is related to the ultimate, then all forms become more sharply defined. This is why Pascal's 'inversion' of the aesthetic life interests Pater, for that halfway position which Pascal derided is for Pater the true sphere of life. The 'either/or' decision, which Pater was always so careful to avoid, involves commitment, which is the exact opposite of the aesthetic life. The aesthetically elevated experience between nothingness and sanctity which Pater longed for, was anathema to Pascal. 'He seems to have little sense of the beauty of holiness. And for his sombre, trenchant, precipitous philosophy there could be no middle terms; irresistible election, irresistible reprobation.'[5] It is the middle terms that Pater embraces, whereas Pascal would obliterate them with his demand for all or nothing.

The Pascal essay is Pater's last attempt to convey the structure of the aesthetic life. While his concept of autonomous art was legitimised by myth and history through his interpretation of phenomena as objective confirmations of his ideas, this essay draws the boundaries of the aesthetic sphere through a study of its counterpart. The fact that at the end of his life he felt impelled to study the aesthetic sphere in the forms of its inversion shows that he had still not abandoned it, even if he sensed that it was only an intermediate stage. Pater is said to have remarked that his purpose in writing *Marius* was to 'show the necessity of religion'.[6] The Pascal essay is the clearest indication of the extent to which the aesthetic sphere, owing to its instability, is only a passageway to the religious sphere. Pascal epitomised for Pater what an 'either/or' decision entails, leaving everything behind in order to give life a religious destination. But Pater conceived of this inconceivability in aesthetic terms.

The aesthetic life, then, is indeterminate, and for its shape it therefore requires constant negative delineation. It is situated between the inadequacy and incompleteness of experience and the religious destination of life. The aesthete lives in contradiction to reality, and herein lies the revolutionary aspect of his attitude, for his approach breaks up existing, solidified forms of life. But he can go no further than this negative contradiction, being unable to devise new forms and ideals. This is why all Pater's characters perish in the end. The absoluteness of the aesthetic life expresses itself in moods, which fluctuate between longing and deep melancholy.

For in the final analysis this reification of an in-between state rejects all legitimation and comfort, and these are essential if a life in opposition to reality is to be bearable and sustainable. Pater's significance as author and critic lies in his illumination of this condition. Perhaps his work does not have the qualities of truly great art according to his own definition, but it does offer a substantial contribution to human self-understanding. He marks the transition from a nostalgic espousal of the past to its active appropriation at a moment when Late Romanticism was about to give way to Modernism.

Notes

1 Pater criticism

1 Dawson, *Ideas*, p. 27.
2 Edmund Chandler, p. 5; see also Powys, p. 173.
3 Saintsbury, p. 346; see also Powys, pp. 175–6.
4 See Reisdorff, p. 18.
5 See especially P. E. More, pp. 85ff.
6 See Olivero's book. Also the collection of enthusiastic responses to Pater: Iser, pp. 391–2.
7 See e.g. *Gaston de Latour*, pp. 48–9.
8 For a critique of Wright, see Tillotson, 'Pater, Mr. Rose', p.45; B. Newman, 'Walter Pater', p. 633; and Dodds in Baker, *Reinterpretation*, p. 201.
9 See Reisdorff, pp. 21ff.
10 Olivero, p. 1.
11 Ibid., pp. 33 and 364.
12 See Reisdorff, p. 25.
13 See Lord David Cecil, *Walter Pater*, p. 3.
14 Foerster in Baker, *Reinterpretation*, p. 63.
15 *Marius* II, p. 127; see also *'The Guardian'*, pp. 32ff.
16 See also Jacobus, p. 389.

2 Historical preliminaries

1 See the books of Gilbert and Kuhn, Hough, Ladd, Egan, Powell, Bowra, and Wellek, *Criticism*; an important study on this theme is that of Abrams.
2 See Burke I, pp. 164, 192 and 233; see also Ladd, p. 133.
3 Blake III, p. 13.
4 This was also the starting-point of Blake's polemic against Wordsworth; see Adams, p. 26.
5 Blake I, pp. 187–8.
6 Adams, p. 32.
7 Quoted by Powell, p. 73.
8 Coleridge II, pp. 257–8.
9 See ibid., p. 257.
10 Ibid., p. 253.
11 Ibid. I, p. 183.
12 Ibid.
13 Powell, pp. 104–5.

14 See ibid., p. 183.
15 Shelley, p. 58.
16 See ibid., p. 18.
17 Ibid., p. 8.
18 See ibid., pp. 33ff.
19 Ibid., p. 42.
20 Ibid., p. 52.
21 Carlyle V, p. 78.
22 Ibid., p. 81.
23 Ibid., p. 82.
24 Ibid., p. 171.
25 Ibid., p. 155.
26 See ibid., pp. 176, 180 and 192.
27 Wordsworth, *Works* IV, p. 463.
28 See Bowra, pp. 89–90, and Eliot, *Use of Poetry*, pp. 72 and 74–5.
29 Wordsworth, *Criticism*, p. 25; see also Owen and H. Huscher's review of the book: *Anglia* 77, pp. 244ff.
30 Wordsworth, *Criticism*, p. 27.
31 Powell, p. 132.
32 Townsend, p. 7.
33 Ruskin III, p. 623.
34 See Evans, p. 89.
35 See Hough, p. 9.
36 See ibid.
37 Ruskin IV, pp. 215–16.
38 Ruskin III, p. 148.
39 Townsend, p. 50.
40 Ruskin IV, p. 288.
41 See ibid., p. 211.
42 See Hunt I, pp. 86–7, 107, 110–11, 112, 129, 132, 134 and 147.
43 See also Hough, p. 44.
44 Rossetti I, p. 383.
45 Ibid., p. 384.
46 See ibid., p. 385.
47 See ibid., p. 386.
48 See ibid., pp. 386–7.
49 See ibid., p. 387.
50 Ibid.
51 Ibid., p. 388.
52 See ibid., pp. 389–90.
53 See ibid., p. 391.
54 See ibid., p. 393.
55 Ibid., pp. 394–5.
56 See ibid., pp. 395ff.
57 Ibid., p. 398.
58 There is no need to discuss Matthew Arnold's position in this connection, as the links between Arnold and Pater have been well covered; see Eliot, 'Place of Pater', Tillotson, 'Arnold and Pater', and Hough, pp. 134ff.

3 The starting-point

1 *Appreciations*, p. 66.
2 See ibid.
3 Ibid., pp. 68–9. For criticism of Pater's interpretation of Coleridge, see Richards, pp. 38ff, though this goes beyond the scope of our discussion.
4 See *Appreciations*, p. 68.
5 Ibid., p. 103.
6 Löwith, *Wissen, Glaube und Skepsis*, p. 28.
7 See ibid., pp. 26ff.
8 For this definition of resignation see Kierkegaard, *Furcht und Zittern*, pp. 42–3.
9 *Appreciations*, p. 98.
10 See *Marius* I, pp. 149–50.
11 See *Plato and Platonism*, pp. 193ff.
12 See ibid., p. 196.
13 Lukács, 'Die Theorie des Romans', p. 249.
14 *Plato and Platonism*, pp. 175–6.
15 Friedrich, p. 430. Friedrich also alludes to Pater himself in explaining the form; see p. 443.
16 *Plato and Platonism*, p. 188. On the significance of twilight, shade and semi-darkness in Pater, see O'Faoláin, p. 333.
17 *Plato and Platonism*, pp. 183–4.
18 Ibid., p. 174.
19 See *Misc. Studies*, pp. 197ff.
20 See ibid., p. 198.
21 See ibid., p. 230.
22 See Lugowski, pp. 41ff.
23 See *Misc. Studies*, pp. 235ff.
24 See ibid., pp. 243ff.
25 Ibid., p. 207.
26 See ibid., p. 208.
27 Ibid., p. 209.
28 Ibid., p. 217.
29 Ibid., p. 226.
30 See ibid., p. 227.
31 Ibid., p. 211.
32 See ibid., p. 222.
33 Ibid., p. 173.
34 Ibid., p. 177.
35 Ibid., p. 178.
36 Ibid., p. 186.
37 Ibid.
38 'I have remarked how, in the process of our brain-building, as the house of thought in which we live gets itself together, like some airy bird's-nest of floating thistle-down and chance straws, compact at last, little accidents have their consequence.' Ibid., p. 184.
39 Ibid., p. 187.

40 Ibid., pp. 193–4. See Newman, *Apologia*, p. 392, on the infallibility of the Church, which he regards as a necessity.
41 See also Willey, *Nineteenth Century Studies*, pp. 231–2.
42 On the question of the idealising effect, see also Sternberger, *Panorama*, p. 141, though he unfolds the problem in a different context and, in tackling it, unmistakably passes certain value judgements.
43 See, for instance, Wright I, pp. 22–3 and 94–5.
44 *Misc. Studies*, p. 205.
45 Hegel, *Philosophy of Fine Art* I, p. 137.
46 On Pater's knowledge of Hegel, see Fehr, 'Pater und Hegel', pp. 300–1; A. Cecil, *Oxford Thinkers*, p. 222; Proesler, p. 82; Cattan, p. 90; Sander, p. 251; Staub, p. 12; Harrison, 'Pater/Heine', p. 665; L. Johnson, pp. 36–7; Höhne, pp. 34–5, and Powys, p. 173.
47 *Plato and Platonism*, p. 120. On the question of expression in Pater, see Dowden, p. 3; Welby in Abercrombie, *Revaluations*, p. 202; Thomas, p. 58; Benson, p. 164; Greenslet, p. 100 and R. V. Johnson, pp. 47–8.
48 Hegel, *Philosophy of Fine Art* I, p. 234.
49 *Renaissance*, p. 71.
50 *Marius* I, p. 94.
51 See also ibid., pp. 156–7. P. E. More, p. 108, in his critique of Pater, believed this contained an element of exhibitionism. On Pater's theatricality, see Wright I, pp. 134 and 201.
52 Ladd, p. 247.
53 This gives rise to the histrionic form of life proclaimed by Wilde and Swinburne in their prose fiction. Henry Wotton sees theatrical self-presentation as the ultimate reality of life: 'I love acting. It is so much more real than life' (*Dorian Gray*, p. 112). Similarly, Lesbia Brandon, the eponymous heroine of Swinburne's novel, on her deathbed sums up all that she desires: 'I love to die acting' (*Lesbia Brandon*, p. 165). On theatricality as a characteristic of the period, see Willey, *Nineteenth Century Studies*, p. 249; also Sedlmayr, p. 202, and Kassner, p. 306, both of whom make very pronounced value judgements.
54 See Rossetti I, pp. 395 ff.
55 See Nahm, pp. 459ff.
56 See ibid., pp. 464–5.
57 Ibid., p. 468.

4 Defining art

1 On the historical origins of this slogan, see the very informative work of Wilcox, pp. 360 ff; also R. F. Egan's study which traces the links between the theory of 'l'art pour l'art' and German Idealism. Although he occasionally refers to the special nature of the concept in the nineteenth century, Singer tries to pinpoint its general, aesthetic features: 'We have seen that in its most fundamental reference "Art for Art's Sake" meant "Art for Beauty's Sake". Now we shall see that it also meant "Art for Form's Sake" ' (p. 348). This is simply one formula explaining another, and does not shed a great deal of light on the situation. Finally, he calls 'Art for Art's Sake . . . an ethical theory'

(p. 352), but still without offering any real definition. Singer's study, however, is a genuine effort to tackle the problem analytically. Scheffler's pamphlet, on the other hand, is merely a hymn of praise from a devotee:

> In truth that which is expressed by the phrase 'l'art pour l'art' is one of the proudest achievements. With this creed, the artist takes all responsibility upon himself. He no longer feels responsible towards any man, any state authority, or social pressure; but his responsibility is all the greater towards himself, his conscience, and the voice within himself saying 'you should'. This makes him free and uninhibited. It is significant that at the same moment when the artist consciously demanded unlimited self-responsibility, martyrdom began. Society disowned him, he became lonely and learnt at first hand the effects of hunger, misunderstanding, disrespect and scorn. But the moment genius was to a certain extent rejected, it was also responsible for all the art of its time; it stood there as leader and as revolutionary (p. 17).

'Without constraint the expression "l'art pour l'art" can be extended to mean: truth for truth's sake – or unconditional knowledge – or religion for God's sake not for man's. If this is considered a bourgeois assessment, then it is a glorification of what is bourgeois. The objection is false in so far as the great artists, poets, composers who were the true representatives of "l'art pour l'art", were constantly in conflict with the bourgeoisie' (p. 18). 'The few that really live with the great works of art, and for whom Art is a religion, are the spiritual pace-setters; they extend and greatly transform that which they gain from Art in many channels, so that the circles become ever wider and, ultimately, everyone can somehow partake directly of the works of genius' (p. 39).

2 *Renaissance*, p. 234.
3 Ibid., pp. 234–5.
4 See the studies by Auerbach; Brinkmann; and Petriconi, pp. 37–66.
5 *Renaissance*, p. 235.
6 Ibid.
7 Ibid., p. 236.
8 Ibid., pp. 238–9.
9 Ibid., p. 150.
10 Grassi, p. 94.
11 See also Reisdorff, p. 231.
12 See Eliot, *Essays*, p. 442.
13 See ibid., p. 441; also West, p. 115; see also John Morley's accordant judgement of Pater in Willey, *More Nineteenth Century Studies*, pp. 297ff.
14 *Renaissance*, pp. 236–7.
15 See also Rehm, *Kierkegaard*, p. 276.
16 Schopenhauer I, p. 188.
17 Ibid.
18 Sternberger, *Jugendstil*, p. 118.
19 Benjamin I, p. 418.
20 *Renaissance*, pp. 213–14.
21 Ibid., p. 2.
22 *Marius* I, p. 102. At the beginning of the century, Coleridge wrote: 'With

regard to works in all branches of the fine arts, I may remark that the pleasure arising from novelty must of course be allowed its due place and weight' (*Biographia Literaria* II, pp. 261–2). In his self-imposed mission, John Davidson at the end of the century regarded it as his task 'to thunder news of a new dawn . . . he heralded the new day to come with an ardour equalled only by the Futurists of Milan' (Jackson, p. 190). See also Buckley, *Victorian Temper*, p. 240.

23 Sternberger, *Jugendstil*, p. 116.
24 Ruskin X, p. 156.
25 Ruskin III, p. 148.
26 Townsend, p. 15; see also Ruskin III, p. 157.
27 *Misc. Studies*, pp. 12–13.
28 For what the category of 'the interesting' entails, see also *Appreciations*, pp. 244 and 37; *Marius* I, p. 103, and *Plato and Platonism*, p. 90. On 'interest' in Pater, see Saintsbury, p. 354; Tillotson, 'Arnold and Pater', p. 68; *TLS*, 3 February 1927, p. 65; Jacobus, p. 393; and Hough, p. 145. For a more detailed explanation of this category and the wide-ranging implications it had in nineteenth-century thought even beyond the realm of art, see Löwith, *Von Hegel zu Nietzsche*, p. 166; Rehm, *Kierkegaard*, p. 121 and Kierkegaard, *Entweder/Oder* I, p. 327.
29 On the concept of art as a stimulus, see Nietzsche, *Wille zur Macht* II, pp. 229–30. For English writers' concepts of the stimulating and the grotesque, see Harris, p. 383; Farmer, *Mouvement esthétique*, p. 70; Jackson, p. 256; Fehr, *Streifzüge*, p. 111 and H. von Hofmannsthal I, pp. 114–15. Francis Adams's book *A Child of the Age* contains a vivid summing-up of the situation: 'Can't you read the signs of the times? Can't you see an Art that becomes day by day more of a drug, less and less of a food for men's souls? A misty dream floating around it, a faint reek of the east and strange unnatural scents breathing from it' (quoted by Burdett, p. 239).
30 See e.g. Ruskin IV, p. 211.
31 See *Appreciations*, p. 253.
32 *Renaissance*, pp. 230–1.
33 See Ruskin XV, pp. 351ff.
34 Ruskin IV, pp. 26 and 98–9.
35 See Roe, p. 278.
36 See ibid.
37 See Malraux, p. 513.
38 Ibid., p. 637.
39 *Appreciations*, p. 62.
40 *Renaissance*, p. 238.
41 *Renaissance*, pp.ix–x.
42 See also Hough, p. 158.
43 Kaufmann, p. 200.
44 *Misc. Studies*, p. 15.
45 Picard, *Impressionismus*, p. 12.
46 See ibid., pp. 72ff.
47 See Malraux, p. 536.
48 *Renaissance*, p. 24.

49 See ibid., p. 25.
50 Haskins is probably the first to have devised this period concept and given it a wide currency.
51 *Renaissance*, p. 156.
52 This is one of the reasons why Picard finds Impressionism an irritant.
53 *Renaissance*, pp. 30 and 47.
54 Burckhardt I, p. 141.
55 *Renaissance*, p. 49.
56 On the question of what the category of the 'interesting' entails see also *Appreciations*, p. 244. For a wider discussion, see Löwith, *Von Hegel zu Nietzsche*, p. 166; Rehm, p. 121; Kierkegaard, *Entweder/Oder* I, p. 327; L. Johnson, p. 7, believes that Pater's constant intention was to stimulate, interest and attract.
57 *Renaissance*, p. 54.
58 Ibid., pp. 55–6.
59 Bollnow, pp. 34–5.
60 *Renaissance*, p. 60. See also ibid., pp. 56 ff, where Pater describes the paintings of Venus and the Madonna in detail.
61 Ibid., p. 61.
62 Ibid., p. 57.
63 Bollnow, p. 26.
64 Ibid., p. 33.
65 See *Plato and Platonism*, p. 282.
66 *Renaissance*, p. 85; see also Powys, p. 179.
67 Bollnow, p. 40.
68 See also Lukács, 'Die Theorie des Romans', p. 252. Joad, p. 108, regards the lack of the object as the true distinguishing trait of decadence. But he simplifies things and makes pronounced value judgements – see esp. p. 122.
69 Bollnow, pp. 245–6.
70 *Renaissance*, p. 95.
71 Ibid.
72 Ibid., pp. 95–6.
73 See esp. *Appreciations*, pp. 67–8. Also Wainwright, p. 448, and Guardini, p. 16.
74 Picard, *Impressionismus*, p. 14.
75 See *Renaissance*, p. 96; also Beardsley's impressionistic tale 'Under the Hill', pp. 5ff and 32.
76 See also Wellek, *Criticism*, p. 198.
77 *Renaissance*, pp. 124ff. Stauffer's not very convincing argument, pp. 89–93, that Dürer's *Melancholia* served as a model for Pater's description of the *Mona Lisa* is irrelevant to the present discussion. Wilde, *Intentions*, pp. 63–4, shows that Wainwright had already dealt with the *Mona Lisa* in a similar way. Regarding the tradition of the concept of the *femme fatale*, to which Pater's description also belongs, see Praz, pp. 187ff and 243–4; also Fehr, 'Paters Beschreibung der Mona Lisa', pp. 87–8.
78 *Renaissance*, pp. 124 and 125.
79 Maugham, p. 281.
80 Malraux, p. 637.

81 *Appreciations*, p. 62.
82 Fehr, 'Paters Beschreibung der Mona Lisa', p. 87. Wilde, *Dorian Gray*, p. 201, has similar visions.
83 *Appreciations*, p. 31.
84 See also Edmund Chandler, p. 10.
85 Apart from 'Style', 'Conclusion' and 'Postscript' are to be regarded as theoretical essays.
86 Edmund Chandler, pp. 79ff and 87.
87 *Appreciations*, pp. 9–10.
88 See ibid., p. 8.
89 See ibid., p. 10.
90 See ibid.
91 Ibid., p. 8.
92 Ibid., pp. 8–9.
93 Malraux, p. 318.
94 *Appreciations*, p. 36.
95 Ibid., p. 18.
96 It is in this respect that Wordsworth became an important model for Pater; see *Appreciations*, pp. 57–8.
97 *Greek Studies*, p. 242.
98 See ibid., pp. 246–7, and *Appreciations*, p. 207.
99 *Appreciations*, p. 29.
100 See also *Marius* II, p. 218.
101 Although Pater's essay on style (1888) appeared eight years after Flaubert's death, it deals almost exclusively with the young Flaubert's correspondence, which was written before the French writer had formulated his ideas on style. On the latter, see Jauss, pp. 96ff. Pater, *Misc. Studies*, pp. 35–6, actually attacks the fiction of 'impersonality in art'. For parallels in Russian Symbolism, see Holthusen, pp. 33–4.
102 *Appreciations*, p. 15.
103 Ibid., p. 34.
104 See also Edmund Chandler, p. 9.
105 *Appreciations*, p. 11; see also esp. p. 10, where the same idea is presented even more decisively.
106 Ibid., p. 12.
107 *Marius* I, p. 96.
108 Ibid., pp. 96–7.
109 Ibid., p. 96.
110 Ibid., p. 97.
111 This controversial term is used here in a phenomenological sense, as has long been the case in art history, and as Curtius, pp. 277ff, has introduced it successfully into literary history.
112 See *Marius* I, p. 98.
113 See ibid., pp. 98–9.
114 Binswanger, p. 176.
115 'English Poet', p. 445.
116 On the basic situation of the Romantic poet, see Auden, p. 151.
117 Benn, *Ausdruckswelt*, p. 89.

118 'English Poet', p. 440.
119 Ibid., p. 442.
120 See also *Marius* I, p. 99, and also Melchiori, p. 23.
121 Pater says expressly in his essay on style that art is a flight 'from a certain vulgarity in the actual world' (*Appreciations*, p. 18).
122 *Marius* I, pp. 94–5.
123 Nietzsche, *Götzendämmerung/Wagner*, p. 23.
124 *Appreciations*, p. 14.
125 Ibid., p. 19.
126 Ibid., p. 18.
127 Ibid., p. 16.
128 Ibid., p. 18.
129 Ibid., p. 17. See also *'Guardian'*, p. 15. Here Pater defines style as the synthetic unity of opposites, and combines the demand for selective perfection with the view that English must be written as 'a learned language'.
130 Kassner, p. 189.
131 *Appreciations*, p. 21.
132 See ibid., pp. 21ff.
133 Ibid., pp. 23–4.
134 See ibid., p. 23.
135 See ibid., pp. 21, 22 and 23.
136 Ibid., p. 26.
137 Ibid., pp. 26–7.
138 Ibid., p. 22.
139 Lukács, 'Subjekt-Objekt-Beziehung', p. 26.
140 See *Plato and Platonism*, pp. 140–5.
141 *Appreciations*, p. 38.
142 Ibid., p. 11.
143 Ibid., p. 182.
144 *Renaissance*, p. 134.
145 Ibid., p. 135.
146 Ibid., p. 138. This idea that all art tends to approximate to the perfection of music was commonly entertained throughout Europe in the 1880s. See Lehmann, p. 66, and Joel II, p. 274. See also Schopenhauer I, p. 264; Hegel, *Philosophy of Fine Art* III, pp. 338ff, and similarly Schleiermacher, pp. 392 and 394; also Kassner, pp. 82 and 305.
147 See Lukács, 'Subjekt-Objekt-Beziehung', p. 39.
148 See Edmund Chandler, p. 86.
149 *Greek Studies*, p. 200.
150 See also Ullmann, pp. 123ff on the style of the Goncourts.
151 *Greek Studies*, pp. 201–2.
152 *Plato and Platonism*, p. 34.
153 *Appreciations* 1889, p. 218. On Pater's atmospheric style, see e.g. A. Cecil, *Oxford Thinkers*, pp. 249–50; Bendz, p. 60; Hunecker, p. 282 and Anon., *Spectator* 104, p. 1076.
154 Hegel, *Philosophy of Fine Art* II, pp. 143–4.
155 Stevenson IX, p. 166.
156 David Cecil, *Ideas*, p. 370, calls Virginia Woolf 'the final exquisite flower of Pater's doctrine'.

5 The problem of orientation

1 See Benjamin I, p. 374.
2 See *Appreciations*, p. 34. On Pater and Keats, see R. V. Johnson, pp. 47–8, although he does not tackle the problem of beauty. In his otherwise useful essay, Johnson is more concerned with the question of Keats's and Pater's attitudes towards sensuous experiences, and also why Pater never wrote a study of Keats.
3 Moore, 'Avowals', p. 101.
4 *Renaissance*, pp. vii–viii. In view of this statement, David Cecil's interpretation, *Pater*, p. 10, seems wide of the mark: 'Beauty, to have the significance he attaches to it, must surely be an incarnation of something absolute and eternal.' Reisdorff, pp. 79–80, also tends to cling to the Platonic concept of beauty.
5 Hegel, *Philosophy of Fine Art* I, p. 78.
6 Ibid., p. 154.
7 See Hough, p. 23.
8 See Ruskin IV, pp. 64 and 75.
9 See ibid., p. 144.
10 Becker, p. 27.
11 *Appreciations*, pp. 247–8. For a wider context of this problem, see F. L. Lucas, pp. 12–13 and 24–5.
12 Malraux, pp. 593–4.
13 Becker, p. 29.
14 *Misc. Studies*, pp. 189–90. See also Cattan, p. 3, and Brie, *Ästhetische Weltanschauung*, p. 48, who delineates similar ideas to be found in Poe.
15 See *Marius* I, p. 92.
16 Becker, p. 48.
17 *Marius* II, p. 17.
18 *Marius* I, p. 93.
19 *Appreciations*, p. 241.
20 Ibid., p. 242.
21 Ibid., p. 247.
22 Ibid., p. 250.
23 See ibid., p. 251.
24 Ibid., pp. 257–8.
25 Ibid., p. 252.
26 Ibid., p. 258.
27 Ibid.
28 Ibid., p. 256.
29 Ibid., p. 241.
30 Malraux, p. 633.

6 What is history?

1 *Renaissance*, p. 206.
2 See ibid., pp. 177 and 211.
3 *Renaissance*, pp. 210ff. Pater follows Hegel sometimes to the very letter:
Sculpture therefore appears to possess the truest means of representing

what is spiritual, whereas both painting and poetry have the contrary appearance of being more remote from Nature for the reason that painting makes use of the mere surface instead of the sensuous totality of the spatial condition, which a human form and all other natural things actually assume; speech, too, to a still less degree, expresses the reality of body, being merely able to transmit ideas of the same by means of tone.

However, the truth of the matter is precisely the reverse of this. For although the image of sculpture appears no doubt to possess from the start the natural form as it stands, it is just this externality of body and nature reproduced in gross material which is not the nature of Spirit as such. If we regard the essential character of it its peculiar existence is that expressed by means of speech, acts, and affairs which develop its ideal or soul-life and disclose its true existence (Hegel, *Philosophy of Fine Art* III, pp. 111–12).

4 Hegel, *Philosophy of Fine Art* I, pp. 141–2.
5 Meinecke, p. 609.
6 Ibid., p. 248.
7 *Renaissance*, p. 222.
8 See ibid., p. 227.
9 Ibid., p. 229.
10 Ibid., p. 231.
11 Ibid., p. 232.
12 Troeltsch, p. 32.
13 See Collingwood, pp. 228 and 282ff.
14 See ibid., p. 132.
15 See *Plato and Platonism*, p. 9.
16 *Renaissance*, p. 237.
17 Hegel, *Philosophie der Weltgeschichte* I, p. 130.
18 *Plato and Platonism*, pp. 19ff.
19 Löwith, *Von Hegel zu Nietzsche*, p. 238.
20 Concerning the problem of the philosophy of history, see Löwith, *Weltgeschichte und Heilsgeschehen*.
21 *Uncollected Essays*, p. 117.
22 *Plato and Platonism*, pp. 72–3.
23 Meinecke, p. 430.
24 Collingwood, p. 225.
25 See *Renaissance*, p. 231.
26 See also Cattan, p. 102.
27 See *Renaissance*, p. 223.
28 See *Greek Studies*, p. 251.
29 Ibid., p. 252.
30 *Renaissance*, p. 218.
31 See *Marius* I, pp. 3ff.
32 *Marius* II, p. 116.
33 See *Renaissance*, pp. 225–6.
34 Ibid., pp. 226–7.
35 *Appreciations*, pp. 60ff.
36 *Renaissance*, p. 49. See also Liptzin, p. 273. There is a similar idea in Carlyle: see Wellek, 'Carlyle and the Philosophy of History', p. 69; also in Amiel I, p. 176, and in Baudelaire, see Hess, p. 109.

37 See *Renaissance*, pp. 198–9, and *Marius* I, pp. 142–3. There is a similar definition of culture in Arnold, *Literature and Dogma*, p. xix: culture is 'the acquainting ourselves with the best that has been known and said in the world, and thus with the history of the human spirit'. On the relationship between Pater and Arnold see Tillotson, 'Arnold and Pater'; Eliot, 'Place of Pater'; Burgum, p. 276 and Wright I, p. 174.
38 Quoted by Curtius, p. 398.
39 *Appreciations*, p. 241.
40 See also Arnold, *Culture and Anarchy*, p. viii: 'culture, then, is a study of perfection, and of harmonious perfection, general perfection, and perfection which consists in becoming something rather than in having something, in an inward condition of the mind and spirit, not in an outward set of circumstances'. For a critique of the aesthetic idea of culture, see Eliot, *Essays*, pp. 435ff; also Chesterton, p. 74, and Holloway, pp. 10–11.
41 See Malraux, pp. 11ff. See also *Appreciations*, p. 80. Wellek, 'Pater's Literary Theory', p. 46, rightly points out that Malraux's 'Imaginäres Museum' is more broadly based than Pater's 'House Beautiful'. The needs of the individual have too much influence on the 'House Beautiful' – a restriction that does not apply to Malraux's concept. The latter is to Pater's what Pater's is to Saint-Beuve's 'Temple du goût'.
42 See Curtius, p. 400, discussing Ivanov.
43 *Marius* I, pp. 153ff.
44 See also Curtius, p. 400, who sees Pater's concept as having overcome the 'Tyranny of standard classicism'.

7 The limits of historical legitimation

1 See Benson, p. 162.
2 See ibid., p. 20.
3 On Pater's 'misinterpretation' of Plato, see P. E. More, p. 112; Benson, p. 20; L. Johnson, pp. 2–3; Cattan, p. 172; Campbell, pp. 265–6 and Huppé, p. 317.
4 *Plato and Platonism*, pp. 9ff; see also Campbell, p. 264.
5 *Plato and Platonism*, p. 8.
6 Ibid., p. 15.
7 Ibid., p. 32.
8 Ibid., p. 46.
9 Ibid., p. 52.
10 Ibid., pp. 52–3.
11 Ibid., p. 81.
12 See ibid., p. 83.
13 Ibid., p. 86.
14 Ibid., p. 90.
15 Ibid., pp. 112–13.
16 Ibid., pp. 117–18.
17 Ibid., p. 123.
18 On the composite nature of Platonic philosophy, see also Nietzsche, *Nachgelassene Werke 1872–6*, p. 16; also Ransome, p. 140.
19 For a wider context relating to the concept of becoming, see Perry, pp. 26–7.

20 *Plato and Platonism*, pp. 139–40.
21 For the transvaluation of Platonic philosophy, see Huppé's informative essay.
22 *Plato and Platonism*, p. 146.
23 Ibid., p. 159.
24 See ibid., pp. 162–3.
25 Ibid., p. 167.
26 See ibid., pp. 168–9.
27 See ibid., p. 169.
28 Ibid., p. 164.
29 See e.g. ibid., p. 166.
30 Novalis II, p. 293.
31 *Plato and Platonism*, pp. 179–80.
32 Ibid., p. 188.
33 Ibid., p. 185.
34 See ibid., pp. 192ff.
35 Ibid., pp. 235 and 238. Law, p. 581, points out that half of Pater's allusions to Plato refer to the *Republic*.
36 *Plato and Platonism*, pp. 275–6.
37 On the importance of the state, see Willey, *Nineteenth Century Studies*, pp. 257ff; Arnold, *Culture and Anarchy*, pp. 158–9 and Brown, p. 137.
38 Benn, *Essays*, p. 43; see also Hegel, *Philosophie der Weltgeschichte* I, p. 92.
39 *Plato and Platonism*, p. 273.
40 Ibid., p. 282.
41 See ibid., pp. 255 and 273.
42 *Plato and Platonism*, pp. 124–5.
43 *Gaston de Latour*, p. vi.
44 Ibid., pp. 82–3.
45 See ibid., pp. 1ff.
46 Ibid., p. 22.
47 See esp. ibid., pp. 8ff.
48 Ibid., p. 34. Elsewhere, *Misc. Studies*, p. 28, Pater writes: 'Were there not survivals of the wild creatures in the gentlest, the politest of us?' For a discussion of this problem in a wider context, see Joel II, p. 748.
49 *Gaston de Latour*, p. 38.
50 Ibid., pp. 41–2.
51 '*Guardian*', p. 28.
52 On the significance of the numinous, see also F. G. Jünger, pp. 232 and 235. For a view in contrast to Pater's landscape, see the description of a Romantic landscape as detailed by Abercrombie, *Romanticism*, p. 128.
53 *Gaston de Latour*, p. 42.
54 Ibid., p. 25.
55 See ibid., p. 47.
56 See ibid., p. 18.
57 Ibid., p. 109.
58 Ibid., p. 67.
59 Ibid., p. 25.
60 Ibid., p. 52.
61 See ibid., pp. 52–3.

62 Ibid., p. 55.
63 Ibid., p. 60.
64 See ibid., pp. 71–2.
65 Ibid., pp. 78–9.
66 See ibid., p. 96.
67 Ibid., p. 100.
68 Ibid., pp. 94–5.
69 Ibid., p. 107.
70 Ibid., p. 132.
71 See ibid., p. 143.
72 Ibid., p. 144.
73 Ibid., p. 147.
74 Ibid., p. 148.
75 See ibid., p. 156.
76 See esp. ibid., pp. 16ff, and several paragraphs in the chapter 'Shadows of Events'.
77 See ibid., p. 159. Kassner, p. 33, remarked: 'He was a striver, this 19th Century individualist with his need for deliverance, half Faust, half bourgeois, all Protestant, a striver . . . for the sake of striving, without a model or with constantly changing models. That's what he was, and in that he distinguishes himself from the other individualists of the Renaissance, with which at times he seemed incidentally as if he were in love.'

8 The ancient gods

1 Kierkegaard, *Entweder/Oder* II, p. 17. Picard, *Flucht vor Gott*, pp. 98–9, suggests that 'a world in which nothing is left feels itself related to the beginnings in which there is still nothing'.
2 See Dockhorn, pp. 49ff. On the revival of Celtic myth, see Arnold, *Celtic Literature*, pp. 2, 106 and 174ff; Hough, p. 236 and Wilson, p. 29. On Pre-Raphaelite concepts of myth, see Farmer, *Pater as Critic*, p. 63, and Hough, p. 50. On the importance of a 'working mythology' for Davidson, see Buckley, *Victorian Temper*, p. 241. The inclination towards the elemental is particularly noticeable in Swinburne. In *Lesbia Brandon*, p. 8, we read of Herbert Seyton, one of the main characters: 'Water and wind and darkness and light made friends with him; he went among beautiful things without wonder or fear. For months he lived and grew on like an animal or a fruit; and things seemed to deal with him as with one of these; earth set herself to caress and amuse him; air blew and rain fell and leaves changed to his great delight.' See also Wilde, *De Profundis*, p. 16, *Dorian Gray*, pp. 187–8, and *House of Pomegranates*, pp. 68ff. In *Confessions*, p. 116, George Moore states with an undertone of satisfaction that 'In old days, when a people became too highly civilized, the barbarians came down from the north and regenerated that nation with darkness.' On the subject generally, see also Jackson, p. 190, and Willey, *Nineteenth Century Studies*, p. 30.
3 See e.g. Young, p. 109, and Wright I, p. 201, and II, pp. 27 and 37.
4 Wilde, *De Profundis*, p. 62. Before his 'conversion' Wilde was quite open to the aesthetic charm of ritual: see *Dorian Gray*, p. 184. On the importance of ceremony and ritual for late-nineteenth-century poets, see Burdett, p. 177;

Somervell, p. 167 and esp. the very detailed description of religious rites and Church ceremonies in Moore, *Evelyn Innes*, pp. 331–2. It was Yeats who deliberately turned away from the aesthetic effects of religious rituals and symbols (see Hough, p. 227). 'If we accept the theory that the myths of the world are descriptions of the rituals that preceded them, and not distorted accounts of historical events, Yeats was actually leading both myth and drama back to their common ritual cradle' (Ure, p. 89). For an attack on the aesthetic view of ritual, see Newman, *Apologia*, Appendix, p. 31. Here Newman also explains why he wrote his novel *Loss and Gain*, which was directed against the 'gilt-gingerbread school'.

5 *Renaissance*, p. 203.
6 Ibid., p. 202.
7 See Otto, *Dionysos*, pp. 19ff.
8 Ibid., p. 22.
9 Jung and Kerényi, p. 20.
10 Ibid., p. 16.
11 See esp. *Marius* I, pp. 3ff, 7–8, 10, 97 and 105ff; *Marius* II, pp. 98ff and 123ff; *Greek Studies*, pp. 124ff; *Misc. Studies*, p. 87. Also Wright I, pp. 64, 70, 109 and 179; II, pp. 38 and 198.
12 *Appreciations*, 1889, pp. 221–2.
13 Picard, *Impressionismus*, pp. 72–3.
14 '*Guardian*', p. 13.
15 *Appreciations*, pp. 48–9; see also '*Guardian*', pp. 99–100.
16 For a discussion of this relationship in a more general context, see Klages, *Mensch und Erde*, p. 25; Dacqué, *Natur und Erlösung*, p. 56 and Klages, *Geist als Widersacher* III, 2, p. 1363.
17 Löwith, 'Weltgeschichte und Heilsgeschehen': *Anteile*, p. 106.
18 Klages, *Mensch und Erde*, p. 40.
19 See also Otto, *Götter Griechenlands*, p. 20.
20 *Greek Studies*, pp. 96–7; see also Klages, *Kosmogonischer Eros*, p. 199, and Dacqué, *Natur und Seele*, p. 23.
21 See also Ruskin XIX, p. 294.
22 On the relationship between consciousness and instinct, see also Nietzsche, *Wille zur Macht* II, p. 8, and I, p. 449; also Amiel II, p. 142.
23 Kierkegaard, *Begriff der Angst*, p. 41.
24 Jung and Kerényi, p. 25.
25 Otto, *Dionysos*, p. 112.
26 *Marius* I, p. 104.
27 *Greek Studies*, pp. 81–2.
28 Jung and Kerényi, p. 129.
29 *Greek Studies*, p. 91.
30 Ibid., p. 93.
31 Ibid., pp. 103–4.
32 Ibid., pp. 102–3.
33 See ibid., pp. 103–4.
34 See ibid., pp. 108–9.
35 Ibid., p. 114. Klages, *Geist als Widersacher* III, 2, p. 1329, stresses the fact that 'motherliness means the place of shelter and protection both for future and for past life'.

36 *Greek Studies*, p. 93.
37 See ibid., pp. 113ff.
38 Jung and Kerényi, p. 192.
39 See *Greek Studies*, p. 91.
40 Ibid., p. 93.
41 See ibid., p. 147.
42 Ibid., pp. 147ff. See also Richard Wagner X, p. 281, and Kierkegaard, *Entweder/Oder* II, p. 200.
43 Jung and Kerényi, p. 167.
44 See *Greek Studies*, p. 82.
45 Jung and Kerényi, p. 225.
46 *Greek Studies*, p. 151.
47 Ibid., p. 121.
48 See ibid., pp. 103–4.
49 Ibid., p. 112.
50 Ibid.
51 Ibid., pp. 110–11. See also Nietzsche, *Birth of Tragedy*, pp. 6 and 40–1. Wilde, *De Profundis*, pp. 53 and 25, stresses: 'I now see that sorrow, being the supreme emotion of which man is capable, is at once the type and the test of all great art . . . Where there is sorrow there is holy ground.' In Swinburne I, pp. 228, 230 and 336ff, the cult of sorrow is given a revolutionary twist which at times resembles Nietzsche's. See also Swinburne's 'Notre Dame des Sept Douleurs' in the poem *Dolores*, I, pp. 285ff.
52 See *Renaissance*, pp. 238–9.
53 *Greek Studies*, p. 149.
54 Ibid., p. 147.
55 Ibid., p. 101.
56 *Greek Studies*, p. 53. Wilde, *De Profundis*, p. 76, also follows Pater in this respect when he regards Demeter and Dionysus as the two central figures of Greek mythology: 'The two most deeply suggestive figures of Greek mythology were, for religion, Demeter, an earth goddess, not one of the Olympians, and for art, Dionysos, the son of a mortal woman to whom the moment of his birth had also proved the moment of her death.'
57 Dowden, p. 12. See also Bush, pp. 532–3; David Cecil, *Pater*, p. 22 and Harrison, 'Pater/Heine', p. 659.
58 *Greek Studies*, p. 10.
59 See *Imaginary Portraits*, pp. 47ff.
60 See *Greek Studies*, pp. 9 and 14.
61 See ibid., p. 11.
62 Ibid., p. 14.
63 Ibid.
64 Ibid., p. 18.
65 Ibid., pp. 18–19. See also Kassner, p. 304, and Klages, *Mensch und Erde*, p. 109. Mrs Humphrey Ward writes in *Robert Elsmere* III, p. 218: 'Paradise is here, visible and tangible by mortal eyes and hands, whenever self is lost in loving; whenever the narrow limits of personality are beaten down by the inrush of the divine spirit.' This obliteration of the self, however, relates to Christian and not to pagan ideas of ecstasy. The notion that Dionysian ravings can be combined with Christian attitudes is not altogether alien to

Mrs Humphrey Ward, and can also be found in Yeats. 'Unlike Nietzsche, Yeats saw Christianity as the triumph of Dionysus' (Ure, p. 44). On the Dionysian background to Swinburne's poetry, see Brie, *Exotismus*, p. 70.
66 Nietzsche, *Birth of Tragedy*, pp. 25–6.
67 *Greek Studies*, p. 43.
68 See ibid., p. 45.
69 See ibid., pp. 40, 42–3 and 44.
70 See ibid., pp. 45ff.
71 See ibid., pp. 40ff and 49.
72 See *Imaginary Portraits*, pp. 57ff, 60 and 66.
73 Otto, *Dionysos*, pp. 130ff.
74 Jünger, p. 187, emphasises: 'The more . . . life is subjected to time, the more questionable it becomes . . . Dionysus, however, lifts us out of time; his feast makes us free of it.'
75 *Greek Studies*, pp. 49–50.
76 On the conception of time as a circular and recurrent movement, see Löwith, *Weltgeschichte und Heilsgeschehen*, p. 26, and Klages, *Geist als Widersacher* III, 2, p. 1329.
77 Bollnow, p. 224.
78 See *Greek Studies*, p. 9.
79 Ibid., pp. 26–7.
80 Ibid., pp. 32ff.
81 Ibid., p. 34.
82 Ibid., p. 37.

9 The limits of mythical legitimation

1 Harrison, 'Pater/Heine', p. 685.
2 See ibid., p. 655; Hecht, p. 576, and Liptzin, pp. 267ff.
3 Heine VIII, p. 70.
4 See ibid.
5 *Misc. Studies*, pp. 155–6.
6 See ibid., p. 142.
7 See ibid., p. 169.
8 Ibid., pp. 145–6.
9 See Heine VIII, p. 68.
10 See Fletcher, *Apollyonists* I, p. 142.
11 See Bunyan, *Pilgrim's Progress* I, pp. 184ff.
12 Ibid., p. 184.
13 See Otto, *Götter Griechenlands*, p. 67.
14 *Misc. Studies*, p. 143.
15 See Otto, *Götter Griechenlands*, p. 68.
16 See *Misc. Studies*, p. 150.
17 See Otto, *Götter Griechenlands*, p. 69.
18 See *Misc. Studies*, p. 170.
19 Ibid., p. 144.
20 See ibid., p. 164.
21 Ibid., pp. 164–5.
22 Ibid., p. 147.

23 Ibid., p. 165.
24 See ibid.
25 See ibid.
26 See also Kierkegaard, *Entweder/Oder* I, p. 55, and *Renaissance*, p. 222.
27 See *Misc. Studies*, pp. 169–70.
28 Ibid., p. 157.
29 Ibid., p. 159.
30 Ibid., p. 160. On cruelty as a trait of Pater's, see Sharp, *Papers*, p. 226; Welby, p. 208; Gaunt, p. 206 and Wright I, pp. 134–5. Chesterton, p. 231, describes the literature of his time as follows: 'It is . . . notable of the Victorian writers that the only supernatural note they can strike assuredly is the tragic and almost the diabolic.' H. von Hofmannsthal I, pp. 117ff, epitomises the mood of Swinburne's poetry in the following terms:

> Like maenads the passions ran with naked feet and dishevelled hair; life put on the mask of Medusa, with its mysterious and frightening eyes; as in the cult of mourning for Adonis, and in the cult of Cybele, the horrors of ripest life and death flowed together . . . What is called love here is a divinity with many names . . . it is Notre dame des sept douleurs, the lust of torment, the intoxication of sorrow; it is in every colour and in every tremble and every glow and every scent of existence.

There is a striking example of Swinburne's Satanism in the scene between Denham and Lady Wariston in *Lesbia Brandon*, pp. 38–9:

> Deeply he desired to die by her, if that could be; and more deeply if this could be, to destroy her: scourge her into swooning and absorb the blood with kisses; caress and lacerate her loveliness, alleviate and heighten her pains; to feel her foot upon his throat, and wound her own with his teeth; submit his body and soul for a little to her lightest will, and satiate upon hers the desperate caprice of his immeasurable desire; to inflict careful torture on limbs too tender to embrace, suck the tears off her laden eyelids, bite through her sweet and shuddering lips.

See also Swinburne, *Lesbia Brandon*, pp. 19, 23, 31, 32, 33–4, 66, 67, 172, 173–4 and 175. On Beardsley's Satanism, see Jackson, p. 102. George Moore, *Confessions*, pp. 93–4, offers a typical variation on the theme:

> the great pagan world of marble and pomp and lust and cruelty, that my soul goes out to and hails as the grandest . . . Oh, for the silence of marble courts, for the shadow of great pillars, for gold, for reticulated canopies of lilies; to see the great gladiators pass, to hear them cry the famous 'Ave Caesar', to hold the thumb down, to see the blood flow, to fill the languid hours with the agonies of poisoned slaves! Oh, for excess, for crime.

For a more general discussion of the problem see Praz's informative study, pp. 51ff and 413ff. Praz says of Rossetti, p. 218: 'In Rossetti there is to be found a conspicuous preference for the sad and the cruel; the Middle Ages, to him, are a legend of blood; beside his Beata Beatrix stand magical, evil creatures.'

31 See *Misc. Studies*, pp. 155 and 156.
32 There are times in Praz's otherwise informative study when the different varieties of Satanism are not sufficiently distinguished. On pp. 380–1, for instance, he offers the following somewhat summary judgement: 'One is forced to the conclusion that perhaps the unlimited licence to deal with sub-

jects of vice and cruelty, which was introduced into literature together with Romanticism, created an atmosphere favourable to the expression of individual feeling, which, in different circumstances, would have remained latent and repressed.' It is certainly true that Satanism offers a form of self-expression, but within this 'fashion' (Praz, p. 381) it is precisely the different nuances that are the most revealing, as we can see from the satanical scenes in Pater.

33 *Misc. Studies*, p. 158.
34 See Ransome, p. 135; Anon., *Spectator* 104, p. 1076; Staub, p. 77 and Powys, p. 174.
35 See *Greek Studies*, pp. 110–11, and Nietzsche, *Birth of Tragedy*, pp. 6 and 40–1.
36 See *Greek Studies*, pp. 252–3, and Nietzsche, *Birth of Tragedy*, p. 21.
37 See *Greek Studies*, pp. 39–40, and Nietzsche, *Birth of Tragedy*, pp. 81ff.
38 See *Greek Studies*, pp. 55, 75, 76ff and 128, and Nietzsche, *Birth of Tragedy*, p. 94.
39 Nietzsche, *Birth of Tragedy*, p. 174.
40 See e.g. Nietzsche, *Wille zur Macht* II, pp. 386–7.
41 *Greek Studies*, p. 53.
42 Ibid., p. 151.

10 *Marius the Epicurean*

1 Lubbock, p. 195.
2 David Cecil, *Pater*, p. 24.
3 On the importance of narrative techniques, see Lubbock's extrapolations from the ideas of Henry James; also Lugowski, pp. 15ff; Forster, p. 75 and Stanzel, pp. 1ff.
4 *Marius* I, p. 153.
5 Forster, p. 29.
6 Ibid., p. 31.
7 *Marius* I, p. 45.
8 *Marius* II, p. 109.
9 *Marius* I, p. 32.
10 Ibid., p. 241.
11 See Forster, pp. 65ff.
12 See ibid., and Muir, pp. 25ff.
13 See Forster, pp. 65 and 68.
14 See Muir, p. 47.
15 *Marius* II, p. 172.
16 See esp. ibid., p. 175.
17 See also Lugowski, pp. 167ff and 176–7.
18 See the chapter 'Stoicism at Court', *Marius* II, pp. 3ff, and 'Conversation Not Imaginary', ibid., pp. 144ff.
19 *Marius* II, p. 14.
20 See ibid., p. 198.
21 See *Marius* I, p. 5.
22 On the importance of this problem for narration, see Benjamin II, pp. 229 and 233.

23 *Marius* II, p. 183.
24 See esp. the chapters 'Animula Vagula' and 'New Cyrenaicism', *Marius* I, pp. 123ff and 144ff; 'Second Thoughts', 'The Will as Vision', and 'The Minor Peace of the Church', *Marius* II, pp. 14ff, 57ff and 109ff.
25 See *Marius* I, p. 8.
26 Ibid., p. 9.
27 Ibid., p. 18.
28 Ibid., p. 43.
29 See also Part II, pp. 49–50.
30 See *Marius* I, pp. 55–6.
31 See ibid., p. 96.
32 See ibid., p. 52.
33 Ibid.
34 Ibid., p. 53.
35 Ibid., pp. 53–4.
36 See e.g. ibid., pp. 183ff and 233; *Marius* II, pp. 25, 68ff, 77–8, 96ff, 132ff, 137–8, 140, 215–16, and 223–4.
37 See ibid., pp. 125–6.
38 Ibid., p. 126.
39 Ibid., p. 130.
40 Ibid., p. 133.
41 See ibid., pp. 24–5.
42 See ibid., pp. 134ff.
43 See ibid., pp. 138 and 146.
44 Ibid., p 138.
45 Ibid., p. 139. In view of Pater's 'Conclusion', both Cecil, *Oxford Thinkers*, p. 238, and Jacobus, p. 43, seem a little wide of the mark in regarding the philosophy of the moment as being nothing but an historical representation of Cyrenaicism.
46 See *Marius* I, p. 131.
47 On the general concept of the moment, see V. Woolf, *Common Reader. First Series*, pp. 190–1, and *Moment*, pp. 9–10. See also Auerbach, pp. 467ff. A concept of the moment similar to Pater's is to be found in Stevenson (see Hicks, p. 61), Henley (see Buckley, *Henley*, p. 50), Beardsley (see Jackson, p. 95), Le Gallienne, p. 131 and Wilde, *De Profundis*, p. 90 (see also Harris, p. 309). On the philosophical significance of the moment in Nettleship's circle, see Young, p. 91.
48 *Marius* I, p. 139.
49 *Renaissance*, p. 236.
50 *Marius*, I, p. 149. See also Kermode, pp. 20 and 21–2.
51 *Marius* I, pp. 151–2.
52 Ibid., pp. 154–5.
53 Ibid., p. 163.
54 Ibid., p. 166.
55 Kierkegaard, *Entweder/Oder* I, p. 140.
56 See the chapters 'The Most Religious City in the World', 'The Divinity That Doth Hedge a King', and 'Manly Amusement', *Marius* I, pp. 172ff, 188ff and 230ff.
57 Ibid., p. 201.

58 Ibid., p. 205.
59 Ibid., p. 201.
60 Ibid., p. 213.
61 Ibid., p. 241.
62 Ibid., pp. 241–2.
63 Ibid., p. 241.
64 See ibid., p. 151.
65 Kierkegaard, *Entweder/Oder* II, p. 139.
66 *Marius* II, p. 6. See also Moore, *Evelyn Innes*, p. 370. Amiel II, p. 239, confesses: 'Indecision being my principle defect'; see also Barry, p. 116. Cardinal Newman's attitude towards the problem of decision assumes an almost emblematical significance for the present discussion. He is completely opposed to the aesthetic concept, despite the fact that in his earlier years he was very open to aesthetic phenomena (see Tillotson, *Criticism*, pp. 147ff). Uncertainty also marks Newman's beginnings: 'Alas! it was my portion for whole years to remain without any satisfactory basis for my religious profession, in a state of moral sickness, neither able to acquiesce in Anglicanism, nor able to go to Rome' (*Apologia*, p. 143). From this emerges his dialectic of salvation: 'there are but two alternatives, the way to Rome, and the way to Atheism: Anglicanism is the half-way house on the one side, and Liberalism is the half-way house on the other' (*Apologia*, p. 329). This was the way in which the Anglican Newman experienced the 'Entweder/Oder' (the Either/Or), for whenever a decision is taken, choice is automatically cut, and so all alternative possibilities come together in a total opposition. For 'a partial truth is in some sense a lie, and so also is a representative truth' (*Apologia*, p. 413). It is the half-way position, the not only . . . but also, that Newman regards as the insidious disease of his time: 'Has all our misery, as a Church, arisen from people being afraid to look difficulties in the face? They have palliated acts, when they should have denounced them' (*Apologia*, p. 274). Such evasion, diminution and falsification of basic facts forced Newman to take his decision. What he accomplished was a true realisation of existence, for this was the part of the journey that he had to make entirely on his own. 'My own soul was my first concern, and it seemed an absurdity to my reason to be converted in partnership. I wished to go to my Lord by myself, and in my own way, or rather His way' (*Apologia*, p. 349). Thrown back upon himself, and utterly alone, Newman took the decisive step along the path to salvation. He left everything behind him, cutting himself off in order to follow the dictates of his conscience (see *Apologia*, p. 377). 'Faith ever begins with a venture, and is rewarded by sight' (*Loss and Gain*, p. 305). Anyone not prepared to take this risk is 'a coward' (*Loss and Gain*, p. 108), but anyone prepared to fulfil his existence, as Newman does, will gain security: 'From the time that I became a Catholic . . . I have been in perfect peace and contentment, I never have had one doubt . . . it was like coming into a port after a rough sea; and my happiness on that shore remains to this day without interruption' (*Apologia*, p. 373). For Newman there is a craving for authority in human nature (see Waddington, p. 66) to be satisfied only by following the dictates of conscience (see also Willey, *Nineteenth Century Studies*, p. 96). His decision brought him freedom from the shackles of temporality to which human existence is otherwise tied. The aesthete's longing for authority, on

the other hand, is shown by his dependence on historical figures. Instead of deciding, the aesthete tries to find security in history and myth.

67 *Marius* II, p. 15.
68 Ibid.
69 Ibid., p. 27.
70 Ibid., p. 72.
71 Hofmannsthal I, p. 238; see also Eliot, 'Place of Pater', pp. 105–6.
72 See *Marius* II, pp. 64–5, 67, 68–9 and 70.
73 Ibid., p. 67.
74 Ibid., p. 70.
75 Ibid.
76 Ibid., p. 68. Carlyle's concept of God has a similarly composite character, see Willey, *Nineteenth Century Studies*, p. 113.
77 See *Marius* II, pp. 76 and 85ff.
78 Ibid., p. 91.
79 Ibid., p. 90.
80 Ibid., p. 95.
81 Ibid., p. 100.
82 Ibid., p. 102.
83 Ibid., p. 112.
84 Ibid., p. 115.
85 See ibid., pp. 149–50.
86 See ibid., pp. 166ff.
87 Kierkegaard, *Stadien*, p. 442.
88 *Marius* II, pp. 219–20.
89 Ibid., p. 175.
90 Ibid., p. 182.
91 This interpretation is confirmed by the end of the novel, and there can be no doubt that *Marius* is not the history of conversion. The end has always aroused controversy among Pater scholars. The following critics see Marius as a Christian: Highet, p. 464; Eaker, p. 32; Thomas, p. 56; Wainwright, p. 445; St J. Lucas, p. 405; Somervell, p. 329; Greenslet, pp. 133–4; Barry, p. 388; Osbourn, p. 400; Sander, p. 243; Young, p. 101; Benson, p. 91 and Vollrath, p. 49. Critics who, like myself, do not regard *Marius* as the history of a conversion are: P. E. More, p. 96; Rosenblatt, 'Marius', p. 106; Cattan, p. 146; Hough, p. 154; Burgum, p. 291; Gaunt, p. 155; Shuster, p. 175 and Lahey, p. 545.
92 See *Marius* II, p. 183.
93 *Marius* I, p. 45.
94 See *Marius* II, p. 212.
95 Ibid.
96 Ibid., pp. 212–13. On the problem of decision, see the revealing sections in G. Moore's *Evelyn Innes*, pp. 371–2 and 374. For a contrasting view, see Newman, *Loss and Gain*, p. 303. For Arnold's attitude, see *Culture and Anarchy*, p. xxxvi. Somervell, p. 186, describes the same problem with regard to Clough.
97 *Marius* II, p. 220.
98 See Rehm, p. 276.

11 *Imaginary Portraits*

1 *Marius* II, p. 65.
2 See Lukács, 'Die Theorie des Romans', p. 248.
3 Vischer, VI, pp. 192–3.
4 See *Imaginary Portraits*, p. 42.
5 Ibid., pp. 14–15. Staub, pp. 61ff, only describes the historical background of the diary, without offering any interpretation.
6 *Imaginary Portraits*, p. 32.
7 Ibid., p. 27.
8 Ibid., pp. 34–5.
9 Ibid., p. 35.
10 Ibid., p. 31.
11 Ibid., p. 35.
12 Ibid., pp. 41 and 44. On the concept of melancholy, see also Pater's disagreement with Amiel, '*Guardian*, pp. 24 and 31ff. He confronts Amiel with Pascal, see p. 34, suggesting that melancholy can only be overcome by religion. On the melancholy of the aesthete at the end of the century, see Gaunt, p. 186, and Hicks, p. 248.
13 See *Renaissance*, pp. 238–9.
14 Ibid., p. 238.
15 *Imaginary Portraits*, p. 47. For historical details, see Staub, pp. 77ff.
16 See *Imaginary Portraits*, pp. 48ff.
17 See ibid., pp. 51–2.
18 See ibid., p. 52.
19 See ibid., pp. 53–4.
20 See ibid., pp. 58–9, 61–2, 63, 64–5, 66–7 and 67–8.
21 See ibid., p. 59.
22 See ibid., pp. 60–1.
23 See ibid., pp. 64–5.
24 Ibid., p. 60.
25 Ibid., pp. 61–2.
26 Ibid., p. 66.
27 Ibid.
28 See ibid., pp. 67–8.
29 See ibid., p. 69.
30 Ibid.
31 See ibid., pp. 75–6.
32 See *Marius* I, p. 151.
33 See also Harrison, 'Pater/Heine', p. 672, with particular emphasis on the importance of melancholy.
34 See *Imaginary Portraits*, pp. 84–5, 86–7 and 90ff. On the historical background see Staub, pp. 89ff.
35 *Imaginary Portraits*, pp. 98–9.
36 See ibid., pp. 90–1 and 86ff. Sedlmayr, p. 116, suggests that in 'the endless breadths of Dutch lowland and sea-scapes, man was nevertheless at home'.
37 *Imaginary Portraits*, p. 94.
38 See ibid., p. 90.
39 See ibid., p. 110.

40 Ibid., p. 107.
41 Ibid., p. 110.
42 See ibid., pp. 107–8.
43 See *Renaissance*, pp. 237–8.
44 See *Imaginary Portraits*, p. 108.
45 Ibid.
46 Ibid.
47 See ibid., pp. 104–5.
48 See ibid., pp. 88 and 96.
49 See ibid., pp. 94ff.
50 Ibid., p. 88.
51 Ibid., p. 89.
52 See Millhauser, p. 220.
53 *Renaissance*, p. 236.
54 See *Imaginary Portraits*, pp. 114–15.
55 See ibid., pp. 119–20.
56 The discovery was made at the beginning of the nineteenth century, see ibid., p. 119.
57 Ibid., p. 124; for local and historical details, see Staub, pp. 100ff.
58 *Imaginary Portraits*, p. 125.
59 See ibid., pp. 124ff.
60 See ibid., pp. 140ff.
61 Ibid., p. 124.
62 Ibid., pp. 144–5.
63 See Part III, pp. 81–3.
64 *Imaginary Portraits*, pp. 145–6.
65 See Parts III and IV.
66 *Imaginary Portraits*, p. 147.
67 See ibid., pp. 147–8.
68 See ibid., pp. 148 and 150ff. See also Staub, p. 106, footnote 12.
69 *Imaginary Portraits*, p. 152. See Millhauser, p. 219.
70 See also Rehm, p. 18.

Conclusion

1 *Misc. Studies*, p. 80.
2 See ibid., pp. 62–3.
3 Ibid., p. 86.
4 Ibid., p. 87.
5 Ibid.
6 Quoted by Wright II, p. 87; see also ibid. I, p. 190; II, pp. 104–5, and Benson, p. 90.

Bibliography

Abercrombie, Lascelles, *Romanticism*. London 1927.

Abrams, M. H., *The Mirror and the Lamp. Romantic Theory and the Critical Tradition*. New York 1953.

Adams, Hazard, *Blake and Yeats: The Contrary Vision* (Cornell Studies in English 40). Ithaca, New York 1955.

Amiel, Henri-Frédéric, *The Journal Intime*. Transl. by Mrs Humphrey Ward. 2 vols. London 1885.

Anon., 'Walter Pater': *Spectator* 104 (1910), pp. 1075–6.

Arnold, Matthew, *On the Study of Celtic Literature*. London 1867.

Literature and Dogma. London 1883.

Culture and Anarchy. London 1889.

Auden, W. H., *The Enchafèd Flood*. New York 1950.

Auerbach, Erich, *Mimesis*. Bern 1946.

Baker, Joseph E., *The Reinterpretation of Victorian Literature*. New Jersey 1950.

Barry, William, *Heralds of Revolt*. London 1909.

Beardsley, Aubrey, *Under the Hill and Other Essays in Prose and Verse*. London and New York 1904.

Becker, Oskar, 'Von der Hinfälligkeit des Schönen und der Abenteuerlichkeit des Künstlers': *Ergänzungsband zum Jahrbuch für Philosophie und Phänomenologische Forschung* (Festschrift for Edmund Husserl). 1929, pp. 27–52.

Bendz, Ernst, *The Influence of Pater and Matthew Arnold in the Prose Writings of Oscar Wilde*. Gothenburg and London 1914.

Benjamin, Walter, *Schriften*. 2 vols. Frankfurt 1955.

Benn, Gottfried, *Ausdruckswelt*. Wiesbaden 1949.

Essays. Wiesbaden 1951.

Benson, A. C., *Walter Pater* (English Men of Letters 59). London 1906.

Beyer, Arthur, *Walter Paters Beziehungen zur französischen Literatur und Kultur* (Studien zur englischen Philologie 73). Halle 1931.

Binswanger, Ludwig, *Drei Formen mißglückten Daseins*. Tübingen 1956.

Blake, William, *The Writings*. Ed. by Geoffrey Keynes. 3 vols. London 1925.

Bock, Eduard J., *Walter Pater's Einfluß auf Oscar Wilde* (Bonner Studien zur englischen Philologie 8). Bonn 1913.

Bollnow, Otto Friedrich, *Das Wesen der Stimmungen*. Frankfurt 1956.

Bowra, C. M., *The Romantic Imagination*. Cambridge: Harvard University Press 1949.

Brie, Friedrich, *Exotismus der Sinne* (Sitzungsberichte der Heidelberger Akademie der Wissenschaften. Phil.-Hist. Klasse 1920, 3. Abhandlung). Heidelberg 1920.

Ästhetische Weltanschauung in der Literatur des XIX. Jahrhunderts. Freiburg 1921.
Brinkmann, Richard, *Wirklichkeit und Illusion.* Tübingen 1957.
Brown, E. K., *Matthew Arnold. A Study in Conflict.* Chicago 1948.
Buckley, Jerome Hamilton, *William Ernest Henley. A Study in the 'Counter-Decadence' in the 'Nineties.* New Jersey 1945.
The Victorian Temper. A Study in Literary Culture. London 1952.
Bunyan, John, *Grace Abounding* and *The Pilgrim's Progress.* Ed. by John Brown. Cambridge 1907.
Burckhardt, Jacob, *Die Kultur der Renaissance in Italien.* Edited by L. Geiger. 2 vols. Leipzig 1904.
Burdett, Osbert, *The Beardsley Period. An Essay in Perspective.* London 1925.
Burgum, Edwin Berry, 'Walter Pater and the Good Life': *Sewanee Review* 40 (1932), pp. 276–93.
Burke, Edmund, *The Works.* 12 vols. London 1899.
Bush, Douglas, *Mythology and the Romantic Tradition.* New York 1957.
Campbell, Lewis, 'Pater's Plato and Platonism': *Classical Review* VII (1893), pp. 263–6.
Carlyle, Thomas, *The Works* (Centenary Edition). 30 vols. London 1896–8.
Cattan, Lucien, *Essai sur Walter Pater.* Paris 1936.
Cecil, Algernon, *Six Oxford Thinkers.* London 1909.
Cecil, Lord David, 'Introducing the Ideas and Beliefs of the Victorians': *Ideas and Beliefs of the Victorians.* BBC, London 1950.
'Fin de Siècle': *Ideas and Beliefs of the Victorians.* BBC, London 1950.
Walter Pater. The Scholar–Artist. Cambridge 1955.
Chandler, Edmund, *Pater on Style* (Anglistica 11). Copenhagen 1958.
Chandler, Zilpha E., *An Analysis of the Stylistic Technique of Addison, Johnson, Hazlitt, and Pater* (University of Iowa Humanistic Studies IV, 3). Iowa 1928.
Chesterton, G. K., *The Victorian Age in Literature* (Home University Library). London 1925.
Coleridge, S. T., *Biographia Literaria.* Ed. by J. Shawcross. 2 vols. Oxford 1907.
Collingwood, R. G., *The Idea of History.* Oxford 1951.
Curtius, Ernst Robert, *Europäische Literatur und Lateinisches Mittelalter.* Bern 1954.
Dacqué, Edgar, *Natur und Seele. Ein Beitrag zur magischen Weltlehre.* Munich 1926.
Natur und Erlösung. Munich 1933.
Dawson, Christopher, 'Introducing the Ideas and Beliefs of the Victorians': *Ideas and Beliefs of the Victorians.* BBC, London 1950.
Dockhorn, Klaus, *Der deutsche Historismus in England. Ein Beitrag zur Geistesgeschichte des 19. Jahrhunderts* (Hesperia Ergänzungsreihe: Schriften zur englischen Philologie 14). Göttingen 1950.
Dodds, John W., 'New Territories in Victorian Biography': Baker, *The Reinterpretation of Victorian Literature.* New Jersey 1950.
Dowden, Edward, *Essays Modern and Elizabethan.* London 1910.
Eaker, J. Gordon, *Walter Pater. A Study in Methods and Effects* (University of Iowa Humanistic Studies V, 4). Iowa 1933.
Egan, Rose Frances, *The Genesis of the Theory of 'Art for Art's Sake' in Germany*

and in England (Smith College Studies in Modern Languages II, 4 and V, 3). Northampton and Paris 1921 and 1924.

Eliot, T. S., 'The Place of Pater': *The Eighteen-Eighties. Essays by Fellows of the Royal Society of Literature*. Ed. by Walter de la Mare. Cambridge 1930.

Selected Essays. London 1949.

The Use of Poetry and the Use of Criticism. London 1950.

Evans, Joan, *John Ruskin*. London 1954.

Farmer, Albert J., *Walter Pater as a Critic of English Literature. A Study of 'Appreciations'*. Grenoble 1931.

Le Mouvement esthétique et 'décadent' en Angleterre (1873–1900). Paris 1931.

Fehr, Bernhard, 'Walter Pater und Hegel': *Englische Studien* 50 (1916), pp. 300–8.

Streifzüge durch die neueste englische Literatur. Straßburg 1912.

'Walter Paters Beschreibung der Mona Lisa und Théophile Gautiers romantischer Orientalismus': *Archiv* 135 (1916), pp. 80–102.

Fletcher, Phineas, *The Poetical Works of Giles and Phineas Fletcher* (Cambridge English Classics). Ed. by Frederick S. Boas, vol. I. Cambridge 1908.

Foerster, Norman, 'The Critical Study of the Victorian Age': Baker, *The Reinterpretation of Victorian Literature*. New Jersey 1950.

Forster, E. M., *Aspects of the Novel* (Pocket Edition). London 1958.

Friedrich, Hugo, *Montaigne*. Bern 1949.

Gaunt, William, *Das ästhetische Abenteuer*. Transl. by Anneliese Schmundt-Wyneken. Hanover 1948.

Gilbert, Katherine and Kuhn, Helmut, *A History of Esthetics*. New York 1939.

Glücksmann, Hedwig Luise, 'Die Gegenüberstellung von Antike-Christentum in der englischen Literatur des 19. Jahrhunderts': Dissertation. Freiburg 1932.

Grassi, Ernesto, *Kunst und Mythos* (rowohlts deutsche enzyklopädie 36). Hamburg 1957.

Greenslet, Ferris, *Walter Pater*. London 1905.

Guardini, Romano, *Über das Wesen des Kunstwerks*. Tübingen and Stuttgart 1952.

Harris, Frank, *Oscar Wilde. Eine Lebensbeichte*. Berlin 1923.

Harrison, John Smith, 'Pater, Heine, and the Old Gods of Greece': *PMLA* 39 (1924), pp. 655–86.

Haskins, Charles Homer, *The Renaissance of the Twelfth Century*. Cambridge: Harvard University Press 1927.

Hecht, Hans, 'Walter Pater. Eine Würdigung': *Deutsche Vierteljahrsschrift für Literaturwissenschaft und Geistesgeschichte* 5 (1937), pp. 550–82.

Hegel, G. W. F., *The Philosophy of Fine Art*. Transl. by F. P. B. Osmaston. 4 vols. London 1916–20.

Philosophie der Weltgeschichte. 4 vols. (Meiners Philosophische Bibliothek). Leipzig 1930.

Ästhetik. Ed. by Friedrich Bassenge. Berlin 1955.

Heine, Heinrich, *Werke*. Ed. by Ewald A. Boucke. Vol. 8. Berlin no date.

Hess, Gerhard, *Die Landschaft in Baudelaires 'Fleurs du Mal'* (Sitzungsberichte der Heidelberger Akademie der Wissenschaften. Phil.-Hist. Klasse 1953, 1. Abhandlung). Heidelberg 1953.

Hicks, Granville, *Figures of Transition. A Study of British Literature at the End of the Nineteenth Century*. New York 1939.

Highet, Gilbert, *The Classical Tradition. Greek and Roman Influences on Western Literature*. Oxford 1949.
Hofmannsthal, Hugo von, *Gesammelte Werke*. Edited by Herbert Steiner. Vols. 1 and 2. Frankfurt 1950–1.
Höhne, Horst, *Der Hegelianismus in der englischen Philosophie* (Junge Forschung II). Halle 1936.
Holloway, John, 'Matthew Arnold and the Modern Dilemma': *Essays in Criticism* 1 (1951), pp. 1–16.
Holthusen, Johannes, *Studien zur Ästhetik und Poetik des russischen Symbolismus*. Göttingen 1957.
Hough, Graham, *The Last Romantics*. London 1949.
Huneker, James, *The Pathos of Distance*. London no date.
Hunt, Holman W., *Pre-Raphaelitism and the Pre-Raphaelite Brotherhood*. 2 vols. London 1905.
Huppé, Bernard F., 'Walter Pater on Plato's Aesthetics': *Modern Language Quarterly* 9 (1948), pp. 315–21.
Ideas and Beliefs of the Victorians. An Historic Revaluation of the Victorian Age. BBC, London 1950.
Iser, Wolfgang, 'Walter Pater und T. S. Eliot. Der Übergang zur Modernität': *Germanisch-romanische Monatsschrift* 40 (1959), pp. 391–408.
Jackson, Holbrook, *The Eighteen Nineties* (Penguin Books). Harmondsworth 1950.
Jacobus, Russell P., 'The Blessedness of Egoism. Maurice Barrès and Walter Pater': *Fortnightly Review* LIX New Series (January–June 1896), pp. 40–57 and 384–96.
Jauss, Hans Robert, 'Die beiden Fassungen von Flauberts *Education Sentimentale*': *Heidelberger Jahrbücher* 2 (1958), pp. 96–116.
Joad, C. E. M., *Decadence. A Philosophical Inquiry*. London 1948.
Joel, Karl, *Wandlungen der Weltanschauungen*. 2 vols. Tübingen 1929.
Johnson, Lionel, *Post Liminium. Essays and Critical Papers*. Ed. by Thomas Whittemore. London 1911.
Johnson, R. V., 'Pater and the Victorian Anti-Romantics': *Essays in Criticism* 4 (1954), pp. 42–57.
Jung, C. G. and Kerényi, K., *Einführung in das Wesen der Mythologie. Gottkindmythos. Eleusinische Mysterien*. Zürich 1941.
Jünger, F. G., *Griechische Mythen*. Frankfurt 1947.
Kassner, Rudolf, *Das Neunzehnte Jahrhundert*. Erlenbach–Zürich 1947.
Kaufmann, Fritz, 'Die Bedeutung der künstlerischen Stimmung': *Ergänzungsband zum Jahrbuch für Philosophie und Phänomenologische Forschung* (Festschrift for Edmund Husserl). 1929, pp. 191–223.
Kermode, Frank, *Romantic Image*. London 1957.
Kierkegaard, Sören, *Stadien auf dem Lebensweg*. Transl. by C. Schrempf and W. Pfleiderer. Jena 1922.
Entweder/Oder. Transl. by W. Pfleiderer and C. Schrempf. 2 vols. Jena 1922.
Furcht und Zittern. Die Wiederholung. Transl. by H. C. Ketels, H. Gottsched and C. Schrempf. Jena 1923.
Der Begriff der Angst. Transl. by C. Schrempf. Jena 1923.
Klages, Ludwig, *Mensch und Erde*. Munich 1920.

Vom kosmogonischen Eros. Stuttgart no date.

Der Geist als Widersacher der Seele. 3 vols. Leipzig 1929–33.

Ladd, Henry, *The Victorian Morality of Art. An Analysis of Ruskin's Esthetic*. New York 1932.

Lahey, G. F., 'Walter Pater and the Catholic Church': *The Month* (1927), pp. 542–5.

Law, Helen H., 'Pater's Use of Greek Quotations': *Modern Language Notes* 58 (1943), pp. 575–85.

Le Gallienne, Richard, *The Romantic '90s*. London 1951.

Lehmann, A. G., *The Symbolist Aesthetic in France 1885–1895* (Modern Language Studies). Oxford no date.

Liptzin, Sol, 'Heinrich Heine, Hellenist and Cultural Pessimist. A Late Victorian Legend': *Philological Quarterly* XXII (1943), pp. 267–77.

Löwith, Karl, 'Weltgeschichte und Heilsgeschehen': *Anteile*. Martin Heidegger zum 60. Geburstag. Frankfurt 1950, pp. 106–53.

Von Hegel zu Nietzsche. Stuttgart 1950.

Weltgeschichte und Heilsgeschehen. Die theologischen Voraussetzungen der Geschichtsphilosophie. Stuttgart 1953.

Wissen, Glaube und Skepsis (Kleine Vandenhoek-Reihe 30). Göttingen 1956.

Lubbock, Percy, *The Craft of Fiction*. London 1957.

Lucas, F. L., *The Decline and Fall of the Romantic Ideal*. Cambridge 1954.

Lucas, St John, 'Vagabond Impressions. Walter Pater and the Army': *Blackwood's Magazine* CCIX (January–June 1921), pp. 405–8.

Lugowski, Clemens, *Die Form der Individualität im Roman* (Neue Forschung 14). Berlin 1932.

Lukács, Georg von, 'Die Theorie des Romans': *Zeitschrift für Ästhetik und allgemeine Kunstwissenschaft* 11 (1916), pp.225–71 and 390–431.

'Die Subjekt-Objekt-Beziehung in der Ästhetik': *Logos* 7 (1917/18), pp. 1–39.

Malraux, André, *Les Voix du Silence*. Paris 1953.

Maugham, Somerset W., *Of Human Bondage* (The Collected Edition of the Works). London 1956.

Meinecke, Friedrich, *Die Entstehung des Historismus*. Munich 1946.

Melchiori, Giorgio, *The Tightrope Walkers. Studies of Mannerisms in Modern English Literature*. London 1957.

Millhauser, Milton, 'Walter Pater and the Flux': *The Journal of Aesthetics and Art Criticism* 11 (1952), pp. 214–23.

Moore, George, 'Avowals, VI. Walter Pater': *Pall Mall Magazine* 33 (1904), pp. 527–33.

Evelyn Innes. London 1908.

Confessions of a Young Man. London 1952.

More, Paul Elmer, *The Drift of Romanticism*. Shelbourne Essays. Eighth Series. London 1913.

Muir, Edwin, *The Structure of the Novel* (7th imp.). London 1957.

Nahm, Milton C., 'The Philosophy of Aesthetic Expression': *The Journal of Aesthetics and Art Criticism* 13 (1954), pp. 458–68.

Needham, H. A., *Le Développement de l'esthétique sociologique en France et en Angleterre au XIXe siècle*. Paris 1926.

Newman, Bertram, 'Walter Pater. A Revaluation': *Nineteenth Century and After* III (1932), pp. 633–40.

Newman, John Henry, *Apologia pro vita sua*. London 1864.
Loss and Gain. London 1869.
Nietzsche, Friedrich, *Nachgelassene Werke aus den Jahren 1872/73–1875/76* (Werke: 2. Abteilung, 10. Band). Leipzig 1903.
Der Fall Wagner. Götzen-Dämmerung. Nietzsche contra Wagner. Umwerthung aller Wenthe I. Dichtungen (Werke: 1. Abteilung, 8. Band). Leipzig 1906.
Nachgelassene Werke. Der Wille zur Macht (Werke: 2. Abteilung, 15. und 16. Band). Leipzig 1911.
Birth of Tragedy (Complete Works vol. I). Ed. by O. Levy, transl. by William A. Haussmann, New York 1925.
Novalis, *Schriften. Fragmente*. Jena 1923.
O'Faoláin, Seán, 'Pater and Moore': *London Mercury* 34 (1936), pp. 330–8.
Olivero, Frederico, *Il Pensiero Religioso ed Estetico di Walter Pater* (Società Editrice Internazionale XVII). Torino 1939.
Osbourn, R. V., 'Marius the Epicurean': *Essays in Criticism* 1 (1951), pp. 387–403.
Otto, Walter F., *Dionysos. Mythos und Kultus* (Frankfurter Studien zur Religion und Kultur der Antike 4). Frankfurt 1933.
Die Götter Griechenlands. Frankfurt 1947.
Owen, W. J. B., *Wordsworth's Preface to Lyrical Ballads* (Anglistica IX). Copenhagen 1957.
Pater, Walter, 'M. Lemaitre's Serenus, and other Tales': *Macmillan's Magazine* LVII (1887/88), pp. 71–80.
Appreciations. With an Essay on Style. London 1889.
'Introduction to The Purgatory of Dante Alighieri', translated by Charles L. Shadwell. London 1892.
Uncollected Essays. Ed. by Thomas B. Mosher. Maine 1903.
Appreciations. With an Essay on Style (Library Edition). London 1910.
Essays from 'The Guardian' (Library Edition). London 1910.
Gaston de Latour. An unfinished Romance (Library Edition). Ed. by Charles L. Shadwell. London 1910.
Greek Studies (Library Edition). London 1910.
Imaginary Portraits (Library Edition). London 1910.
Marius the Epicurean. His Sensations and Ideas. 2 vols. (Library Edition). London 1910.
Miscellaneous Studies (Library Edition). London 1910.
Plato and Platonism (Library Edition). London 1910.
The Renaissance. Studies in Art and Poetry (Library Edition). London 1910.
Sketches and Reviews. New York 1919.
'Imaginary Portraits 2. An English Poet'. Ed. by Mary Ottley: *Fortnightly Review* CXXIX New Series (January–June 1931), pp. 433–48.
Perry, Ralph Barton, *Philosophy of the Recent Past*. London 1927.
Petriconi, Hellmuth, *Das Reich des Untergangs. Bemerkungen über ein mythologisches Thema* (Untersuchungen zur vergleichenden Literaturgeschichte 1). Hamburg 1958.
Picard, Max, *Das Ende des Impressionismus*. Munich 1916.
Die Flucht vor Gott. Erlenbach-Zürich and Leipzig 1934.
Powell, A. E., *The Romantic Theory of Poetry*. London 1926.
Powys, John Cowper, *Visions and Revisions*. London 1955.
Praz, Mario, *The Romantic Agony*. London 1933.

Proesler, Hans, 'Walter Pater und sein Verhältnis zur deutschen Literatur'. Dissertation. Freiburg 1917.

Ransome, Arthur, *Portraits and Speculations*. London 1913.

Rehm, Walther, *Kierkegaard und der Verführer*. Munich 1949.

Reisdorff, Julius, 'Die ästhetische Idee in Walter Paters Kunstkritik'. Dissertation. Bonn 1952.

Richards, I. A., *Coleridge on Imagination*. London 1950.

Roe, F. W., 'Ruskin and the Sense of Beauty': *Studies by Members of the Department of English* (University of Wisconsin Studies in Language and Literature 2). Madison 1918, pp. 270–99.

Rosenblatt, Louise, *L'idée de l'art pour l'art dans la littérature anglaise pendant la période victorienne*. Paris 1931.

'Marius l'Epicurean de Walter Pater et ses points de départ français': *Revue de Littérature Comparée* 15 (1935), pp. 97–106.

Rossetti, Dante Gabriel, *The Collected Works*. 2 vols. Ed. by William M. Rossetti. London 1890.

Ruskin, John, *The Works* (Library Edition). Ed. by E. T. Cook and Alexander Wedderburn. 39 vols. London 1903–12.

Saintsbury, George, *Prefaces and Essays*. London 1933.

Sander, Ernst, *Walter Pater, Imaginäre Portraits. Übertragen und mit einem Nachwort*. Hamburg 1946.

Scheffler, Karl, *L'Art pour l'Art*. Leipzig 1929.

Schleiermacher, Friedrich, *Sämtliche Werke*. Ed. by Carl Lommatzsch. *Vorlesungen über die Ästhetik* (3. Abteilung, 7. Band). Berlin 1842.

Schopenhauer, Arthur, *Die Welt als Wille und Vorstellung*. 2 vols. Berlin and Vienna 1924.

Sedlmayr, Hans, *Verlust der Mitte*. Salzburg 1948.

Sharp, William, *Papers Critical and Reminiscent*. (Selected Writings vol. III.) Arranged by Mrs William Sharp. London 1912.

Shelley, Percy Bysshe, *Defence of Poetry* (Belles-Lettres-Series). Ed. by L. Winstanley. Boston no date.

Shuster, George N., *The Catholic Spirit in Modern English Literature*. New York 1922.

Singer, Irving, 'The Aesthetics of "Art for Art's Sake" ': *The Journal of Aesthetics and Art Criticism* 12 (1953), pp. 343–59.

Somervell, D. C., *Geistige Strömungen in England im 19. Jahrhundert*. Transl. by Otto Funke (Sammlung Dalp 9). Bern 1946.

Stanzel, Franz, *Die typischen Erzählsituationen im Roman* (Wiener Beiträge zur englischen Philologie 63). Vienna 1955.

Staub, Friedrich, 'Das imaginäre Portrait Walter Paters'. Dissertation. Zürich 1926.

Stauffer, Donald A., 'Monna Melancholia. A Study in Pater's Sources': *Sewanee Review* 40 (1932), pp. 89–93.

Sternberger, Dolf, *Panorama oder Ansichten vom 19. Jahrhundert*. Hamburg 1955.

Über den Jugendstil und andere Essays. Hamburg 1956.

Stevenson, Robert Louis, *The Works* (Pentland Edition). 20 vols. London 1906/07.

Swinburne, Algernon Charles, *Lesbia Brandon*. Ed. by Randolph Hughes. London 1952.
The Complete Works (The Bonchurch Edition). Ed. by E. Gosse and Th. J. Wise. 20 vols. London 1925–27.
Thomas, Edward, *Walter Pater. A Critical Study*. London 1913.
Tillotson, Geoffrey, 'Pater, Mr. Rose, and the "Conclusion" of the Renaissance': *Essays and Studies* XXXII (1946). Coll. by Basil Willey. Oxford 1947.
'Arnold and Pater. Critics Historical, Aesthetic and Otherwise': *Essays and Studies* III, New Series (1950). Ed. by G. Rostrevor Hamilton. London 1950.
Criticism and the Nineteenth Century. London 1951.
Times Literary Supplement, 'On re-reading Pater'. 3.2.1927, pp. 65–6.
Townsend, Francis G., *Ruskin and the Landscape Feeling* (Illinois Studies in Language and Literature 35, 3). Urbana 1951.
Troeltsch, Ernst, *Der Historismus und seine Probleme* (Gesammelte Schriften 3). Tübingen 1922.
Ullmann, Stephen, *Style in the French Novel*. Cambridge 1957.
Ure, Peter, *Towards a Mythology. Studies in the Poetry of W. B. Yeats*. Liverpool 1946.
Vischer, Friedrich Theodor, *Ästhetik oder Wissenschaft des Schönen*. 6 vols. Munich 1922/23.
Vollrath, Wilhelm, *Verschwiegenes Oxford. Matthew Arnold, Goethe und Walter Pater, Fellow of Brasenose*. Heidelberg 1955.
Waddington, M. M., *The Development of British Thought from 1820 to 1890. With Special Reference to German Influences*. Toronto 1919.
Wagner, Richard, *Sämtliche Schriften und Dichtungen*. Leipzig no date.
Wainwright, Benjamin B., 'A centenary query: Is Pater outmoded?': *English Journal, College Edition* 28 (1939), pp. 441–9.
Ward, Mrs Humphrey, *Robert Elsmere*. 3 vols. Leipzig 1888.
Welby, T. Earle, 'Walter Pater': Abercrombie, L., *Revaluations. Studies in Biography*. Oxford 1939.
Wellek, René, 'Carlyle and the Philosophy of History': *Philological Quarterly* 23 (1944), pp. 55–76.
History of Modern Criticism: 1750–1950. London 1955.
'Walter Pater's Literary Theory and Criticism': *Victorian Studies* 1 (1957), pp. 29–46.
West, Alick, *The Mountain in the Sunlight. Studies in Conflict and Unity*. London 1958.
Wilcox, John, 'The Beginnings of l'Art pour l'Art': *The Journal of Aesthetics and Art Criticism* 11 (1952), pp. 360–77.
Wilde, Oscar, *The Picture of Dorian Gray*. Paris 1908–1910.
A House of Pomegranates. The Happy Prince and other Tales. London 1908.
De Profundis. London 1909.
Intentions. London 1909.
Willey, Basil, *Nineteenth Century Studies. Coleridge to Matthew Arnold*. New York 1949.
More Nineteenth Century Studies. A Group of Honest Doubters. London 1956.
Wilson, Edmund, *Axel's Castle. A Study in the Imaginative Literature of 1870–1930*. New York and London 1936.

Woolf, Virginia, *The Moment and Other Essays*. London 1947.
The Common Reader. First Series. London 1951.
Wordsworth, William, *Literary Criticism*. Ed. by Nowell C. Smith. London 1925.
The Poetical Works. Ed. by E. de Selincourt. 5 vols. Oxford 1940–49.
Wright, Thomas, *The Life of Walter Pater*. 2 vols. London 1907.
Young, Helen Hawthorne, 'The Writings of Walter Pater. A Reflection of British Philosophical Opinion from 1860 to 1890. Dissertation. Bryn Mawr. Lancaster 1933.

Bibliographical addendum: selected works on Pater since 1959

(For a full account up to 1973, see Franklin E. Court, *Walter Pater. An Annotated Bibliography of Writings about Him*, De Kalb, Illinois 1980)

Beppu, Keiko, *The Educated Sensibility of Henry James and Walter Pater*, Tokyo 1979.

Bloom, Harold, *The Ringers in the Tower: Studies in Romantic Tradition*, Chicago 1971.

Charlesworth, Barbara, *Dark Passages: The Decadent Consciousness in Victorian Literature*, Madison and Milwaukee 1965.

Conlon, John J., *Walter Pater and the French Tradition*, Lewisburg 1982.

Crinkley, Richmond, *Walter Pater: Humanist*, Lexington 1970.

Dale, Peter Allan, *The Victorian Critic and the Idea of History: Carlyle, Arnold, Pater*, Cambridge, Mass. 1977.

DeLaura, David J., *Hebrew and Hellene in Victorian England: Newman, Arnold and Pater*, Austin 1969.

Dodd, Philipp (ed.), *Walter Pater: An Imaginative Sense of Fact*, London 1981.

Downes, David A., *Victorian Portraits: Hopkins and Pater*, New York 1965.

The Temper of Victorian Belief: Studies in the Religious Novels of Pater, Kingsley and Newman, New York 1972.

Fishman, Salomon, *The Interpretation of Art: Essays on the Art Criticism of John Ruskin, Walter Pater, Clive Bell, Roger Fry and Herbert Read*, Berkeley 1963.

Fletcher, Ian, *Walter Pater*, London 1959.

Frank, Ellen Eve, *Literary Architecture: Essays Toward a Tradition – Walter Pater, Gerard Manley Hopkins, Marcel Proust, Henry James*, Berkeley 1979.

d'Hangest, Germain, *Walter Pater: L'Homme et l'Œuvre*, Paris 1961.

Johnson, Robert V., *Walter Pater: A Study of his Critical Outlook and Achievement* (Australian Humanities Research Council Monographs 6), Melbourne 1961.

Knoepflmacher, U. C., *Religious Humanism and the Victorian Novel: George Eliot, Walter Pater, and Samuel Butler*, Princeton 1966.

Levey, Michael, *The Case of Walter Pater*, London 1978.

McKenzie, Gordon, *The Literary Character of Walter Pater*, Berkeley 1967.

Meisel, Perry, *The Absent Father: Virginia Woolf and Walter Pater*, New Haven 1980.

Monsman, Gerald C., *Pater's Portraits: Mythic Pattern in the Fiction of Walter Pater*, Baltimore 1967.

Walter Pater, Boston 1977.

Walter Pater's Art of Autobiography, New Haven 1980.

Seiler, R. M. (ed.), *Walter Pater: The Critical Heritage*, London 1980.

Stein, Richard L., *The Ritual of Interpretation: The Fine Arts as Literature in Ruskin, Rossetti, and Pater*, Cambridge, Mass. 1975.
Ward, Anthony, *Walter Pater: The Idea in Nature*, London 1966.

Index of names*

*Both indexes compiled by Monika Reif-Hülser.

Index of subjects